HEALING OF THE SELF

THE NEGATIVES

THE NOTEBOOKS OF PAUL BRUNTON
(VOLUME 7)

HEALING OF THE SELF

THE NEGATIVES

PAUL BRUNTON
(1898–1981)

An in-depth study of
categories ten and eleven
from the notebooks

Published for the
PAUL BRUNTON PHILOSOPHIC FOUNDATION
by Larson Publications

International Standard Book Number (cloth) 0-943914-26-4
International Standard Book Number (paper) 0-943914-27-2
International Standard Book Number (series, cloth) 0-943914-17-5
International Standard Book Number (series, paper) 0-943914-23-X
Library of Congress Catalog Card Number: 87-80403

Manufactured in the United States of America

Published for the
Paul Brunton Philosophic Foundation
by
Larson Publications
4936 Route 414
Burdett, New York 14818

Third printing, 1996

The works of Paul Brunton

A Search in Secret India
The Secret Path
A Search in Secret Egypt
A Message from Arunachala
A Hermit in the Himalayas
The Quest of the Overself
The Inner Reality
(*also titled* Discover Yourself)
Indian Philosophy and Modern Culture
The Hidden Teaching Beyond Yoga
The Wisdom of the Overself
The Spiritual Crisis of Man

Published posthumously

Essays on the Quest

The Notebooks of Paul Brunton

(continued next page)

CONTENTS

EDITORS' INTRODUCTION

This seventh volume in *The Notebooks of Paul Brunton* is an in-depth presentation of the tenth and eleventh (of twenty-eight) major categories in the personal notebooks Dr. Paul Brunton (1898–1981) reserved for posthumous publication. Both sections of this volume are immediately useful. Each deals with a topic currently receiving a great deal of attention on both the personal and the professional levels.

Part 1, *Healing of the Self*, will be useful to private individuals and to members of the healing community. It examines mind-body relationships in health and sickness. Contrasting conventional, psychic, and spiritual approaches to healing, it clarifies basic principles of healing and recommends a combination of conventional and alternative methods. It also offers a variety of practical techniques that have proven useful both in self-healing and in assisting conventional treatment.

Because of the "datedness" of *some* of the medical and psychological terminology that appears in this section, we would like to remind the reader that these notes were written and compiled during a period that spanned approximately forty years. During that period, the fields of medicine and psychology underwent a great many changes—not only in terminology but also in technique. In keeping with his lifelong interest in current events, P.B. wrote many of his paras in response to events and ideas as they developed within the evolution of the healing community itself. He seldom took the time to go back and update such notes, and even more rarely did he record the time at which they were composed.

As P.B. concerned himself primarily, however, with the salient issues and philosophic implications of such ideas, the *meanings* he addresses are still clear and timely—even when the language carrying them seems somewhat dated to professionals in the field. For that reason, we have made no attempt to update older terminology. We suspect that readers familiar with more current terminology will find it fruitful, as we have, to approach the more technical sections as excerpts from a researcher's workbook which parallels developments in the healing arts since the early 1940s.

Part 2, *The Negatives*, examines the nature and roots of evil in both the individual and the world. Tracing the activity of sinister forces in previous and possible future world war, it emphasizes the urgency with which the current world-situation demands clear recognition of—and intelligent individual response to—the intensification of these destructive forces both within and around us. The section suggests a number of constructive alternatives, both at the individual and at the social level, to our present course.

Some readers may wonder at the juxtaposition of these two categories—*Healing of the Self* and *The Negatives*—in a single volume. They are certainly an odd pair if one approaches them from a materialistic viewpoint. From the perspective of Mentalism, however, both address the powerful influence of thought (technically including attitudes and emotions) upon our lives. In Part 1, P.B. points out that the reciprocal influence of body and psyche suggests a common ground—Mind. Were it not for this "mental" nature of both psyche and body, many illnesses and their causes would remain mysteries. This section focuses as well on how *conscious* thought-processes may positively (or negatively) modify bodily health—within certain limits that it also clarifies. Similarly, in Part 2, P.B. addresses the power of negative thought to produce adverse effects not only upon ourselves but also upon our fellow human beings and our environment. In both sections we see also the power of human thought to attract from beyond its own normal range the influences—either for healing or for evil—of forces greater than that of our own personal selves. These two sections, then, are both pointed applications of the principles of Mentalism, which P.B. introduced in *The Hidden Teaching Beyond Yoga* and considers further in category twenty-one of the current *Notebooks* series.

Readers who have come this far into *The Notebooks* series will have noticed direct relationships among some of the twenty-eight "categories" in P.B.'s overall outline. (This outline appears as the table of contents for *Perspectives* and is printed at the end of each subsequent volume.) Both sections of the present volume stand in direct relationship to certain categories appearing in other volumes. *Healing of the Self* relates directly not only to its companion category in this volume, but also to *Relax and Retreat* and *The Body* (in volumes two and four, respectively). *The Negatives* relates directly to *Emotions and Ethics*, *The Ego*, and *Human Experience* (in volumes five, six, and nine, respectively). To discover P.B.'s full thought on issues common to these distinct sections, it is worthwhile to study them in relation to one another.

   Editorial conventions with regard to the quantity of material chosen, as with regard to spelling, capitalization, hyphenation, and other copy-editing considerations, are the same as stated in introductions to earlier volumes. Likewise, (P) at the end of a para indicates that it is one of the relatively few paras we felt it was necessary to repeat here from *Perspectives*, the introductory volume to this series.

   We are profoundly grateful for the continuing support and expertise of friends and co-workers at Wisdom's Goldenrod and The Paul Brunton Philosophic Foundation, and to the continually expanding number of *Notebooks* readers throughout the world who are responsible for yet another volume in this series going to press. Further information about *The Notebooks* and related activities may be obtained by writing the

Paul Brunton Philosophic Foundation
P.O. Box 89
Hector, New York 14841

Part 1:
HEALING OF THE SELF

It comes to this—that much of human disease and sickness is traceable to the faulty functioning of the human self. Learn how to use that self correctly in its physical, emotional, intellectual, and spiritual aspects and you learn how to prevent or cure part, or most, or even all of your ill health.

1

THE LAWS OF NATURE

The spiritual importance of health

When a man's health has broken down, nothing seems so important to him as its restoration. It is only then that he really realizes the value of good health. This has been stated from the merely conventional and worldly standpoint. But what of the spiritual standpoint? The aspirant whose health has broken down becomes continually preoccupied with the condition of his body, so that the thoughts and time which he gives to it are taken from the thoughts and time which he could have given to his spiritual aspiration. And when he comes to his meditation periods, he may find it difficult to rise above his bodily states, so that even his concentration and power of meditation may be disturbed by it. For after all, the body is the instrument with which he has to work, and through which he has to achieve his high purpose during incarnation on this earth. This is why systems have been created to lay a foundation of health and strength for the spiritual endeavours of the aspirant. Moreover, if he seeks to be of service to his fellow men, his capacity to serve will be limited by the condition of his health, and may even be inhibited on the physical plane altogether. With good health he becomes more valuable to others but with bad health less so.

2

What is wrong with offering physical benefits to the students of philosophy? Why should it not make them healthier and help overcome their difficulties? Why should philosophy be indifferent to their personal welfare? Is it something fit only to be read about in library chairs or meditated upon in mountain caves? That is to say, fit only for dreamers and not for those who have to struggle and suffer in the world? No—it is something to be proud of, not something to be ashamed of, that philosophy shows us how to live so as to prevent avoidable sickness and how to find a path out of perplexing difficulties.

3

There is nothing meritorious in meekly accepting illness and disease because they are God's will. The human being is entitled to defend its body against them.

4

He should be ready to die at any time but not willing to do so. For the need of staying on in the body until a deeper spiritual awareness has been gained should make him care more for his health, fitness, and efficiency.

5

If the body does not become non-existent because, ultimately, it is a thought-form, neither does it become unimportant. For it is only in this body that we can attain and realize the ultimate consciousness. If, as has been explained in *The Wisdom of the Overself*, the physical wakeful state is the only one in which the task of true self-realization can be fully accomplished by the individual, then it is also the only state in which all mankind will ever accomplish it. As the social arrangements and living conditions in the world may accelerate or retard the process of enlightenment, it becomes clear that the nature of those physical arrangements and conditions *is* important in the eyes of those who care for mankind's spiritual welfare. Consequently, true wisdom cannot be indifferent to them but, on the contrary, will always seek to improve the one and ameliorate the other.

6

Why should we refuse, in the name of an other-world sanctity, the healing gifts of Nature because they help the body which belongs to this world? Are we such ethereal creatures already, have we attained the disembodied state, that we can afford to neglect the aches and pains, the ills and malfunctions of this, our earthly body?

7

Most of the individual's health troubles are the result of karma. The body is a source of pleasure and misery to nearly all; but both being temporary, the one balances the other. He should do his utmost to keep his body in good health by following the best program of physical living, diet, and so on, that his own experience and expert advice can suggest. He should try the most reasonable treatment for illness which both the Indian (including hatha yoga) and Western medical systems can offer. After he has done these things then there is nothing more he can do except to take his sufferings as a constant reminder of the necessity of seeking happiness in a spiritual self above the body self.

8

The question you ask about the inevitability of ill health on this path needs a page to itself. Generally speaking, there is no such inevitability.

Indeed the cleansing of the subconscious mind, the discipline of the bodily senses, and the quieting of the emotional nature promote good health. Where, however, the student through ignorance or through outside factors fails to make certain necessary changes in thought, feeling, attitude, or living—necessary at a certain period for his further evolution—then his higher self forces those changes upon him through upheavals or upsets in his environment or in his body. This is done by sending down some karma. In the latter case it means, of course, illness or disease—sometimes "accident." This covers certain individual cases, but there are many others where ill health is only the ordinary karmic result of earlier transgressions of the laws of physical, emotional, moral, or mental health, and not the result of special Overself intervention. Finally, there is the third group where it is the result of the natural imperfection of life on this earth where everything, as Buddha said, is doomed to decay and perish. Nobody escapes this general law. Mrs. Eddy could not escape it nor could Buddha himself escape it, as he once explained when he fell ill with fever. Such imperfection is, however, one of the causes which drive mankind to seek a higher life, a diviner better existence; so it is not useless. This earth is not our true home. We belong elsewhere, nearer to God's perfection, beauty, harmony.

Disease has hidden causes

9

Diseased conditions in the human body are often traceable, by a subtle and penetrating analysis, to diseased conditions in the human soul. Medical science deals chiefly with the physical organism, and so long as it persists in regarding only that part of the being of man, so long will it continue to find its theories falsified, its carefully prepared experiments turned into blind guesses, and its high percentage of failures maintained. I might make my point clearer, perhaps, by stating that the body is after all only a sensitive machine, and that if the thinking and feeling man who uses that machine in self-expression is distorted, unbalanced, or discordant in any way, then these undesirable qualities will reproduce themselves in the physical organism as appropriate disease or functional derangements.

10

The causes of disease with which conventional medicos deal are too often themselves the effects of still deeper causes. It is because unconventional healers recognize this that they are able to achieve so much higher a proportion of dramatically successful cures than the medicos can achieve.

And their principal recognition is of the spiritual nature of man, along with the mental emotional influence on the body.

11

When plague broke like a wave over the heads of mankind in the fifteenth century and spread with startling rapidity through the nations of Europe, the obvious physical causes were in themselves but agents of the less obvious soul-causes, defects in the very character of humanity. Insomnia and cancer, to take but two of the representative illnesses of our own epoch, are no less plaguelike in their menace to people of today, no less the products of causes inherent in imperfect human character, habit, or environment.(P)

12

Although we can often find the physical causes of physical ailments, behind these physical causes there are quite often maladies of the soul. Heal the soul and the bodily healing may follow. Obviously there are many cases where no success would result.

13

The first step in healing, for both the healer and the patient, is to pray, to ask for enlightenment about the true and first cause of the sickness. What act or what thought of the patient was primarily responsible? Once learnt, it must be corrected.

14

A disease may well be the outer expression of an inner conflict, or an inner weakness, or an inner misery.

15

He may push the problem away for a time, but it will be only for a time. One day it will return and he will have to deal with it again.

16

Those who violate the laws of their own being will suffer in health.

17

When Jesus told the woman he healed to sin no more, he added that it was her sinning which brought her ill-health upon her. Here then is one of the potent causes of sickness.

18

So long as we remain alienated from the Overself, so long shall we suffer misery and spoil life.

19

The claims of the inner life for attention and satisfaction are too often thrust aside, with a consequent unbalance. This deplorable condition increases until in middle life bodily malfunctions and maladies begin to appear, nervous and emotional stresses begin to cause trouble. It is then that the little "I" starts to break down. But because those claims are still, consciously or unconsciously, resisted, the cures are either temporary or followed, later, by new forms of ill health. This is not to say that there is only this single origin of sickness or disease, but it is certainly a very modern one.

20

If the change begins in the body's behaviour it may influence the mind to a very limited extent, but if it begins in the mind's thinking it will influence the body to a very large extent. That is the difference.

21

If, when we consider a subject from the standpoint of medicine, psychology, biology, or philosophy, we treat the body and the mind as two entirely separable things, it would be a mistake. They have a common origin.

22

We agree with all those virile advocates of health who assert that it is the foundation of human happiness. But we would widen its definition and make it include mental, emotional, and spiritual health.

23

The psychological causes of disease have only recently come under investigation by the strict methods of modern science, but the general fact of their existence was known thousands of years ago. Plato, for instance, said: "This is the great error of our day, that physicians separate the inner being from the body."(P)

24

What needs to be learned and accepted is the mentalist law of reproduction—as apart from the biological law—which teaches that sustained thoughts or violent feelings may produce physical-body effects.

25

Many of the conventional ideas prevalent in the medical profession are still materialistic, although some members of that profession do not shut their eyes to the dominant role of mind in the mind-body relationship. When the perceptions of the inner being are developed, the all-importance of healing wrong thought-emotion becomes clear.

26

The belief that disease exists entirely in the mind is an exaggerated one. The opposite belief that it exists entirely in the body is equally carried too far. In both cases experience and reflection must ultimately produce a reaction, provided prejudice is not stronger than the spirit of truth-seeking.

27

Nothing that happens to a man happens to his flesh alone or to his mind alone. The one can never exclude the other, for both have to suffer together, or enjoy together, or progress together.

28

Here again mentalism makes it possible for us to understand the basic principle which is at work. The entire body being a mental construct, it is occasionally possible to apply mental forces so as to repair wastage, heal disease, and restore healthy functioning. We say "occasionally" advisedly, for reasons which will shortly be given.

29

Psychosomatic medicine deals with physical diseases caused by emotional or mental factors, by moods or fears, by hidden conflicts or repressions. It has steadily been rising into an influential place of its own in recent years.

30

Mentalism affirms the true nature of the body, and hence of the nerves in the body. Pain is a condition of those nerves and hence must ultimately be what the body is—an idea in the mind.

31

What healing agent can be used successfully to cure a pathological condition whose first origin is in the mind? Should it not also be mental?

32

The power of bodily conditions to control thinking is admittedly true. Experience tells us that this is so, that physical causes are effectual in producing mental-emotional results. But this is not the whole truth. The reverse fact, that spiritual and psychic forces can heal or injure the body, that thoughts and feelings can affect its functioning, must also be admitted into consideration.

33

Even if it be hard to grant by sceptics that the mind is the whole cause of a particular sickness, they may be willing to grant that it is at least a contributing cause.

34

If the individual mind were completely cut off from the Universal Mind, if it really lived in a realm composed only of its own thoughts, then the formation and continuation of the world-image would be fully under its control. But this is not the case. Consequently it lacks the freedom to mold the body-thought as it would or prolong its life at will.

Physical mortality

35

The treatment of unpleasant realities by not including them in his picture of the world comforts but at the same time befools a man. None of the great prophets like Jesus and Buddha denied the existence of sickness, the reality of pain, or the significance of suffering in the cosmos. No—they acknowledged them as being inseparable from human life but pitied the victims and offered them an inward comfort which was based on truth and reality.

36

The animal part of us is doomed to oblivion, the spiritual part is ageless and deathless. The physical body belongs to the animal part. All attempts to perpetuate it must fail and arise from confusing the two levels of being, the transient and the eternal.

37

People ask Why, if all is mind, if—as you say—our bodies are only ideas, can we not control regulate and improve our bodies by controlling regulating and improving our minds? Why not go further still, with Christian Science, and play with the possibility, not only of these achievements, but also of rendering the body immortal by thinking it so?

The answer is that nobody can deny the creative power of the mind. It may do all these things, except the last. That it will never do. Why? Because we live in a world whose fundamental law of being—as Buddha discovered and Jesus taught—is decay and death, change and transition. Indeed, it was because they were so painfully aware of these truths that they sought and found the only *true* way of escape for man and that was into Nirvana, into the Kingdom of Heaven—not into the physical body again! No Christian Scientist from the first founder down to the latest follower has ever achieved physical immortality, nor ever will. "Man will never tire of seeking immortality," wrote Dr. Alexis Carrel, whose biological researches, yet mystical sympathies, entitle him to speak with high authority. "He will not attain it, because he is bound by certain laws of his organic constitution. . . . Never will he vanquish death. Death is the price he has to pay for his brain and his personality."

Now as for the other things, the possibilities of spiritual healings of pathological conditions, miraculous mental cures of disease, and rapid acceleration of organic repairs through concentrated thinking, I repeat that we do not deny them. They have always existed, always been demonstrated. The relation between psychological and physical processes must certainly exist if our doctrine is true. But there are two other factors at work in human life which must also be considered and must not be ignored. What are they? The first is the factor of destiny, self-earned in previous lives and now awaiting physical expression in the present life. It has something to say, whether we like it or not. The second is the factor of renunciation. When you accept the doctrine that all is mind and each individual thing is but an ephemeral idea, you must perforce accept the doctrine that you as an individual, as the ego, are also an ephemeral idea. Now when you go further and declare that you want reality, you want to find eternal and not ephemeral life, you will have to abandon the fleeting idea for the eternal Mind in which it occurs: that is, you will have to sink the ego and merge its will in the greater universal will of the Infinite Being. Do this! What will you find next? That your personal desires have sunk with it, that your individual wishes and hopes and fears have dissolved and disappeared. The desire for bodily betterment, however very attractive, would have gone too. You cannot have a single desire and yet enter the Kingdom of Heaven, as Jesus pointed out. So good health, the care of your painful diseases, the healing of your disturbed organs—right, necessary, and desirable as they undoubtedly are—are nevertheless matters which you must try to effect in a desireless way; you may try to cure them but you must leave the result to the higher will. If you insist that the body must yield to your desires of a cure, to your personal desires, then your ego, not the real universal self, has got the upper hand and is directing you. In that case you will be no better off, for you have no guarantee of success even then. Most Christian Scientists experience a score of failures for every cure. Whereas if you do your best mentally *and* physically to put your body right, but do it impersonally—accepting failure, if it comes, with as much equanimity as you can—you will certainly be no worse off than the Christian Scientist so far as the possibilities of cure are concerned, and you will be infinitely better off so far as realizing truth is concerned, with all the wonderful peace that will bring in its train. This is one meaning of the words "Not my will but Thine be done" which Mrs. Eddy failed to learn.

38

Don't you think, having seen so much illness around you for so many years, that life is forever striving to instill into us through pain what Buddha learned through reflection—that both body and world are doomed to decay and die, being subject to the law of universal incessant change? The experiences of life are the lessons of a guru, for we get just the kind of karma whose silent instruction is needed at the time. The whole world, more or less, is having to learn this great truth at present but it is too blind and too ignorant to grasp the lesson in its clarity and entirety.

39

How far the duration of human life can be extended is not known. The claims of hatha yogis are unauthenticated, while the theories of Christian Science and the experiment of Sri Aurobindo have still left it an uncertain matter. It is true that stories of centenarians being found in different parts of the world are not few and often pass unquestioned. But the difficulty of proving the date of birth usually remains. Most centenarians belong to the illiterate peasant class, to those who have not taken care to retain a correct knowledge of their age, for it was not so important to them as it is to the educated classes. There is hardly a record of payment by life insurance companies for the life of a centenarian. It is reasonable to ask, however, why, if the reparative and destructive elements in the body could be balanced, men should not live for centuries. In the absence of authenticated cases, we may only take the stand that Nature seems to have set her own limits to human life.

40

Some "back-to-nature" schools of therapy assert that all diseases are the consequences of transgressing the laws of health, just as some esoteric schools assert they are the consequences of incurring karmic debts. The first often point to the wild beasts as being perfectly healthy examples of living according to Nature. But those who have firsthand acquaintance with jungle life will refute this claim. Not only are all animals—whether domesticated or wild—subject to sickness, but even plants, grain crops, trees, fruits, and vegetables are subject to it by blight and rust.

41

The young and the strong may glory in the satisfaction of being alive, but the old and decrepit, the sick and the infirm, feel no such response to their existence.

42

The pain and unpleasantness which beset human experience at times—mentally or physically—are not without their complementary pleasure and joy at other times.

43

We would all like a happy beginning, a happy middle, and a happy ending to our story, but life betrays us: only in fiction is the craving really fulfilled.

44

If the pain is there, racking the physical life, the peace exists behind it, permeating the inner life.

45

Another of the great errors for which Mrs. Eddy was responsible is the idea that physical death will ultimately be conquered by the practice of Christian Science. Mrs. Eddy herself, the foremost exponent of her own system, could not demonstrate that conquest. No other Christian Scientist has yet demonstrated it. And I might add the prediction that no Scientist will ever do so. Here again there is a basis of actual truth behind the erroneous teaching, and the whole doctrine provides an apt illustration of the tendency of Christian Science to enter a region of misunderstanding the moment it attempts to apply its true principles to things of this earth.

There was a time in the far past of the human race, a time now lost in the dim mists of antiquity, when the life of man was stretched to a number of years far in excess of what it is today. That time has been hinted at by hoary legends of a Golden Age and by biblical stories of a pre-Flood race. Such a time will return in the cyclic course of our planet's history, but naturally it is far-off in the future. Nature herself is in no hurry. She has plenty of time to accomplish her purposes. And in those days men will again have a normal life-span of hundreds of years.

There exists in Asia a certain ancient knowledge—whose name may conveniently be translated as "The Art of Yogic Body Control"—which promises its votaries astonishing benefits in longevity. This age-old art is not the same as the alchemy of medieval Europe, when men sought vainly in experiments for the elixir of life. It is of such antiquity that those who hand it down tell us that it was born just after the time when the fabled gods had ceased to walk this earth. The exponents have almost disappeared from the world, but the tradition is so widespread throughout the East that solitary individuals still practise it in remote and unfrequented places. So difficult are the exercises which belong to this system, so laborious are its practices, so ascetic the self-discipline which it involves, that one can understand why it has almost faded out of existence. It performs strange feats such as stopping blood circulation and lung action, permitting knives and daggers to be run like skewers through the living flesh without harming it and with an extremely rapid drying of blood, and even the burial alive of an entranced body beneath the ground and its safe resurrection several hours or some days later. The principal basis of these feats consists in making certain changes in the breath rhythm, changes which involve such risk to life and health that we are not prepared to assume the responsibility of describing here the exercises for the development of such powers. It is also necessary to live a celibate and chaste existence, to refrain from expending energy in worldly work and business, and to reduce diet to an astonishing minimum.

Because they demand a special and severely ascetic training which is the work of several years devoted wholly to this austere task, such feats are necessarily uncommon. The ordinary layman could hardly be expected to find the time for such training, nor is there any necessity for him to do so. These displays are certainly spectacular but have primarily only scientific, medical, and theatrical values rather than a general one. Meanwhile, Nature has set her brief term to the human body, and those whose attachment to the body is not overweening will resignedly accept that term while the others must do so unwillingly.

But this is a different matter—living in the fleshly body for ever and ever, a notion which must seem insupportable to many who find the present brief term of man's existence quite enough for them to cope with. If Nature cared so much to preserve the physical body of man, she would not introduce earthquakes, eruptions, hurricanes, famines, pestilences, and floods into the scheme of things. The fact that she does do so indicates rather that she regards his body as being only a fragment of the man, not as the full man himself. It was Mrs. Eddy's idea, of course, that in those days sin and sickness would also have disappeared from the world, so that our existence would be a halcyon one. It is a pretty picture, but man's true home is not in the tabernacle of flesh; it is elsewhere. The fleshly body is but a temporary abiding place at best, and when man has arrived at a state of perfect spirituality he will abandon it and use a vehicle more consonant with his high condition, an electromagnetic body that will more easily and more faithfully represent him. Yes, death will be conquered, but not in the way that Christian Scientists imagine. It will be conquered firstly, by extending the duration of human life to a constantly increasing period; and secondly, by completely abandoning the physical body for a subtler one.

Mary Baker Eddy saw clearly enough that the real inner man—his spiritual being—is undying and immortal. For her statement of this truth, she deserves much credit, although it is certainly not a novel one. But when she began to consider that inner being in relation to its transient earthly tenement, the body, she became confused and misunderstood the nature of that relationship. The hour of every man's death is fixed by a higher will than his own, by that power which some call destiny but which itself takes its rise out of the Infinite Power, and no Christian Science practitioner or ordinary physician has ever "saved" the life of anyone. A man's own Overself fixes the dates of certain major events in his life prior to the moment when he utters his first cry as a babe, and the date of his death is but one of those appointed hours.

The *Dhammapada* says: "Not in the sky, nor in the depths of the ocean, nor by entering the caverns of the mountain, nowhere in the world can such a place be found where a man might dwell without being over-powered by death."

We are as flies on the wheel of the Universe. For all our loud buzzing it still rolls along on its own path. And yet these people confidently imagine they set the great Laws of Destiny at naught, and interfere with the workings of the Cosmic Plan.

46

Christian Science, like Sri Aurobindo, sets up the goal of physical im-mortality. Neither has yet succeeded in turning this from a theoretical into a demonstrable achievement. I believe, with the Buddha, that neither of them ever will. But this is something which the future must settle. What we can settle with certainty now is that the goal is inconsistent with the general teaching. For in the case of Christian Science, matter is ardently proclaimed to be unreal. Why then all this bother to immortalize a mate-rial body? Why should any consistent Christian Scientist be so attached to an admittedly false concept of his own consciousness as to wish to per-petuate it for all eternity? And in the case of Sri Aurobindo, the arch-exponent of yoga, we ask why, if the attainment of the divine conscious-ness is the declared goal of yoga, death should not be regarded as being the failure to seek this consciousness and true immortality as being its success-ful realization? It is perfectly true, as Christian Science asserts, that there is a world of being where error, evil, and sickness are quite unknown and also true that man can penetrate and dwell in this world. It is, however, quite untrue to assert that he can thereby abolish his life in the lower world where error, evil, and sickness do exist all around him. He will, in fact, have to carry on a double-sided existence. Within, all will be harmony, goodness, health. Without, much will be discord, baseness, and disease. He can liberate himself from the flesh and its environment, but only in his attitude towards them. Both will still be there. He can, by intense inward concentration resulting in a trance-like state, think them out of his exis-tence completely for a time, but not for all time. Nor can he change their character; that is, he cannot convert the body into a tree in actuality, nor a tree into a river.

47

Whereas Christian Science denies the reality of a diseased condition and doesn't deny the physical body altogether, philosophy denies only the *materiality* of the physical body and accepts the *existence* of the condition. Again, whereas Christian Science asserts that physical sickness was never given a place in God's scheme of things, philosophy says that it was given a place and fulfils a part of the divine purpose in our human evolution from a lower to a higher state of consciousness.

48

There is no disease which can affect the man's divine soul, no sickness which can lay it low. It is his incorruptible element. Hence it is certainly true to say that the perfect man does not suffer from these things. But what is usually ignored or generally unknown is that "the perfect man" does not exist on earth, only "in heaven"; never in the flesh, only in the spirit. This earth and this body have been given over to the alternations of decay and growth, of death and birth—in short, to processes of change involving corruptibility. There is only one sure, permanent, and impecca-ble way of overcoming disease or sickness, and that is to live consciously in the Overself as well as the body. Whoever understands all this will find it easy to understand that the same causes prevent the possibility of living forever in identically the same body, and thus of attaining physical immor-tality. The laws which influence the building up of the body are precisely the laws which also influence its eventual breaking down. There is no trustworthy record in history that any human being has so far evaded the operation of these laws and survived the planet's vast evolutionary cycles. That man may discover how to prolong his life beyond the present average span or how to preserve his body in good functional and organic health is, however, a possibility which need not in any way be denied by these statements.

49

That alone can exist forever which is not compounded together out of different elements, for it is a law which we see everywhere at work in the universe that all such composite things must become decomposed again in time. We may be able to devise means to prolong the body's life, but we shall never be able to immortalize it.

50

When so many others fall victim at some time to sickness or accident, there is no certainty that he will remain indefinitely immune.

51

The truth is with Jesus, who said that flesh and blood will not inherit eternal life.

52

Life brings its sufferings to every quester, as to every nonquester, as to all beings who move on this earth. Successful completion of the quest may free him from some of them but could it ever free him from all of them? The happiness he may find cannot be an absolute; it must be qualified.

53

The characteristics stamped upon earthly life are in part unpleasant, miserable, and painful. Sickness and struggle are not merely the result of wrong thinking, as Christian Science avers, but native to and almost inevitable in our existence. Were it otherwise, we would be so satisfied that we would never aspire to a higher existence, but anxieties goad us eventually into seeking inner peace, worldly troubles stir us to seeking an unworldly refuge, fated frustrations drive us to seeking diviner satisfactions, and bodily illness to seeking spiritual joy. Ours is the world of the imperfect. The perfect reality could never be expressed amid its limitations. No one has ever "demonstrated" conquest over death, or complete freedom from human afflictions before death. These things are inherent in our lot. Through death's presence we are aroused to the need of eternal life; through afflictions to the need of eternal serenity. They exist only in the spirit. So the health and prosperity we can demonstrate are essentially spiritual.

54

Out of this physical suffering he should have learned the lessons of a deep wisdom: first, that this earth is not his home but only a camp; second, that this body is not his true self but only a garment; third, that suffering, disappointment, or discontent is inseparable from earthly life, real happiness is to be found only in the super-earthly life; fourth, that the full force of the mind must be developed by renunciation, sacrifice, concentration, and aspiration so that it can even here to a large extent create an inner life that continues peacefully in whatever state the body may find itself.

The Philosopher's body

55

The pains and maladies which accompany and punctuate physical existence are not taken away from the spiritually aware man. Their presence continues to act as a reminder—as much to him as to all other men—that just because they do accompany the body's life, that life is an imperfect and unsatisfying one. His five senses are working like all other men's and so must report the painful as well as pleasurable sensations. But what he does gain is a peace deeper than the body's sensations, and unbreakable by their painful nature. One part of him—the lesser—may suffer; but the other part—the greater—remains undisturbed. In his higher and spiritual nature he is well fortified against these afflictions, sustained by heavenly forces denied to other people.

56

The Buddha was not immune from disease. The austerities he practised during his search for enlightenment permanently affected his health, and his ceaseless activity for forty-five years greatly weakened him towards the end of his life. He often suffered from a severe headache and in his old age he suffered from severe backache which sometimes forced him to stop a sermon halfway and ask one of his disciples to continue from where he left off. The unsuitable meals which he was sometimes forced to eat were responsible for a dyspepsia which persisted throughout his life, culminating in his last fatal illness of dysentery. But none of these ailments prevented him from being always ready with help for those who needed it.

57

Will man ever be able to retain and maintain the same physical form permanently? To some it would be the height of happiness to realize such an aim, whereas to others it would be a sentence of captivity without hope of release. Is the sage able to prolong his physical life far beyond the normal period? Is there any truth in the Indian legends of yogis who live for a thousand years or more? If not, why should such advanced men lack this power? The answer to the first question is in the negative; to the second question probably in the negative. The answer to the third question is that transiency is the law governing all formed things; that death is the inevitable complement of birth because, as Buddha pointed out, whatever has a beginning in time must likewise have an end in time; and that the truth is that the sage does not really die for he persistently reincarnates in order to help mankind.

58

We need also to remember that the attitude of the advanced soul towards personal suffering is not the same as the common one. His standpoint is different. So far as we know human history on this globe, all the facts show that sickness, pain, disease, and death are parts of the conditions governing the physical body's experience because they are inescapable and inevitable parts of all physical-plane experience for highly organized forms, whether human or otherwise. That is, they are part of the divine plan for man. We humans resent such experiences, but it may be that they are necessary to our rounded development and that the Illuminated who have approached closer to the infinite wisdom perceive this and drop their resentment. Here we may recall Sri Ramakrishna's attitude towards the cancer in the throat from which he died, Saint Bernadette of Lourdes' attitude towards her painful lingering and fatal disease of consumption, Ramana Maharshi's fatalism about his bodily pains and ailments, and Sri Aurobindo's reply to the physician who attended him for a broken knee after a fall: "How is it that you, a Mahatma, could not foresee and prevent this accident?" "I still have to carry this human body about me and it is subject to ordinary human limitations and physical laws."(P)

59

With time, the body deteriorates, its youth and beauty vanish, its health becomes uncertain or, worse, precarious. The young Gautama, over-whelmed by this sudden realization, sought in the mind a better and more lasting condition.

60

The vain delusion that death will have no power over the prophet, and over those followers who faithfully practise the prophet's teaching, has appeared in modern times in Western as well as Oriental mystical circles.

61

Even Gandhi shared and propagated the view that a sinless man would necessarily have a perfectly healthy body. When, later, he suffered from appendicitis, he blamed his own failure to control passion and thought for its appearance.

62

If he can succeed in refusing to identify himself with the suffering body, he will not suffer with it.

63

When Buddha's favorite disciple, Ananda, remarked that his master no longer looked so fine and well as formerly, Buddha replied with the instruction: "Thus it is Ananda that upon youth follows age, upon health sickness, and upon life death."

64

The Buddha himself could not escape from suffering various illnesses; H.P. Blavatsky was a notorious sufferer of the most painful maladies; and even Mrs. Eddy herself suffered from pneumonia in her old age, although her illness was kept secret.

65

All the high-sounding babble will not remove the stark fact staring them in the face; all the glib consolatory theorizing will not waft away the terrible spectacle of the guru stricken by cancer.

66

Because he is not a hatha yogi he will feel the pain of his body when it suffers, but he will also feel that the pain is itself enclosed by a sea of serenity. The ordinary man feels the pain alone. The philosopher feels both the pain and its antidote—Being.

67

Such is our ignorance that we weep when one man, who is weary with age, escapes from his body, and we perform a dismal ceremony of lament when another man, tired with sickness, separates himself from it. We pretend to believe in God, in a Mind infinitely wise, and yet we have not learned to accept death as a wise event in nature and one as proper as birth. These cults which seek to perpetuate earthly life thereby question the divine wisdom and reveal their own materialistic and egoistic attachments.

68

The attainment of spiritual consciousness does not automatically bring with it the attainment of healing powers, any more than it brings mathematical powers or musical powers.

69

The fallacy that the body is automatically healed of its diseases when the mind is healed of its ignorance, needs to be exposed because it is so specious and so attractive.

70

I prefer to take truth from Buddha rather than from Mrs. Eddy. As against her claim that Christian Science could demonstrate immortality in the flesh, Buddha declared: "That which, whether conscious or unconscious, is not subject to decay and death, that you will not find."

71

It is a curious bifurcated kind of consciousness where he is aware of what the body is suffering but where he can also feel the support of infinite peace at his centre. Thus both pain and peace are within it.

72

Shomo believed it until the very moment that he was killed in a carriage accident in 1871. Benjamin Purnell's cult, the House of David, held to the same silly idea until he was thrown into jail for disgusting crimes and his following fell away. Father Divine claimed to be approaching one hundred years of age and to be exempt from mortal death. The deaths of these leaders were unexpected to the followers, and sometimes even to themselves. Thomas Lake Harris, who founded the community "Brotherhood of the New Life," maintained this delusion until the very year of his own death at the beginning of the century. Mary Baker Eddy taught it as a truth but failed, in her own terminology, to "demonstrate" it when she too died soon after Frederick Howland, leader of the little sect Adonai.

73

"I had a joyous certainty that deafness and blindness were not an essential part of my existence since they were not in any way a part of my immortal mind."—Helen Keller in *Midstream*, her autobiography

74

When Ramana Maharshi was stricken with cancer, his resident disciples were dismayed. When he died in agony, they were stunned.

75

Do these yogic dignitaries contradict each other? "Physical health is essential for true spirituality," says Bhagat Singh Thind, a contemporary Sikh-Indian lecturer and teacher of yoga in the U.S.A. Yogananda, who claimed to have been granted the title of *Paramahamsa* (Great Master) by his guru, stated flatly in one of his lessons on Self-Realization: "The presence of God cannot be felt while the darkness of overpowering disease prevails." Yet Sri Ramana Maharshi, suffering from a fatal cancer, affirmed the contrary and declared the body to be nothing.

76

King Milinda said: "You have declared that the Arhats feel no pain of mind though they are all subject to pain of body, but does not the mind subsist because of the body? Is the Arhat without authority, mastery, or supremacy over the body?"

Nagasena replied: "It is even so."

Milinda said: "This does not appear to be right. Even a bird has authority over his nest."

Nagasena said: "There are ten things that in every birth accompany the body, namely: 1. *Varna* (colour) 2. *Tapa* (heat) 3. *Khuda* (hunger) 4. *Thrisna* (thirst) 5. *Mala* (feces) 6. *Mutra* (urine) 7. *Nidra* (sleep) 8. *Vadi* (disease) 9. *Khaya* (decay) 10. *Mritya* (death). Over these ten an Arhat exercises no power."

Milinda said: "Will you kindly explain to me how it is that this occurs?"
Nagasena said: "Because of the earth all beings exist, the earth cannot be commanded by all these things. In like manner, because of the body the mind exists, the mind cannot command or control the body."

Milinda said: "Why is it that an ordinary person suffers both bodily and mental pain, unlike the Arhat, who suffers only bodily pain?"

Nagasena said: "Because there has been no accomplishment of Vidarsana and other exercises by which the mind is brought into subjection. There is a hungry bull that is tied only by a small withe which it breaks in its anger and then runs away. In the same way, when the mind is not under discipline, it becomes irritated, breaks away from fear and the voice of sorrow; thus there is pain both of body and mind. But the mind of the Arhat is under proper discipline; it does not disturb the body; it is bound as to a pleasure of Nirvana, and the Arhat is therefore free from the pain of mind, whilst he is still subject to the pain of the body."

Milinda said: "But would it not be a thing to be esteemed as a wonder if when the body is quieted or agitated, the mind were to remain tranquil? Kindly explain to me how this can be."

Nagasena said: "The branches of a tree are shaken by the wind but the trunk remains unmoved. In like manner as the mind of the Arhat is bound to the firm pillar of Samadhi by the cord of the Four Paths, it remains unmoved even when the body is suffering pain."

77

Even in the midst of bodily sufferings, he will still keep and not lose this beautiful serenity of mind. And he is able to do so precisely because he is able to differentiate the flesh from the mind. Inevitably, it must counteract, even though it may not obliterate, the body's pain.

78

Pain and suffering, sin and evil, disease and death, exist only in the world of thoughts, not in the world of pure Thought itself. They are not illusions, however, but they are transient. Whoever attains to pure Thought will also attain *in consciousness* to a life that is painless, sorrow-free, sinless, undecaying, and undying. Being above desires and fears, it is necessarily above the miseries caused by unsatisfied desires and realized fears. But at the same time he will also have an *accompanying* consciousness of life in the body, which must obey the laws of its own being, natural laws which set limitations and imperfections upon it. This much can be said to be the element of truth contained in some theoretical doctrines of Vedantic Advaita and Christian Science.(P)

2

THE UNIVERSAL LIFE-FORCE

There is a single source of Life which envelops the universe and pervades man. By its presence in himself he is able to exist physically and function mentally.

2

That Power which brought the body into existence originally maintains its involuntary functions, cures its diseases, and heals its wounds. It is within the body itself; it is the life-force aspect of the Soul, the Overself. Its curative virtue may express itself through various mediums—as herbs and foods, hot, cold, or mud baths, and deep breathings, exercise, and osteopathy—or it may express itself by their complete absence as in fasting, often the quickest and most effective medium. Or, disdaining physical methods entirely, it may act directly and almost miraculously as spiritual healing.(P)

3

The role of physical treatments of any kind is to supply favourable conditions for the action of the universal life-force which does the real healing work, just as food, water, and air supply materials to this same force for the repair of tissue and the regeneration of cells.

4

If it is the heart's activity which enables the whole body to exist and carry out its function in the world, it is the life-force's activity which enables the heart to carry out its function in the body.

5

The body has its own natural intelligence which serves it when the skin is cut or the flesh is wounded, coagulating the blood and forming new tissue. This intelligence heals, repairs, and re-energizes, provided you put no obstructions in its way through wrong diet, excessive activity, or bad habits.

6

Nature is an expression of the Universal Mind. The plants are given to us for medicine or food. It is an insult to Nature to despise these remedies.

7

The physical body attracts solar energies from the surrounding atmosphere, and vital elements from food, air, and water, and incorporates them into itself. This gives it the force whereby its limbs make their movements. But the ultimate sustaining strength is derived from the Overself.

8

It is this intelligent life-force which regulates the hair's growth, keeps the body at an even temperature, and regulates contracting and expanding of the lungs. Man does not do these things consciously or ordinarily, but the force is well able to take care of them.

9

The life-force comes into play automatically when healing is required, but we put so much obstruction in its path that we prolong the disease until it may become chronic.

10

The belief that the body is permeated by a power which heals it when sick was accepted by the Greeks before Christ. The medical man's role is to co-operate with this power.

11

Just as there is one process in the body which decays it with the years and ultimately destroys it, so there is another process which beneficently recuperates and even heals it.

12

After all and in the end, it is Nature which brought us to birth on this planet. Can we not therefore credit her with the power of restoring the health needful to maintain the lives she has taken the trouble to originate?

13

Nature not only soothes troubled minds but heals troubled bodies. She provides them with curative herbs, barks, waters, rays, leaves—the woods are sanitariums.

14

The psychic poisons resulting from civilized man's excessive, exciting, and ego-stimulating activities must be treated on different levels, the antidotes being sleep, mental quiet, diet, rest, and relaxation.

15

The life-force displays one remarkable effect during sleep: it not only recuperates the body but—as in the cases of Napoleon and General Douglas MacArthur—keeps the body strong and tough even though never exercised. For these two men possessed the uncommon power of being able to fall asleep within a minute or two at will.

16

Incubation is the old term applied to the sleeping in a temple—usually a special shrine or sanctuary used for healing and healing-dreams and dream-oracles alone—as a means of healing. This was practised by ancient Greeks and Babylonians. It was also frequently practised in ancient Egypt at the temples of Isis and Serapis with effects similar to those of hypnotism. Five hundred years before Christ at the temple of Epidaurus, where the inspiring spirit or god was Aesculapius (the patron saint of modern medicine still), sick patients were put to sleep by priests at the foot of Aesculapius' statue. In many cases, they awoke suddenly cured.

17

That the real effectiveness of incubation was not the work of a departed spirit but of Nature in the sleep state combined with the sufferer's faith, was shown by the custom which still prevails in Greece. Here sleep in a temple of Aesculapius was simply replaced by sleep in the church associated with a Christian saint.

18

Consider a cut hand and how Nature at once sets to work to repair the damage. The anatomist tells us that the leucocytes in the blood automatically build a bridge of tissue over the wound's surface. But what orders the leucocytes to make the needed adjustment? What shows them how to make it? There is obviously an intelligence behind them, a mind within the body outside and apart from the conscious mind.

19

There are no miracles in Nature, but there are happenings to which science possesses no key. The human consciousness, for instance, is capable of manifesting powers which contradict psychological knowledge, just as the human body is capable of manifesting phenomena which contradict medical knowledge. Both powers and phenomena may seem miraculous, but they really issue forth from the hidden laws of man's own being. The processes take place in the dark only to us.(P)

The vital body

20

This life-force, this invisible energy, is behind and within, around and above the physical body. Under certain circumstances its area can be seen and traced out and its recuperative healing power drawn upon. It forms an aura, the etheric or vital body of light, but not the still more elusive and subtle divine body of Light nor the aura of various colours, the astral body.

21

The life-principle is a nonmaterial reality which manifests as the aura in which the physical body is immersed. It keeps vital organs and vital parts in condition and activity until it vanishes at death and merges with the astral (mental-emotional) form instead. It can also manifest electromagnetically.

22

What are the "higher bodies"? Just as man has a physical body with which to operate in the physical world, so he has a vital body, an emotional body, and a mental body through which to express these other parts of his nature. This is the teaching of Theosophists, Hindus, and occultists. These bodies survive the death of the physical body, but are reduced to seed atoms when, between incarnations, man passes into a state of happy dreamless slumber. But from the philosophical viewpoint, the "higher bodies" are simply thought bodies, or, more correctly, states of consciousness.

23

The body's health or sickness shows only the surface of what is happening: the inner man is concerned with it too. His thought, feeling, attitude, and action—his whole character—reflect it. But the inner man is unseen; hence only fragments get known. For there lies the aura where causes precede the physical effects. Only now in recent years has the aura been clearly photographed, both in black and white and on colour film.

24

Just as a particular body may reject someone else's surgically transplanted organ, so a particular aura may reject someone else's as it impinges in close contact. Repulsion will be strongly felt.

25

Some aura of the owner clings to much-used and much-worn objects.

26

If the physical body has a limb amputated, the etheric body remains whole. If an eye is removed, the etheric eye remains untouched, whole.

27

Behind, within, and around the physical body there is another and invisible body which we may call the vital body. This is a kind of archetype or pattern for the physical body. On several points they coincide, but not on others. This subtler etheric body comes into existence before actual birth and remains for a while after actual death. During incarnation it is closely connected with the physical body and especially with its vitality, health, and sickness. The part of it which surrounds the physical body and which we may call the vital aura should not be confused with the other and larger aura wherein emotions and thoughts are reflected. During experiments which I made with a group of London physicians before the war, it was found that this vital aura extended for about forty-five centimetres beyond the physical body. When the vital aura was in a devitalized, fatigued condition, there was less resistance to sickness; but when it was energized the resistance increased. The life-force which we draw from the universal life-force enters into the vital body. Resistance can be increased by deep breathing, by exercise, and by imagining the life-force as a white light entering through the head and penetrating downwards into every cell of the physical body. This also helps the healing process in sickness. Not only are the cells permeated by these methods, but they are also purified.(P)

Nature's healing power

28

The body does not function blindly like some machine. On the contrary, it is an expression of the divine wisdom and the divine power, which are taking care of every cell within it from head to toe. If the personal ego, with its materialistic ignorance and blind desires, did not wilfully or unknowingly interfere with the body's natural operation in health and in sickness, we would have much less trouble with it. Even so, despite the constant interference of the ego, the body is still a remarkable tribute to the wisdom and power inherent within it.

29

The healing powers of Nature truly exist, quite apart from the medical powers evoked by physicians, but they exist like electricity. To benefit by them we must draw them, focus them, and concentrate them on ourselves. This is done by our strong and sufficient faith, by our own concentration of attention, and by our relaxing and stilling of the whole being.

30

He will feel the Power moving through the flesh of his arm and hand, tingling in his fingers. He will feel the victorious attitude permeating his mind.

31

Because there is such peace revealed by the body, speech, and movements, wrinkles come slower to his face, if at all.

32

The modern man suffers from a certain physical sickness and some mental ailments which are of his own making. This is because his thoughts are forever centering in his personal ego, his emotions forever revolving round his little self. He can help to free himself from the one and heal himself of the other if he will create an oasis in this desert by daily and purposely withdrawing into the impersonal atmosphere of the higher nature.

33

What is the real power that works these cures? Who is competent to probe these workings and explain them accurately?

34

The wonderful truth of reality hidden behind the illusion of this mortal world was the greatest and grandest discovery of Mrs. Eddy; but the belief that the finding of this reality would automatically bring perfect health and give power to bring perfect health to others was her illusion. No Adept who knows what reality is ever regards physical healings or physical miracles as being other than illusion, because he knows whence they proceed. He knows that the powers which work such miracles are hidden and latent powers of the human mind, and not of the divine self, and that you can awaken these powers by concentration or by yoga—if you concentrate deeply enough.

35

The first principle of healing is to stop the obstructive resistance of the little ego so carried away by the belief that it can successfully manage its own life. The method of doing this is to cast out all negative thoughts, all destructive feelings, and all excessive egoisms. The second principle is to attune the individual to the universal life-force. The method of doing this is to learn the art of relaxing body and mind.

36

The life-principle in man can certainly heal his body, but the faulty conditions in that body which he must put right can be put right only by himself. That is his share of the therapeutic work, and not the life-principle's. That is where he must give it his co-operation. If he expects it to do everything, and is too ignorant or indolent to do his part, he may get the healing but it cannot be more than an imperfect one.

37

If he succeeds in arousing the "Spirit-Energy" he may direct it, if he chooses, toward defective bodily structures or toward faulty organic functions. This will effectually supplement whatever remedial agent is being used and perhaps even supplant it.

38

How few have learned that it is not the quantity of medicine they swallow but the degree of contact with Nature's life-force that they establish which cures their diseases.

39

The same power which can illuminate the seeking mind can also heal the suffering body.

40

The practical method which is here presented differs radically from the method of the Christian Scientists, although a superficial reading may give the impression of similarity. The Christian Scientist *asserts* his inner nature to be divine and a part of God, but the assertion remains a mere intellectual statement unless he has previously opened up a channel to that inner nature with the tool of meditation, prayer, or aspiration. If he has done this, then the assertion rises into the realm of reality and may produce remarkable results; if he has not succeeded in doing this, then his assertion remains mere words, one thought out of the multitude which pass and repass through the brain of man. Moreover, so long as he possesses false notions of what constitutes "demonstration," so long as he thinks that he is *entitled* to prosperity, good health, and other desirable worldly things because of his spirituality, so long will he find—as so many Christian Scientists do find—that his successes alternate with startling failures. It would be an unpleasant task to illustrate this statement with instances of such failures, not in the rank and file, but in the foremost ranks of the Christian Scientists, and I shall not attempt it. These failures indicate that we must follow no narrow track of sect-ordained thought, but do some research on our own account.

41

It is a dramatic fact that remedial changes may take place in the organs themselves under the influence of this healing force.

42

The more he comes into harmony with the cosmic order, the more will his health and strength benefit, his thoughts and feelings become positive. But this is not to say that he will be cured of existing maladies or be kept in perfect health. Harmony means that due regard and attention will be given to the body's importance, hygiene, care, and correct feeding. It means that the thoughts and feelings will be constructive.

43

Nature's healing power will do its own work upon the sick body if not obstructed by man's foolish methods. Sometimes it will do this best if left entirely alone—as when he rests in bed and fasts from food. At other times it will be quicker and more effective if assisted by man's intelligent methods.

Exercises and meditations

44

It is possible to direct the healing power of the white light, in imagination and with deep breathing, to any part of the body where pain is felt or to any organ which is not functioning properly. This does not instantly remove the trouble, but it does make a contribution towards the healing process.

45

Amid the tumult of ego-directed thoughts and feelings, the distress brought on by an adverse circumstance which the ego has not been able to endure or set right can be lessened and relieved by relaxing, letting go, pausing, lying physically and mentally still, whether in a prayer for inner peace or a simple meditation, but in any case turning the affair over to the higher power as a sign of having let go. Such temporary withdrawal gives the Overself its chance to break through the ego's crust and to bring its ministering peace, help, guidance, or healing.

46

If you want to heal a man do not concentrate upon the nature of his disease, or you may strengthen it. Concentrate rather upon the nature of his Overself, that its mighty grace may be released to him. Do not even pray that he will be cured. Pray rather that the power of the Overself's grace may work within him, and do what it will.

47

The nape of the neck is one of these important—physically sensitive— centres. It can receive through the hand-touch of a healer the magnetism which affects the health condition.

48

The Arab physicians use the prolonged fast treatment for advanced syphilis; the Hindu fakirs use mud packs for it. Thus both turn to Mother Nature, and do not always turn in vain.

49

After he has felt the divine power and presence within himself as the reward of his meditative search, he may turn it towards the healing of his body's ailments. This would be impossible if he were less than relaxed, peaceful, assured, if either fear or desire introduced their negative presence and thus obstructed his receptivity to the healing-power's penetration. When the contact is successfully made, he should draw the power to every atom of his body and let it be permeated. The cure could be had at a single treatment, if he could sit still and let the work go on to completion. But although the power is unlimited, his patience is not. And so he must treat himself day after day until the outer and physical result matches the inner and spiritual achievement.(P)

50

Healing Exercise and Meditation: (1) Lie flat on back on flat surface (for example, rug on floor). (2) Let body go completely limp. (3) Relax breathing with eyes shut, that is, slow down breathing below normal. Slowly exhale, then inhale; hold breath two seconds, then exhale slowly again. Repeat for three to five minutes. While inhaling, think that you are drawing in curative force from Nature. While exhaling, think that there is being taken out of your body the ill condition. (Note that on the inhaled breath, you—the ego—are referred to as the active agent, whereas in the exhaled breath this is not so and the change is being effected spontaneously.) (4) Let go all personal problems. (5) Reflect on the existence of the soul which is you, and on the infinite life-power surrounding you and in which you dwell and live. (6) Lie with arms outstretched and palms open, so as to draw in life-force either through palms or through head. (This makes contact with higher power through silent meditation, and it draws on the reconstructive and healing life-force attribute of this power.) Draw it into yourself. Let it distribute itself over the entire body. Let its omnintelligence direct it to where it is most needed, whether that be the affected part or some other part that is the first cause of the sickness. (7) Place hands on affected part of body and deliberately direct force through hands to body. A feeling of warmth should be noticeable in palms of hands. (8) Recollect through imagination the all-pervading sense of God and his infinite goodness.(P)

51

Healing Exercise: Inhale deeply but slowly and unhurriedly. With each breath fix the mind in the life-essence pouring in and permeating each part of the body until the whole of it is bathed and held by the stream.

52

Healing Exercise: Hold the thought that all these countless cells which compose your anatomy shall receive this transmuted energy. Along with the concentration inhale deeply, hold the breath, and exhale for an equal amount of time.

53

Acupuncture is a valid acceptable body of knowledge and skill, new only here but not in the ancient Far East. It should be allowed to integrate itself with our own scientific modern knowledge and medical techniques. There are still other techniques worth learning in most Oriental lands.

54

The medicines used in homeopathy include biochemical preparations—that is, minerals—which are generally beneficial, and, as with all homeopathic medicines, need a longer time to work their effects. Among them, there is kali mur, which is useful for colds in the nose, the throat, and the ears. There is natrum mur, which is useful against hives. Such medicines should be mixed with water and swallowed a few times during the day if they are in powder form. If, however, they are in tablet form, they should be dissolved very, very slowly in the mouth.

55

I have often suggested the use of eucalyptus oil, well diluted with warm water, to prevent colds or relieve their beginnings. The diluted oil can be applied externally to the nose and throat, or inhaled by increasing the temperature of the water. It is also useful as an excellent antiseptic for urinary troubles, against mosquitoes, and in other ways.

56

Before attempting to practise magnetic healing, expel the air from the lungs a few times in order to purify them. Only then should you apply the hands near to or nearly touching the patient, or the affected part of your own body.

57

The healing Light seen in vision is bluish-white.

58

As the Egyptian priests knew and as the Greek physicians believed, mental concentration upon symmetrical geometric patterns may help the healers work physically and the patient himself emotionally.

59

If, during the prayer or meditation, he succeeds in lifting himself above his ordinary level and the healing vibration begins to respond, he may find the change signaled by a gentle inner shifting.

60

In the moment when you feel that actual contact with the One Infinite Life-Power has been made, draw it into the body and let it permeate every part, every organ, and every atom. It will tend to dissolve sickness and drive out disease.

61

When visiting Perth, Western Australia, I was told about an interesting case. The wife of a local government scientist had had several operations for cancer until one buttock was almost entirely cut away. But she remained uncured. In despair she decided to invoke higher healing power and practised the sun-gazing exercise (which she had read in *The Wisdom of the Overself*) every day for a year. At the end of this period the doctors pronounced her cured.

62

Direct treatment of the patient is not the only way a healer uses. Absent treatment is also effective. The healing power can cross oceans and traverse continents as readily and as speedily as can radio waves or thought. Telepathy is a fact and the basis of this operation.

63

The ministrations of absent healing are most successful when the patient is passive and receptive to them. Hence the work of its power is most effective when the sufferer is sleeping or relaxing.

64

In the Orient the yogi's touch is deemed a beneficent thing, and many a time while out walking with one in a village I have had to stop as he paused to permit passers-by to touch his feet. The English had a somewhat similar tradition in medieval and even later times, though it was the king who then held "divine power" and it was his hand which bestowed the benediction. The ceremony of touching is taken very seriously in the Orient, and more than once I was reminded of cynical King William III, who would bestow the following gratuitous prayer upon his subjects as he touched them: "May God give you better health and more sense!"

65

After he has done what medical authorities—both orthodox and unorthodox—recommend, or what he may have been guided to do from within, he should place his sick friends or relatives in the hands of God without further anxiety concerning their condition.

66

Nor is it always needful for the healer to see the patient or person; the latter may be cured by correspondence alone.

67

Since this Power is everywhere present and since one's mind can touch the mind of another even though he be far away, use this period of contact to help anyone whom you wish to benefit. You can help him spiritually or you can even help him physically—the distance will not stop the working of the Power flowing through you to him. To what extent your help will go depends on more than one factor and therefore cannot be predicted. It may be little or much.

68

Hindu religion worships light in its intensest form—the sun. The Hindu holy men say that the sun-bath is good for the body; if taken when its rays are mild—that is, at dawn and at dusk—it can cure the body of many diseases. They further claim this practice will re-absorb the semen into the blood stream and thus strengthen the physical body.

69

Homeopathy uses poisons—such as aconite, belladonna, strychnine, and calomel. Hence it represents the dark principle. Also, why does it go out of its way to create the symptoms of disease?

70

Self-healing Relaxation Technique: Allow at least about twenty minutes to a half hour for this practice each day, but you should continue for a much longer period if the desire or capacity for it arises. Select a time of day when you can be alone, free from disturbances, and when you are free from emotional reactions to any personal matters other than this need of being cured. It would be useless to treat these instructions in a merely superficial and external way, for then they could be followed and finished in about sixty seconds. There are two prerequisites that must be satisfied for these instructions to be effective. First, the whole of one's mind and feeling should be concentrated on each of their separate parts as unfolded in each sentence. Second, it is essential that you should not leave any part and pass on to the next one before you have fully soaked yourself in and surrendered yourself to it. There must be no haste.

(1) *Posture*: Assume supine posture, lie flat on your back on a couch, completely limp, no tenseness in the body, entirely comfortable, quiet, and relax all muscles from head to foot. Merely lying down is not enough; loosen also the muscles in your lips, eyes, and hands. Close the eyes.

(2) *Breathing*: Concentrate on the rhythm of breathing for a couple of minutes. Give it all your attention for this period until you are so immersed as to become unified with it. While concentrating, make the inhalation and exhalation breaths of equal duration. They should be long deep

slow and even, not jerky and not strained. This slowing down of respiration should result in a lessening of tension.

(3) *Making contact on the physical level*: Begin to think of and dwell upon the One Infinite Life-Power, filling all space and pervading the entire universe, existing everywhere, containing and permeating all creatures, all humanity, including one's self. Accept and stress its existence. Next call on its help, then concentrate on the idea of its recuperative power, which develops and sustains every cell of the body from birth, heals its wounds and knits its broken bones, for your own case.

(4) *Treating the body*: Imagine this Power to be flowing into you as a White Light. Mentally draw the current into the body, through the forehead, the palms, and the solar plexus. Lastly, bring it to the diseased part of the body needing healing and concentrate it there. Place a hand lightly over this part and bathe both hands and affected part with the White Light, trying to feel this intensely, for about two minutes. Forget the rest of the body, and hold full intense attention here. Then with the mind's eye, forget the sick part. Become relaxed again, letting the Light immerse in and distribute itself throughout the entire body.

(5) *Reaching to the soul*: Think of the whole body as being a manifestation of Creative Intelligence and as a projection of the higher self. Next regard it as a perfect thought in the World-Mind. Finally forget it entirely. Lift consciousness above the plane of the physical world. Immerse thought in the concept of the higher self alone, forgetting its projected personal self. Next, empty the mind as far as possible of all thoughts and seek inward sacred stillness.

(6) *Supplementary work*: (a) At fixed or odd times during the day he stops the pressure of life and people on himself and learns by repeated recollection to remain consciously relaxed throughout the day, even if it be only for a minute or two. (b) Whenever possible, take off five minutes every hour for relaxation practice at fixed times.

71

"I practised the self-healing technique for some weeks before going into the hospital. Faith is essential and I had it in full. I prayed for strength and later saw a great white light—heard beautiful voices calling. I passed consciously out of the body—falling into deep sleep for several hours. I awoke refreshed and was pronounced cured by the amazed physicians. Since then I feel sustained, guided, and protected by a higher power." This was related to me by a woman who suffered from terribly destructive diseases. When she first approached me she was on the verge of suicide.

72
Exercise I: To Relieve Tension and Cultivate Relaxation

(a) Sit upright on a chair of comfortable height, with the knees and legs together, if comfortable, or slightly apart if not. Lean slightly forward, keeping the spine straight, and allow both the arms to hang down full length and lifeless, like heavy weights, from the shoulders completely relaxed.

(b) Both hands are then lifted very slowly at the elbows, almost to shoulder height, then abruptly dropped, palms upright, on the upper thighs. Keep the feeling of limpness and heaviness in the arms, with the lower part of the body utterly relaxed.

(c) Picture an ethereal aura of pure, white, electrifying Light all around you. Then, imagine this magnificent Light is actually pulling you upright by the top of your head. Its compelling force should, as a result, automatically straighten the spine, and the back of your trunk, neck, and head form a perfectly erect line. Finally, imagine the Light is pervading inside the whole of your body.

This exercise should give a feeling of physical refreshment and complete physical relaxation. It is also useful when having to listen to lengthy talks, lectures, and so on, or when reluctantly trying to practise meditation after a fatiguing day.

Exercise II: To Promote Harmony

Repeat Exercise I, then add:

(a) Try to see and feel that the aura of Light has an actual substance and that It is becoming part of you, that you are melting into It, becoming one with It. Next, think of it as being the pure essence of Love, especially in the region of the heart.

(b) When this Love has been experienced as a sensation of heart-melting happiness, let it then extend outwards to embrace all the world.

This exercise should give a feeling of being in harmony with Nature, the universe, with all living beings, and with humanity as a part of Nature.

Exercise III: To Heal Sickness

Repeat Exercises I and II, then add:

(a) Think of the white Light as being Nature's intelligent and recuperative Life-Force.

(b) Let it pour in, through the top of your head, passing directly to the solar plexus centre, which is the region which must first be worked on and affected if the healing force is to become efficacious. Thence send it to any afflicted area, remaining there. Feel Its benevolent, restorative, and healing presence working upon it.

(c) *In order to be fully effective this exercise must be accompanied by intense faith in the recuperative powers of this Light.*

Astonishing proof of its effectiveness in relieving a troubled organ or curing a diseased part of the body, when persevered in for a sufficient period of weeks or months, has been clearly shown by results. In some cases, paralytics have regained full use of their disabled limbs by following the outline given here.

Exercise IV: To Establish Telepathic Harmony or Help

Repeat Exercise I, II, and III(a), then add:

(a) Let the White Light enter the region of the heart, remaining there.

(b) Form a mental image of the face of the individual you wish to contact, and reduce it in size until it is small enough to fit into the palm of your hand.

(c) Place this tiny image in the centre of the white Light permeating your heart.

(d) Endeavour actually to *see* the individual there in your heart. This exercise should be used to promote physical or mental help to a distant friend, to bring about goodwill from one who has expressed enmity, or to establish a deeper spiritual relationship. It is also useful in the student-teacher relationship, because it promotes better sympathy and affinity, as well as strengthening the telepathic link.

Note: Where imagination is well developed the attempt to visualize light may be used, but where either the intellectual or the instinctive preponderates over it, the attempt need not be made—only the unseen power invoked and directed by faith.

3

THE ORIGINS OF ILLNESS

The karma of the body

There is certainly evidence to indicate that man is dependent on his physical nature. There is also metaphysical evidence which reveals that the body is strongly influenced by the psyche. Materialist medicos are right so far as they go, but they cannot explain why such-and-such a person has a particular kind of physique, for example, which metaphysics can and does. That reason lies in former incarnations where concentration upon the present form took place. The quality of thought, plus the capacity to rise above it, are special keys to this problem.

2

All diseases are not, however, caused by soul illness. Destiny looms more largely in this matter than any physician is likely to admit, although it is equally true in the long run that man is the arbiter of his own fate, that the real self bestows every boon or ill upon its fragmentary expression, the personality, and bestows them with a just impersonal hand. But I must be content to leave the explanation of such a seeming paradox for another place and another time. Suffice it to hint that the *past* of individual men is infinitely more extended than is apparent at first glance.

3

As he penetrates deeper and deeper into that subtle world of his inner being, he finds that thought, feeling, and even speech affect its condition as powerfully as outer conditions affect his physical being. A complete falsehood or a gross exaggeration, when conscious and deliberate, stuns or inflames the delicate psyche. If persisted in and made habitual, the psyche becomes diseased and falls sick. This may be followed, soon or late according to the sensitivity of the man, by physical sickness. If sickness does not come, then he will be exposed to it in the form of a karma shadowing some future incarnation.

4

Where there is no obvious transgression of the laws of bodily hygiene to account for a case of ill health, there may still be a hidden one not yet uncovered. Where there is no hidden one, the line of connection from a physical effect may be traced to a mental cause—that is, the sickness may be a psychosomatic one. Where this in turn is also not obvious, there may still be a hidden mental one. Where all these classes of cause do not exist, then the origin of the sickness must necessarily be derived from the karma of the previous reincarnation—sometimes even from a still earlier one, although that is less likely. Under the law of recompense, the very type of body with which the patient was born contains latently, and was predisposed to reveal eventually, the sickness itself. The cause may be any one of widely varying kinds, may even be a moral transgression in the earlier life which could not find any other way of expiation and so had to be expiated in this way. Therefore it would be an error to believe that all cases of ill health directly arise from the transgression of physical hygienic laws.

5

It is possible to be quite enlightened without being quite free from physical maladies. For the body's karma does not end until the body's life ends.

6

It is hardly true that the attainment of spiritual consciousness automatically brings perfect health, only partly true that it brings better health, and only in certain cases does it do even that. The present-day human body too often has a toxic condition and a poisoned environment. The spiritual disciplines for attainment purify body and mind, thus leading to less sickness. It will not be until a future and better race of humanity has worked out these bad qualities and created a purer environment that a state of perfect health will be actualized.

7

In a broad general division, philosophy finds three causes of sickness. They are wrong thinking, wrong living, and bad karma. But because karma merely brings back to us the results of the other two, we may even limit the causes of disease to them. And again because conduct is ultimately the expression of thought, we may limit the cause of disease finally to a single one of wrong thinking. But this is to deal with the matter in a metaphysical, abstract, and ultimate way. It is best when dealing with sickness in a practical way to keep to the threefold analysis of possible causes. Yet the matter must not be oversimplified as certain schools of unorthodox healing have oversimplified it, for the thinking which produced the sickness may belong to the far past, to some earlier reincarnation, and not necessarily to the present one, or it may belong to the earlier years of the present incarnation. In those cases, there is the fruit of an unknown earlier sowing, not necessarily of a known present one. Therefore, it may not be enough merely to alter one's present mode of thought to insure the immediate obliteration of the sickness. If we shoot a bullet in the wrong direction, we cannot control its course once it has left the gun. But we can change the direction of a second shot if we realize our error. We can continue our efforts, however, to change our first thinking, to get rid of negative harmful thoughts and feelings and thus improve our character. For if we do this, the type of physical karma manifesting as the sickness which they create will at least not come to us in the future, even if we cannot avoid inheriting it in the present from our former lives. Study of this picture would reveal what sickness as a karma of wrong thinking really means and why it often cannot be healed by a mere change of present thought alone. The proof of this statement lies in the fact that some people are born with certain sicknesses or with liability to certain diseases, or else acquire them as infants or as children before they have even had the opportunity to think wrongly at all and while they are still in a state of youthful innocence and purity of thought. Therefore it is not the wrong thoughts of this present incarnation which could have brought on such sickness in their case. Nor can it be correct to suggest that they have inherited these sicknesses, for the parents may be right-thinking and high-living people. By depriving themselves of faith in the belief in successive lives on earth, the Christian Scientists deprive themselves of a more satisfactory explanation of the problem of sickness than the one they have. They say that it was caused by wrong thinking, and yet they cannot say how it is that a baby or a child has been thinking wrongly to have been born with or to have acquired at an early age a sickness for which it is not responsible and for which its parents are not responsible.(P)

8

It might be said that most *organic* physical disease is karmically caused and most functional physical sickness is mentally caused.(P)

9

The recognition that he is a victim of serious disease embitters one man but humbles another. Which of these two effects will arise depends on his past life-experience and present mentality.

10

It is said that Ramakrishna died because he took on the karma of others. This is also offered by some disciples as an explanation of why Ramana Maharshi, like Ramakrishna, died of cancer. But the truth about this matter is not known; only opinions and theories about it prevail.

11

Deep hurts and bitter experiences from a former unknown incarnation throw their shadows on the present one.

12

Some are aroused from their thraldom to sexual slavery, or to dietetic sensuality, by the sudden descent of illness, trouble, or impending disaster. From this suffering they derive some strength to amend their ways.

13

Plotinus was born in Egypt, studied with Ammonius Saccas, planned to travel to Persia and India, but was brought by fate to Rome instead. There he passed his life, writing and lecturing with great success on Neoplatonism. He was a sage, an ascetic, and a rapt concentrated genius. Yet why was he so often sick? He could not care for his own body, could not do like his near-contemporaries Jesus Christ and Apollonius of Tyana did—heal his own body.

14

The man who follows an evil course habitually and determinedly must one day suffer a moral and emotional and mental collapse.

15

Another cause of illness is that God sends us tests and ordeals on this path, which may take the form of illness. But in that case we emerge spiritually stronger and wiser, if they are passed, and so benefit.

16

There is no inevitability of physical suffering on this path generally, but there is for certain individuals. Karma comes down more plentifully at certain times for certain aspirants, but as mind and body are highly interrelated, this is offset by the purification of body and emotions. Hence students need not be afraid of this. Again, spiritual healing is a real fact, but it works in a mysterious way dependent on divine grace; but here also it applies only to certain individuals.

17

The karmic relation between undisciplined passion and physical disease is obvious in the sphere of sex. It is not so obvious in other spheres.

18

It is a mistake to believe that because any art of healing—whether it be a material or a spiritual one—is able to heal a particular kind of sickness once, it is consequently able to heal all similar cases of sickness by its own merits. Forces outside it have something to do with the matter. There are some cases where failure by material methods is preordained by the higher power of destiny. There are others where failure by spiritual methods is also inevitable, because the heart of the sick man has not been touched. As elsewhere, there are limits to human effort set here by certain laws.

19

Disease may re-emerge again at some later time, or if it doesn't, it will do so in the next birth. We are not saying here however that all sickness and all disease are caused by wrong thinking in this present reincarnation but that some of them are. How great or how small that part is depends entirely upon the individuals concerned. With some, it is a very high proportion, with others it is a small one. In the former case, therefore, we must look back to anterior lives for the wrong thought or wrong conduct which produced the sickness of the present physical body as bad karma.

20

Although Mary Baker Eddy—of whom I am a great admirer—was quite correct in saying that the Real Self is free from sickness, pain, and suffering, the simple denial—by the individual—of these obviously present symptoms will often fail to banish them. Philosophy takes a broader view: it does not attempt to deny the undeniable. It recognizes that all prolonged or intense suffering, being karmically self-earned—whether in this lifetime or in a former one—carries with it a message. This message must be learned and actively taken to heart while, at the same time, every available means—physical, mental, and spiritual—within reason should also be applied in the hope of relieving the suffering and restoring normalcy. The practice of Christian Science is one part of these means, and a most valuable part, but still only a part.

21

We earlier mentioned that successful healing could never be guaranteed and was only occasionally possible. The healing cults are quite correct in looking for a practical demonstration of successful spirituality in the affairs of daily living, but they are quite wrong in believing that this demonstration always takes the form of perfect health. It is so far from fact that some adept yogis and sages have been known to take on their own shoulders the diseases karmically incurred by disciples closely associated with them, for just as such a one can transfer his own karmic merit to others in order to help them, so he may take from them their karmic demerits. But ordinarily man is not entirely a free agent in this matter, whatever credulous enthusiasts may assert to the contrary, and does not have the last word to say in it, karmic and cosmic evolutionary forces being also at work.

Again, these enthusiasts have to face this problem. The thoughts of God must necessarily be expressive of the will of God. It is quite impossible to separate the one from the other. It logically follows that suffering and sickness being present in the world, they must also be the expressions of God's will.

22

We have inherited a body which, after ages of mistreatment, degradation, and wrong feeding, cannot quickly change itself and accept the new habits and the new feeding with its organs in their present condition.

23

If the millions spent on research for cancer cures have so far failed, and if a simple change of faulty thought, belief, conduct, and goal cures it, the worth of this method is thereby demonstrated. If Sai Baba will take twenty cases of advanced cancer and cure them, under world inspection, he will do more to bring humanity out of the threatening danger of total war than all his preaching. For part of his message must be abandonment of war.

24

Metaphysical or faith cure is an oversimplification of the healing problem and consequently yields only a part-truth. Bodily healing is an occasional by-product of the healing of thought and feeling, or the re-education of moral character; it is not at all the invariable result of such processes. Sickness may come to advanced students for a variety of causes, some of which arise from outside the individual. Karma is the commonest, but one such cause might be the application of a test or ordeal from the divine soul to the human ego that aspires to evolve more rapidly.

25

If wrong living breaks hygienic laws and provokes disease, wrong-doing also breaks karmic laws and provokes disease, as one form of retribution out of several possible forms. A hereditary affliction would obviously be of karmic origin ultimately.

26

It is not possible for me to agree with the statement that mentalist doctrine could banish disease if it were firmly established in the race consciousness. Is this also the Christian Science view? Such a statement would be quite correct if the body-idea were wholly a human creation. But it is not, for the World-Mind (God, if you like) or Nature is also responsible for it. The individual mind and the cosmic mind are in indissoluble connection, and out of their combined activity the human world-idea is produced. It would be correct to say, however, that the redirection of thought and feeling would largely help to eliminate disease. As the race learns to substitute positive for negative thoughts, aspiration for passion, and concentration for distraction, it will inevitably throw off many maladies that originate in wrong attitudes.

27

Certain maladies in the physical being may quite easily be directly traced to evil impulses in the mental being. It is not only man's diseases which are the consequence of his bad thinking, however, but also man's misfortunes. If he is healthy in body he may be unhealthy in fortune. Karma's retribution expresses itself in a variety of ways. It is a mistake to narrow this linking of wrong thinking and ill feeling with the body's sicknesses alone. They are to be linked with all forms of bad karma. Disease is only one form. Their effects may appear in other forms instead. Disease is merely one of them.

Mental states and physical conditions

28

States of mind are directly or indirectly connected with states of health. A mind sinking under the heavy weight of responsibilities, or filled with the heavy stresses and pressures of business, or depressed by frustration unhappiness or unrest, or shaken by the ending of a close relationship, may soon or late reflect itself in disease, sickness, or breakdown as in a mirror.

29

Wrong thinking expresses itself in the end in wrong functioning of some organ of the body. The nature of the thoughts and the nature of the malady correspond to each other.

30

The man who gives himself up to negative destructive thoughts or a feverish tempo of living for years and, later, finds himself sick or diseased, usually fails to think there is any mutual connection between the mental thoughts or unrelaxed way of life and the physical state. He does not even dream that he has been called to account.

31

Quite clearly, it is as disorders of the various organs, as functional troubles, or as abnormal conditions in one or another part of the body that emotional, nervous, and mental disharmonies first show themselves physically.

32

Definitions: A sickness develops into an ailment, which if not cured becomes a disease.

33

There is dissension between heart and head, between feeling and reasoning, and there is disease in the body itself.

34

There is an undesirable physical reaction for every undesirable emotional activity.

35

Most people are careless about their mental habits because these seem of trivial importance by contrast with their physical habits. They do not know that sinning against the mind's hygiene may manifest in the physical body itself.

36

The body's organs are affected by the mind's states. Worry or fear, shock or excessive emotion may disturb, reduce, increase, or even paralyse their working for a time—in some cases for all time.

37

The clouds of adverse fortune and ill health pass and change over the earth of man's body. In that body there is ultimately reflected his own mental and emotional reactions to them.

38

The human being is a whole, but has different aspects. What manifests itself as an emotional disturbance in one aspect may also manifest itself later as a bodily sickness.

39

The body's health and the ego's fortunes eventually match the good or ill shape of the ego's thought.

40

To overlook the psychological factor in the cause of sickness and to concentrate solely on the physical factor is much too narrow-minded and not truly scientific. At the present stage of human knowledge, it is too simple and naïve an attitude to cover all cases.

41

Mental causes cannot be put in a test tube and examined; this is one reason why they have been overlooked.

42

What we have been saying does not deny the physical causes of disease; it only refers them back to an earlier start in the mind.

43

We know that a person can worry himself into a state of physical sickness, but there seems to be less acceptance for the opposite idea that emotions and thoughts can also produce healing and not injury.

44

When fears and doubts, negative thoughts and pessimistic moods strongly dominate the inner life for long periods, or for a shorter one more strongly, they may provoke repercussions in the physical body and create disease.

45

The subconscious activity of mind provides the working link between thinking feeling and the flesh through brain and spine, through sympathetic nerve system and delicate nerve plexus. In this way the interplay of character health and fortune is brought about.

46

When a man is ever bitter, resentful, unkind, and critical; never gentle, constructive, praising, and compassionate; then poison trickles through his inner being and must in the end reappear in his bodily being.

47

Some of the thoughts which poison mind and blood, negatives to be cast out and kept out, are: spite, ill will, unforgiveness, violent conduct, and constant fault-finding.

48

The sins of the heart bring on a diseased psychic being and this in turn, if not changed, brings on a diseased physical being.

49

All negative states of mind and emotions are destructive. They work harm to some one of the body's organs or interfere with its functions. If those states are continuous, they sink into the subconscious and the results appear as disease. This is possible because the sympathetic nervous system, which controls the automatic functions of the body, such as circulation and elimination, digestion and nutrition, is open to influence by the subconscious mind.

50

The emotions and moods which work destructively on the physical body and may be the real origin of its sickness include fear, hatred, anger, jealousy, despondency, anxiety, worry, doubt, and inordinate excitement.

51

It is not his occasional thoughts which create sickness or affect fortune, but his habitual ones.

52

Those who nurture hate or vow revenge, slowly shorten the life period of their physical body.

53

The overactive hyper-irritable nerve and brain fatiguing kind of life in which civilized man has entangled himself builds up much inner tension and loads him with useless psychic burdens of negative feelings.

54

Depression, melancholia, and despair have been known to bring on wasting ailments and even death. The mind's suffering, if too intense and too prolonged, may shift to the flesh.

55

Of these lower emotional causes of ill health, fear and shock are perhaps the commonest.

56

Many an illness or the malfunctioning of an organ or a disease begins with a strong negative thought, and, by the latter's constant repetition until it hardens into a chronic mental-emotional condition, builds up to a crisis in a subsequent year.

57

It is the routine activity of the brain, and especially the mental tendency toward anxiety and fear which is expressed through it, which interferes with Nature's healing processes—whether these be spiritual or physical or both—or obstructs them or delays them or defeats them completely. This anxiety arises through the sufferer's confinement to his personal ego and through his ignorance of the arrangements in the World-Idea's body-pattern for the human body's protective care. The remedy is in his own hands. It is twofold: first to change from negative to positive thinking through acquiring either faith in this care or else knowledge of it; second, to give body and brain as total a rest as his capacity allows, which is achieved through fasting and in meditation. The first change is more easily made by immediately substituting the positive and opposite idea as soon as the negative one appears in his field of consciousness. He trains himself not to accept any harmful thought and watches his mind during this period of training. This constructive thought must be held and nourished with firm concentration for as long as possible. The second change calls for an abstinence from all thoughts, a mental quiet, as well as an abstinence from all food for one to three days.(P)

58

To the extent that he can release himself by inner discipline from his negatives, to that extent will he release himself from many troubles which might otherwise descend upon him. As irritations fall away from his personal feelings, ills of body, circumstance, or relationship fall away from threatening his personal fortunes.

59

If the mind of a spiritual healer can help to remove disease, it is equally true that the mind of some other person can contribute to cause it. If one's own wrong thinking may be partly or wholly responsible for one's diseases, others who are thinking constantly or powerfully about one may be partly or even wholly responsible for them too. This is the basis of sorcery in the Orient and of witchcraft in the medieval West.

60

The mental and emotional adjustment to frustration or loss which philosophy brings about is definitely therapeutic.

61

If ignorance of the laws of our psychophysical being causes many people to contravene those laws and become sick, carelessness about obeying them brings illness to some who do know them.

62

Selfish people, worrying people, negative people, complaining people, venomous people need to find this inner peace. It will heal them of their moral maladies, which in turn may be the causes of their physical maladies.

63

Psychosomatic illnesses are curable by physical means. But either the cures are temporary or other symptoms of a different kind appear and replace those which have disappeared.

64

Merely to express belief in faith healing is not enough to receive healing. There must also be willingness to make needed moral and psychological adjustments, if they are directed towards the inner causes of the illness.

65

Everyone without a single exception wants to be healed of his diseases but how few want just as much to be healed of their hatreds, their rages, and their lusts?

66

It is sometimes possible to deduce the nature of the wrong-doing from the nature of the subsequent affliction.

67

People do not understand how their destructive moods, thoughts, and emotions affect the cerebro-spinal system and through that eventually the intestinal organs to the degree of creating poisons within those organs. It is not enough to take care of the diet and to eliminate foods which are harmful to physical health. It is equally necessary to take care of thoughts and feelings, and to eliminate all those which are harmful both to spiritual and physical health.

68

To cover up an unhealthy condition is not to cure it. And so long as a man is immersed in an entirely separative and selfish outlook, so long as he habitually fears, worries, holds grudges, or hates, so long must he be regarded as "sick" and "unwell."

69

Theory left unapplied is only one-third of knowledge. A surgeon knew and taught that anger would raise the pressure of the blood and strain the heart in proportion to its severity. Yet it was anger that eventually killed him.

70

The influence of body on mind is shown by the efficacy—in his case at least—of Socrates' method of smiling at himself when counterattacking a negative emotion while it was yet in its slender beginning.

71

There is a corrective purpose in the existence of disease. Any cure which removes the symptoms but fails to correct the inner mental or physical cause of them is merely a temporary expedient, not a real cure. It serves the ego's present convenience. But the future must necessarily be menaced by a reappearance of the same disease, or of a different one which will also express the cause. And this may happen either in the same lifetime or in the next.

72

A disease whose origin is physical will not need more than a physical remedy to cure it. But one of a psychical, mental, or moral nature can be reached and overcome only by corresponding means.

73

The long walk which might fatigue your strength and become difficult drudgery becomes easy and endurable if, at the same time, your mind is deeply absorbed in concentration on some lofty matter. Why? Because you are not then thinking of your ego. Such is the power of the mind over the body.

74

If a man lives only and wholly in positive harmonious feelings, if he consistently rejects all negative and destructive ones, the result must certainly be that he will enjoy better health in the body as he already enjoys the best in the mind.

75

The materialist who tries to find a physical explanation for every sickness is nevertheless forced to admit that the mind does have at the very least a limited influence upon the body. This is proven by mental shock hastening the heartbeat; by worry acting on the nervous system and affecting the flow of secretions, thus contributing towards indigestion; by violent anger raising the blood pressure. Because fear liberates toxic poisons, the expression "died of fright" may be literally true.

76

If one emotion brings a blush of blood to the face, another takes the blood away and leaves pallor. In the first case, it has led the minute arteries of the skin to expand; in the second case, it has led them to contract. If this is what a momentary state of mind can do to the body, imagine what a persistent state can do!

77

Intense happiness felt on hearing some important good news will start a smile on the face. Intense anxiety wrinkles the forehead and depresses the mouth; if it becomes habitual and chronic, the bowels become constipated. These two facts about wholly opposite moods are known to nearly everyone, because the line of causality is straight, obvious, and universally witnessed. What is less known because harder to discern is the third fact that selfish inconsiderate stubbornness and constant hatred create the poison of uric acid in the bloodstream and this indirectly leads to rheumatism. What is first felt mentally is almost immediately reflected physically.

78

The Chinese system lists the following inner causes of functional sickness: fear and untruthfulness weaken the kidneys; anger affects the liver; depression and worry affect the lungs; excessive joy affects the heart; overactive mentality affects the stomach; timidity, indecision, and cowardice affect the liver by producing insufficient bile.

79

A mother who is overwhelmed by powerful negative emotions like anger or grief while nursing her infant, could be the cause of its spasms and convulsions.

80

Even medical science admits that a depressive kind of emotionalism contributes towards causing hardening of the arteries and hence earlier old age.

81

Whenever Gandhi had an important decision to make, and went through protracted self-wrangling in the process, the physician who attended him noted that his blood pressure rose considerably. Once Gandhi went to sleep in such a condition. Next morning the pressure had fallen to normal. During the night he had ended the mental pressure and arrived at a decision!

82

Angina pectoris is recognized by many physicians now as a very serious disease, often fatal and always painful, mostly brought on by extreme nervous tension.

83

The power of the mind over flesh is proved convincingly even by such simple, everyday experiences as the vomiting caused by a horrible sight, the weeping caused by a tragic one, the loss of appetite or positive indigestion caused by bad news, and the headache caused by quarreling.

84

The need to take care of the nature of our thoughts was illustrated by the life-story of Eugene O'Neill. The gloomy themes of his plays, the gaunt tragedy and overhanging doom with which he deliberately permeated them, brought him down in his later years with an incurable disease. His palsied hand could not write, and dictated material always dissatisfied him. Those who deny the line of relevant connection between his grim thinking and his sickness ignore the fact that he was an ultrasensitive man—so sensitive that a large part of his life was occupied with the search for a solitary place where no people could interrupt him and where he could live entirely within himself.

85

Why is it that in the stage of heavy sleeping trance a hypnotic subject's nervous system fails to make the usual reactions to a burning match applied to the hand or a pointed pin stuck into the flesh? Why does the usual sensitivity to pain vanish so largely, often completely? If consciousness really lay in the nerves themselves it could never really be divorced from them. It is because consciousness does not arise out of the material body, but out of the deeper principle of the immaterial, that it can function or fail to function as the bodily thought-series. Hence when the consciousness is turned away from the body, when it is induced to cease holding the nerve system in its embrace, it will naturally cease holding the pleasurable or painful changes within that system too.

86

Fear retards digestion; anger hurts the spleen; excessive lust leads to inflammations, infections, or impotence; jealousy creates excessive bile; a shock caused by bad news may turn hair white.

87

The person who holds such negative feelings as chronic gloom and constant fault-finding, who worries self and nags others, is walking the direct path to either a disordered liver or high blood pressure. Vicious mental and speech habits injure the person's own body and demoralize other people's feeling.

88

How much was Carlyle's bitter, rancorous mind, as expressed in his bitter, epithetical speech, responsible for the malady of dyspepsia which afflicted him for so many years?

89

Anger brings the liver's function to a standstill; this throws its bile back into the system, and bilious indigestion follows.

90

Vincent Sheean, in his autobiography, says of his intensely ardent friend Raynal Prohme, "She died of inflammation of the brain, thus literally, and all too aptly, burning away."

91

The tears which well up in the eyes are physical, yet the self-pity which causes them is plainly mental.

92

The connection between breathing and thinking has been noted by the yoga of physical control. The connection between breathing and feeling also exists. Apoplexy—a fit of choking, the inability to breathe at all—may seize and kill a man during frustrated rage. The breath catches and almost ceases when bad news is suddenly heard.

93

There is a direct line between emotional shocks fears or worries, and stomach ulcers.

94

Saliva may become poisonous in anger. Gastric juice may stop flowing in shock of bad news.

95

A Berlin opera singer went to the United States on a visit. While there she received the unexpected news of her husband's sudden death. The shock severely affected her feelings. That same week she became afflicted with diabetes and suffered greatly from it for several years until she died.

96

The emotion of fear may bring on a cold sweat even in an environment of tropic heat.

97

At last medical science is coming to recognize the power of feeling to make disease in the flesh, the contribution of mind and mood to the body's sickness. In deep-seated emotional anxiety it has found the primary cause of diabetes, the manifestation of excess sugar in the system being a legacy from that.

The importance of hygiene

98

Both common sense and practical experience inform us that some sicknesses come solely from physical causes. The proper way to treat them is to use physical methods, that is, to find those causes and remove them, and to apply physical remedies.

99

Those who transgress against the body's law of being and suffer the penalty in ill health, cannot reasonably blame God's will when they ought to blame their own abuse, neglect, or ignorance.

100

The penalties of violating hygienic laws may in some cases be escaped by spiritual means, but the penalties of *continuing* to violate them may not. The cause which engenders a malady must be itself removed, or else the removal of the symptoms which are merely its effects will be followed eventually by their reappearance or by those of a different malady. Wisdom here tells us to obey the laws and to regard disease as a warning of our transgression of them.

101

Those who seek healing only to be restored to sensual courses and selfish designs, may commit further errors and be worse off in the end.(P)

102

It would be just as wrong to argue that *every* physical disease proves a moral fault or mental deformity to exist, as it would be to argue that the absence of such disease proves moral or mental perfection to have been attained. Many animals are quite healthy too!(P)

103

Where physical laws of hygiene have been broken and continue to be broken, where gluttonous or ill-informed eating and intemperate living have led to bodily disturbance, the sufferer must still rectify his physical errors whether his spiritual healing is successful or not.(P)

104

Nature has implanted true instincts in our body to sustain and protect it. If we, through slavish acceptance of society's bad habits, pervert those instincts or dull their sensitivity and poison our body, Nature forces us to suffer sickness and pain as the warning consequences of such perversion.

105

Insofar as man through ignorance fails to observe nature's laws or through weakness persistently disobeys them, he is everywhere suffering the penalties attached to his wrong habits.

106

The truth is that no man is free to please himself and eat what he fancies. All men, including all teachers and members of the cults which claim this freedom and who trespass against themselves in this matter, will have to pay the penalty in some way or at some time.

107

The man who revels in his sensuality will naturally defend it. But when some form of great suffering comes to him as a direct consequence, and he sees it for the first time as a sin, he will cease doing so.

108

Ill health disturbs the mind and, if prolonged or serious, may bring on neuroses.

109

The way one views oneself and others, one's life and the world, has too often been affected by chronic disagreeable sensations in a small part of the body, too often been improved by improving the physical condition, to assert that physical causes are unimportant.

110

Why is it that the number of deaths from cancer has been increasing so rapidly in our times, and so disproportionately to the increase in population? Why is it that this is happening in all those parts of the world where civilization has been spread? Why is it that those people who live in the most modern way—the Americans—have the most cancer? Is there not a hint here that our present way of living contributes something to its cause?

111

How many people who would never dream of committing murder upon someone else, commit it upon themselves!

112

Health troubles show up the value of good health, since the physical body's condition has a strong influence upon the mind's condition. It is worth the trouble of studying the body's true needs to keep it a useful and efficient servant.

113

To take up an air of indifference to the actual and physical surroundings, to assert to oneself that the circumstances do not matter, may be mere pretension or pathetic self-deception. Environmental conditions *do* matter. Flesh and blood, nerve and body have reactions and responses which laugh at our theory.

114

The search for mental, moral, and emotional causes of bodily effects is valid only in a proportion of cases, not in all cases. For there are physical laws governing the physical body, laws which, when broken, automatically bring punishment.

115

Those who neglect the body and break the laws of its health can gain no cure by mental means but only a temporary respite.

116

Philosophy grants at once that physical causes like bad environment, faulty heredity, broken hygienic laws, germ infections, and improper feeding may cause disease.

117

The emptiness of conventional salutations and the futility of conventional greetings are not realized because they are not thought about. What is the use of formally wishing anyone good health when he is constantly breaking hygienic laws and thus moving nearer towards ill health? Instead of writing such phrases in letters to him or uttering them on parting from him, it might be more beneficial in the end to draw his attention to those neglected laws. But to do that would be to sin against the sacredness of convention. The shock of such reminders might hurt his feelings but it might also arouse him to take a different course.

118

If so many sicknesses are the effects of preventable abuses, is it not rational to tie oneself down to a regime which prevents those causes? Then, so far as humanly possible, we have done what we can to gain and retain good health, and if sickness comes it will be "by an act of God" and not by our own.

Dangers of drugs and alcohol

119

Alcoholic drinks must be banned not only for obvious reasons—their effect upon the mind, the emotions, and the passions—but also for their effect upon the body itself. The man who is trying to purify it cannot afford to admit into his organism the foul microbes of decomposition which they contain.

120

Those who have witnessed the ghastly results of becoming addicted to drugs may not know that at a certain point the addict may become involved very easily with what is called "black magic." This is the forbidden path which seeks to obtain a higher spiritual result by the wrong means, by forbidden means and, in the end, causes a man to lose his own soul and become a slave of evil forces.

121

Strong alcohol paralyses the brain centre controlling spiritual and intuitive activity for two hours, and so nullifies meditation, which should not be practised within two hours of drinking it. Those who take such stimulants and still want to unfold spiritually should restrict their drinks to light wine or beer.(P)

122

Smoking not only harms the body but also depresses the mind. The cumulative and ultimate effect of the poison which it introduces is to lower the emotional state by periodic moods of depression.(P)

123

Drug experience may lead to hallucination, obsession, paranoid monstrous prehuman evolutionary images, or highly overdrawn images of human experience.

124

It is the strong spirits which influence a man more dangerously than the light wines. It is they which tend to drag him downward to the animal plane of development.

125

"The illumination-contemplations which visited me daily for several months disappeared for a few hours if I drank alcohol," a very advanced European meditator told me.

126

A narcotic experience may give a distorted reflection of the real; it cannot give the real itself. Even so, the price that must be paid for the mirrored images is even greater than the attendant perils.

127

The United States government has, for some time, made efforts to reduce the use of tobacco in order to improve public health. These efforts have not succeeded at all. Why? For that same reason that women took to smoking and that men still smoke even though they know it is harmful. They will tell you, or you will see, that they resort to the cigarette, the cigar, or the pipe because it soothes their nerves, and they feel a need of achieving this result. The tobacco plant itself was used long ago in the antique period of both North and South America and on the other side of the world in the Near, Middle, and Far East. But tobacco was not the only plant they used. They had several others which have come down to us, such as the poppy plant and a certain mushroom. And from them modern knowledge has created chemical drugs. What does this mean? The stress which produces nervousness is more common among the moderns than it was among the ancients. What were, and are, all of them seeking? It was either relief for the ego or uplift of conscience or the attainment of the spiritual awakening.

128

Drugs weaken and may eventually even destroy reason.

129

Alcohol is a drug which removes symptoms. But, like most drugs, it removes them only temporarily.

130

Even a little liquor may excite a man, and much liquor makes him mentally unbalanced.

131

G.K. Chesterton wrote voluminously in defense of drinking wine and beer (he never touched spirits), yet he drank himself into a long serious illness which nearly cost him his life and after which he was forbidden for some years to take any alcohol at all.

132

Do not confound the drugged vision of God with an authentic one.

133

It is not only intoxicating drinks which can cause man to become heedless and lose self-control; certain drugs can have the same result even though the symptoms are different. Therefore they are banned except when used medically in some situations.

134

Contrary to common belief, the drinking of alcohol does not make a man more "human." It deprives him of truly human characteristics and makes him more animal.

135

Those who try to find the kingdom of heaven through drugs, whether plants like Mexican mushrooms or Indian hashish, or chemicals like lysergic acid, may gain glimpses, get signs, and receive hints, but they will not, cannot, escape paying the price of inner deterioration in the end.

136

The fascination which follows the taking of those drugs which seem to have given instant mystic experience is deceptive. A scrutiny of such experience shows that there are liabilities because the seeming enlightenment is illusory, and the taker has no control over the drug and its effects—some of which can be quite bad. He has no means of judging in advance how tolerant his body and mind are towards it, whether it will give him nausea, sickness, headaches, nightmares, or momentary insanity instead of the alleged enlightenment.

137

The drug hashish affects the brain centre which controls the speed of the pictures which pass through consciousness, as well as the dimensions of those pictures. Caffeine affects a different centre in a different way. But neither drug affects consciousness itself; it affects the mechanism which conditions a *product* of consciousness—the ego in its wakeful state.

138

Both drugs and alcohol interfere with the proper practice of meditation, and after taking one or the other one would have to wait a period until the effect wore off before the real practice of meditation could begin.

139

Just as the imagination can weave all kinds of phantasies and experiences in dream which are simply not true, so can it do precisely the same during drug usage.

140

The mystic who meditates with open eyes and is able to sink himself into the last stage of contemplation, staring with glassy but unseeing orbs, is duplicated for the observer in outward appearance only by the drug addict who takes stronger drugs and who has been taking them for quite a time. He too shows the symptoms in his eyes, in the paleness of his skin, and in the trance-like, coma-like condition into which he often falls.

141

The resort to drugs for spiritual purposes can never be justified, for the same drug which raises or widens the taker's consciousness today may cast him into a pit of devils and horrors the next week.

142

One of the bad effects of drugs, in certain cases, is to create schizo-phrenia.

143

To gain apparent serenity at the cost of real sanity is hardly a profitable transaction.

144

In their impatience and eagerness to get the mystical experience, some resort to taking either infusions of drugs like Indian hemp or ingestions of them like lysergic acid. The effect is usually euphoric at first but startlingly fantastic afterwards. LSD is the latest of them all and probably the most powerful of all—certainly the most amazing of all.

145

We know that there are drugs which enhance the movement of time twofold and threefold until impatience arises in them at what seems the extraordinary slowness of others around them.

146

Because chemical drugs can affect the mind, can induce states of con-sciousness, it is claimed that the excesses or the horrors which have been produced through their means show that spiritual consciousness is entirely related to the physical brain, that the greatest attainments of the yogis can be produced in a hour or two instead of many years or a lifetime by taking a simple drug, and that therefore modern science has achieved the opening of a door to spiritual self-realization which many would-be yogis have failed to achieve—in other words, that the Kingdom of Heaven is not within you but within a pill or a tablet.

147

It is true that a number of persons who have used a plant (not chemical) drug have had visions of previous embodiment in animal and human forms. But because they got it in an illegitimate way, they often have to suffer a penalty, either in self-damage or in self-entangled karma.

4

HEALERS OF THE BODY
AND MIND

Services of the healing arts

A wise system of healing would coordinate physical and psychological, artificial and natural, dietary and spiritual treatments, using some or all of them as a means to the end—cure. But as the spiritual is the supreme therapeutic agent—if it can be touched—it will always be the one last resort for the desperate and chronic sufferers when all other agents have had to accept defeat.

2

Just as philosophy seeks a full rounded development of the psyche in its approach to spiritual self-realization, so does it seek a full adequate treatment in its approach to the problem of curing sickness. It recognizes that even if a sickness began with evil thoughts or wrong feelings or disharmonious courses of action, these have already worked their way into and affected the physical body and brought about harmful changes in it, either causing its organs to work badly, or introducing poisons into its blood system, or even creating malignant growths in its tissues. Therefore physical means must also be used to treat these physical conditions, as well as the spiritual means to get rid of wrong thoughts and discordant feelings. Both methods should be applied together to make an adequate treatment. Consequently philosophy does not, like Christian Science, deny the utility or necessity of ordinary medical treatment. On the contrary, it welcomes such treatment, provided it is not narrow-minded, materialistic, or selfishly concerned more with fees than with healing.

3

Why should we not unite working on the body by physical means with working on it by the healing power of the higher self? Why not give the latter a chance to repair its own work, since the physical-mental ego is its own projection?

4

There is no need to make the mistake of those cults which avoid mention of the body and its sicknesses, which pretend that both are not there. Let the fact of their existence be there but, at the same time, hold the thought of the Overself's superior power over them.

5

The art of healing needs all the contributions it can get, from all the worthy sources it can find. It cannot realize all its potentialities unless it accepts them all: the homeopath along with the allopath, the naturopath along with the chiropractor, the psychiatrist along with the spiritual ministrant. It does not need them all together at one and the same time, of course, but only as parts of its total resources. A philosophic attitude refuses to bind itself exclusively to any single form of cure.(P)

6

The services of a physician skilled in the knowledge of diseases and in the care of their sufferers should never be slighted. Orthodox allopathic medicine deserves our highest respect because of the cautiously scientific way it has proceeded on its course. It has achieved notable cures. But it also has many failures to its debit. This is in part due to the fundamental error which it accepts in common with other sciences like psychology—the materialist error of viewing man as being nothing more than his body. Only by setting this right can it go forward to its fullest possibilities. Its deficiency in this respect has forced the appearance and nourished the spread of unorthodox healing methods, of which there are many. Most of these have something worthwhile to contribute but unfortunately—lacking the caution of science—make exaggerated claims and uphold fanatical attitudes, with the result that they too have their failures and incur public disrepute. The extreme claims made by credulous followers and unscientific leaders of mental healing cults revolt the reason of those outside their fold and lead to distrust of the justifiable claims that should be made. But they have enough successes to justify their existence. Only by a mutual approach and interaction will they modify each other and thus bring a truly complete system of healing. They are already doing this involuntarily and therefore far too slowly. They have to do it willingly and quickly if the world of sick and suffering patients is to benefit by the full extent of present-day human knowledge.(P)

7

The cults which allow healing power only to the Spirit, which would deny it to all other means or media, even as secondary causes, are too extreme and fanatical.

8

When either faith healing or naturopathic treatment is too passive, when it refrains from timely co-operation with nature by the use of positive means, be they nontoxic medicines or essential operations, it becomes guilty of sacrificing the patient to its own narrowness.

9

I consider W.J. Macmillan's view on healing one-sided and incomplete, but thought my foreword to his book [*The Reluctant Healer*] was not the place to criticize him.

10

No healer's treatment is always successful nor is the cure always permanent. Failures are many and relapses are common. Those who shout and splutter from evangelistic public platforms exhibit the ego's arrogance, not the Overself's quiet humility.

11

They hold the view which conforms with their presuppositions, their inborn tendencies and governing prejudices, in short, with their little ego, not their impersonal higher Self. This is why there are so many contesting theories, why the body's ill health may cause the mind to be governed by negative thoughts, why this conflict of authorities shows their worthlessness.

12

All these cults and groups which acknowledge the power of mind over body but which leave out the acknowledgment of the body's power over the mind, are out of balance and so out of truth to that extent. This statement may be a matter of arguable theory with partisan adherents of either side, but it is a matter of tested fact with creative leaders who consciously exercise *both* powers.

13

The physical cure will surely be accelerated and the physical therapy will surely be helped if mental and spiritual healing agents are also joined in. In this way the individual limitations of the method of treatment being used will be overcome and each healing agent will contribute to bringing about a complete and successful result.

14

It is foolish to believe that there is any particular healing method which has only to be applied for it to be universally and equally successful or that there is any particular human healer who has only to be visited for one to be cured.

15

A careful study will elicit the fact that although all these various systems differ in their tenets of belief, they have several similarities of technique. A scientific examination of these similarities will yield the basis for determining the universally correct tenet of belief. Such an examination is necessary because the systems themselves have not sufficient interest in a scientific approach to make it themselves and are too self-interested to check their alleged cures with sufficient care. Even were they truly independent intellectually—which they are not—they are usually tied up to some form of religious creed. All these systems are dogmatic ones, being mostly based on some personal revelation. They depend primarily on faith. The treatments include very much more than faith alone.

16

The nature-curist who denounces all allopathic drugs as being satanic, the homeopath who can see physical salvation only in his own minute doses of medicine, and the conventional allopath who rejects the first as a quack and the second as a fool—each illustrates in his own person the defect of an ill-balanced mind. Suffering humanity needs all the help it can get. It cannot afford to reject either nature-cure, homeopathy, or allopathy. It needs all three and even more.

17

The practice of disidentification from the body detailed in *The Quest of the Overself* is not the same kind of mental treatment as Christian Science. The latter begins and ends with dogmatics, whereas the other is a rising by strict reasoning from the known facts to the unknown. Constant and repeated thinking about these arguments must go on until they are your own, until you have achieved thorough conviction.

18

A defective theory in healing must sooner or later lead to a contradiction in practice. The rejection of natural yet physical methods of supplementing and completing the higher ones explains why so many Christian Scientists have recourse, in hours of desperation, to the medicos they denounce and the systems they despise.

19

A prudent and balanced approach to the question requires us to make use of the services of allopathy as well as homeopathy, psychotherapy as well as physiotherapy, spiritual healing as well as mesmeric treatment, herbalism and even surgery—if and when needed—if we are to make the fullest use of developed human knowledge and skill.

20

Susruta, a Hindu physician and writer who lived in the pre-Christian era, aptly and expertly expressed the philosophic view of healing when he observed, "He who knows but one branch of his art is like a bird with one wing."

21

When comparing one Oriental country's healings with Occidental ones, or pagan centuries' cures with Christian ones, what the diligent student as well as the experienced traveller may find is that the techniques, mediums, and procedures are often the same, only the names of the agents using them are changed.

22

Why should anyone reject the physician and his medicines for the osteopath and his manipulations, or both for the healer and his prayer? The power which cures works through all three; if it did not, if it worked through a single channel alone, the others would never have been needed, found, and used.

23

Whether it is religion or science, official allopathic medicine or less established homeopathic medicine, each can make us its beneficiary and has its contribution to give us. But each also has its undesirable side, too often a sectarian narrow intolerance of the other. The world of knowledge, culture, techniques, skills, arts, and worship should be open to all seekers—whether their quest is for truth, God, information, or healing—and not dictatorially limited in its offering to the established, the traditional, the successful, and the conventional.

24

Is there a science of spiritual healing? If there is, we can discover it only by freeing ourselves from the cultist standpoint; for, with conflicting doctrines and different methods, Christian Science, Spiritism, Roman Catholicism, Hypnotism, and Couéism have yet produced similar results. It follows that these healings do not prove all their claims but may prove a part.

25

Every healer, orthodox and unorthodox, has his percentage of failures, although the figure is generally unknown. Spiritual healing is not a universal cure-all. It is complementary to other systems.

26

From the moment that a healing cult fastens itself to the Bible exclusively, it narrows its vision and limits its power.

27

When truth gets into the hands of fanatics they do it harm. One man teaches that *all* disease is caused by wrong diet only, but another teaches that it is caused by wrong thinking only. But truth says that both these causes are operative in man's world, as well as several others.

28

It will have to be recognized that, since we exist simultaneously on two levels, all our problems of suffering and sickness must be looked at from two points of view if they are to be adequately seen and grasped. There is the common and familiar immediate one, which deals with them as they are in appearance. There is the uncommon and unfamiliar alternate one, which deals with them as they are in reality. An orthodox physician treating a case of disease takes the first viewpoint. A Christian Science practitioner treating the same case takes the second one. Neither takes a wholly adequate and truly philosophical viewpoint.

Medicine and surgery

29

The services of medicine and surgery, despite the harm done by their errors and experiments, have been and are too great not to be appreciated at their true worth.

30

Fanatic followers of naturopathy as well as of Christian Science reject the services of surgery. Yet do the men among them ever stop to think that the act of shaving, which they perform daily, is itself the performance of a minor surgical operation? For the hair is as much a tangible part of their anatomy as is the bony skeleton. This also applies to finger nails, toe nails, calluses, and corns.

Such opposition to surgery on the part of those who are unorthodox in their views of healing is based partly on blind fanaticism and partly on blind ignorance. The excessive attachment to their own particular system prevents them from seeing its true place and surgery's true relation to it. Natural methods should be tried first, surgical methods only last. If natural methods are tried too late or tried without result, then it is quite proper to resort to surgery if any hope lies there. They should be given their chance in the earlier stages of a disease but if they are not, if the disease has advanced to a serious or chronic degree, surgery may fitly be considered, either alone or in conjunction with them.

Even in divine healing, the spiritual force may still use a surgeon through which to express itself. It does not necessarily have to use only a saint to do so. Spiritual healing completes and does not displace the conventional allopathic or the unorthodox physical healing systems. It does not supplant but supplements them.

31

Opposition to the new and powerful drugs is not because of their ineffectiveness. That they produce swift and curative results is admitted. The opposition is instigated by the harmful effects upon other organs or parts of the body subsequent to the cure, and sometimes accompanying it.

32

As the science of medicine becomes more reverent, it will bring the spirit to the healing of the body in addition to its medicine.

33

Life on earth is so short, so beset by dangers of many kinds, so exposed to our own ignorance and Nature's indifference, that we cannot afford to turn our eyes away as do the Christian Scientists from the discoveries and knowledge of men who have devoted their years to patient sacrifice and research for the alleviation of human sickness.

34

It is usually wise to consult a physician, wiser still to consult a specialist. Why reject the knowledge they have accumulated, the experience they have gained? But blindly to follow their advice is quite another matter. Here a critical judgement is needed, for medicine is immensely far from being the perfect science that mathematics is.

35

So long as orthodox medicine fails to recognize the mental or emotional origin of so many cases of sickness, so long will its cures be temporary and incomplete.

36

To reject the valuable contribution of surgical art is to neglect human knowledge of anatomy and human capacity to co-operate with Nature. Thousands of years ago, a gifted Hindu writer and medico even acclaimed it in these words: "Surgery is the first and highest division of the healing art, least liable to fallacy." Exaggerated, perhaps, but it is certain that the ancient Hindus knew and practised a well-developed form of this art— even including plastic surgery—but it mysteriously disappeared in the course of time. The successive foreign invasions and their massacres of intellectuals may have had something to do with it.

37

Gandhi denounced surgical techniques as unnatural and urged his followers to have nothing to do with them. Yet he lived to modify his view, for when stricken by appendicitis he accepted the help of those very techniques. The operation was successful. The medieval Church placed a ban upon those who performed any operation upon the human body that was accompanied by the shedding of blood. The modern Church has removed the ban and in its hospitals permits the extensive practice of surgery. Thus the erroneous theory of Gandhi and the erroneous superstition of the Church were corrected by time, which brought the facts of experience into play.

38

I have always associated hospitals with gloom, with drabness, with ugliness, and with despondency. The association was once falsified in California and again in Denmark. But not till I was taken through the hospital founded by Padre Pio at San Giovanni Rotondo did I associate such intensely positive values as cheerfulness, beauty, hopefulness, and the last word in modernity with such an institution.

39

On transplants: If they have any positive value at all, amid all the negative ones, it is a blind and mistaken attempt to renovate human life—blind, because ignorant of life's higher laws of rebirth and karma, mistaken because leading always to greater evils than those it seeks to remedy.

40

The surgical operations to transfer certain glands from animal bodies to human ones may be successful in their vitalizing results on sexual stimulation, but their karmic results are deplorable. The man who so abuses Nature as to permit a lower grade creature's glands to be engrafted into his higher grade body is himself punished by Nature. He risks causing himself to be reborn with a deformed or even crippled body.

41

Official established and organized medicine is like official established organized religion. It has much that is true but there are also many weeds growing in its garden. We should not be afraid to venture outside its limits.

42

Every teaching which rejects the knowledge and skills gained by science, in order to put forward its own point of view—however "spiritual" this may be—condemns itself in theory and cripples itself in practice. It may do some good and help some people because of the modicum of truth inherent in it, but it would be able to do more good and help more people by accepting the results of science and adding them to its own. This is just as true of scientific medicine itself as it is of a medical-mystical cult.

43

Iconoclastic science came into the world and in a few short centuries turned most of us into sceptics. It may therefore surprise the scientists to be told that within two or three decades their own further experiments and their own new instruments will enable them to penetrate into, and prove the existence of, a superphysical world. But the best worth of these eventual discoveries will be in their positive demonstration of the reality of a moral law pervading man's life—the law that we shall reap after death what we have sown before it, and the law that our own diseased thoughts have created many of our own bodily diseases.(P)

The practices of psychology

44

There are diseases of the mind quite apart from those of the body, yet too often neither the sufferer nor those in his surroundings will recognize the morbid symptoms. He considers himself, and they consider him, normal.

45

The moderns refuse to split up Mind into Consciousness and its Contents and they will not believe that Consciousness *per se* has its pure, unalloyed existence. Hence the utter confusion of modern psychology. Yet it is the light of this Consciousness which enables their own busy intellects to function and their bodies to believe themselves to be conscious entities. Everything in Nature works by Its *reflected* light.

46

The inner nature that is rent by unresolved conflicts and unhappy divisions needs healing just as much as the outer body that is afflicted by pain-bringing disease.

47

Psychoanalysis and psychiatry have to deepen themselves if they are to fulfil their own best possibilities. The emotional vacillations and mental perturbations of the lower self must be studied and understood, but this will never be adequately achieved if the existence of the higher Self is denied or ignored.

48

The psychoanalysts, who are so busy pointing out the complexes of other people, have themselves one supreme complex that dominates and obsesses. It is psychoanalysis itself!

49

The mistake of the analysts is to treat lightly what ought to be taken seriously, to regard as a parental fixation or sex repression what is really the deep spiritual malady of our times—emptiness of soul.(P)

50

It is needful to look into the self in depth, to a level where psychoanalysts are seldom able to reach. For the real aim is to penetrate through thoughts to Thought itself, through the personal being to the impersonal one. Further, according to ancient tradition, not only must meditation penetrate deeply, it must also be continuous.

51

The work of a true psychoanalysis and a wise psychiatry is only preparatory to the work of mysticism. Yet in some cases it is necessary and valuable to a true philosophical mysticism. In clearing the mind from preoccupation with maladjusted personal problems, it makes more possible the opening of the gate of impersonal spiritual consciousness.

52

These complexes and neuroses begin to lose their power from the first moment that we begin clearly to recognize and frankly to acknowledge their existence. This indeed is the primary requisite of successful treatment, whether it be self-applied or whether it be the work of someone else.

53

Without psychological delving into, and treatment of, the emotional conflicts and moral problems, the conscious complexes and the subconscious tensions which absorb so many of the individual's forces and obstruct so much of his spiritual aspirations, any technique remains incomplete. Such a therapeutic activity is not separate from the religio-mystical one, but indeed forms a necessary part of it and confirms its purpose.

54

Half our maladies arise from a sickness which philosophic discipline alone can heal, from a divided, unbalanced, distorted, warped, or unintegrated psyche.

55

There are deformed minds as well as bodies, diseased emotions as well as physiques. Everyone wants to heal the one but few want to heal the other.

56

The psychology which believes its study of man to be complete with its study of his reflexes, complexes, emotions, and behaviour is superficial. It has still to get at and explain his *consciousness* of those things.

57

There are two essential divisions in the psychological constitution of man. The first is the realm of thoughts, the second is that which is aware of the thoughts, the thinker. Modern psychology has done nothing more than grope in the first realm; it has been quite unable to find the final verified truth about the second one, about the mind that is behind all thoughts.

58

The psychoanalyst, the psychological counsellor, and the psychotherapist can all study and practise philosophy with benefit to their professional work. Having done so, they can then play a useful role in treating those who would like to undertake involvement but are emotionally or psychologically too egocentric, too easily upset and unbalanced, or suffering too much from psychoses or neuroses, to be able to rise to its impersonal demands. There is of course a semi-lunatic fringe always around religion, spiritualism, and occultism, with a smaller one around mysticism, for there is some sort of ego satisfaction to be found there. The philosopher is not concerned with this atmosphere.

59

Too many unbalanced persons prematurely occupy themselves with occultism, hypnotism, spiritualism, and even mysticism. It is better not to encourage them, for that will only make their present condition worse. Their first need is to get straightened out and for this they need outside help. The proper help is not easy to find. If it is professional and paid for such as that given by psychologists, psychoanalysts, or psychiatrists, it may have only a very limited value. The kind of help that would be really efficient would be a combination of these professional skills with philosophic, intuitive, and psychic skill.

60

More patients suffering from mental disorders drag out miserable lives in hospitals than those suffering from other forms of sickness, although sickness may kill more people more quickly. This is only a part of the price modern man is paying for his "civilized" way of life.

61

Freud's outlook was too materialistic, his interpretation of psychological processes too mechanistic, his personal experience too one-sided to

permit him to adequately solve the human problem. Nevertheless he presented a good start in opening up a neglected mental hinterland to science.
Adler advanced beyond Freud. Jung advanced beyond Adler. Psychoanalysis has indeed made a useful contribution, amidst all its errors and
exaggerations. It has brought into light what was formerly and unhealthily
hidden in darkness. It has said what needed saying but what nobody had
the courage to say. It has helped people understand their character better.
But this said, its work is useful only on its own level, which is much
inferior to the philosophical one.

62

Insofar as he can bring anyone to see himself as he is, the psychiatrist
may prepare him—at a price—for this quest or, if he is particularly materialistic, may hinder his patient from it.

63

Those who take only a casual interest in their mental health will not take
a serious interest in philosophy.

64

There has never been in incarnation so high a proportion of neurotics,
psychotics, and mildly unbalanced, destructive, violent, or largely mad
persons.

65

Everybody can recognize a bodily deformity—whether it be his own or
another's—in an instant, whereas hardly anybody recognizes a mental
deformity until weeks, months, or even years have passed: sometimes it is
never recognized at all.

66

Ignorance of the laws of psychic well-being is not less dangerous because it is so common.

67

There is a legitimate place for experiment in the applied sciences: it
contributed so much to their development. But in the matter of psychology, consciousness, psychical investigation, and the religious inner life, the
need for guarding sanity and safeguarding morality is surely there.

68

To tell yourself that you are getting better and better every day, when
the *cause* of your sickness is making it worse and worse, is to lead the mind
into illusion, error, and self-deceit. Suggestion has its proper place and
usefulness, but it is only a part and not the whole of psychotherapy.

69

Pseudo-practical psychology is a system for turning thoughts into things, mental images into physical realities, and airy nothings into solid some-things—by believing in them.

70

The psychoanalytic method has only a limited usefulness, as its theory has only a quarter truth. If adopted and followed unrestrainedly it may do as much harm as good, or sometimes even more. It may make the patient so self-absorbed that he is deprived of the broad interest in life necessary to a healthy mind. It may cause him to go on seeking for childhood experiences that never existed, for the alleged roots of his trouble—a process over which people have sometimes wasted years. He may read extreme sexual meanings into his night dreams and his day thoughts, and thus come to absurd attitudes towards life. And finally, the patient may become so dependent on the analyst that he is a helpless creature unable to cope with the world by his own willed and personal response.

71

The psychoanalyst may do useful work in bringing to the surface an earlier happening which gave a suggestion whose work upon the mind and feelings led ultimately to illness.

72

The psychoanalysts work busily on the ego all the time, thus keeping the poor patient still imprisoned in it. But a reference to the Overself might help him really to get rid of some complexes.(P)

73

To how many persons has the average Freudian psychoanalyst brought true inner peace? If statistics were available they would be disillusioning. Why is this? It is not for lack of shrewdness, training, research, and prac-tice on the part of the analysts. The basic answer is that both he and his patients are moving in a vicious circle; all their attention is being kept within the ego, that combination of animal and lesser human traits which has yet to discover its greater self. They seek escape, healing, and freedom where there is none. In that greater self alone the good, the true, the beautiful, and the healthy resides.

74

Psychoanalytic practices may be quite right in their place and for their purpose, but the technique used has no place in philosophy. We do not consider it necessary to delve into an aspirant's childhood in order to explain his present mental condition. For as we believe that his past stretches away into numerous earlier reincarnations, it is obviously insufficient and inadequate merely to take the past of the present reincarnation alone for analysis. Nor do we consider it of any use to try to explain his repressions and frustrations by attempting to interpret his dreams. For we consider most dreams to be merely a worthless melange of thoughts, events, and experiences of the previous twenty-four hours. The really significant dreams are very few.

75

Freud confessed that he had never had any mystical experiences or mystical feelings. He therefore went on to dismiss all such things in purely materialistic terms, making the silly assumption that because he had never had them, therefore it was not possible for anyone else to have them.

76

Freud thought that by searching in the darkest corners of our souls, by putting the most sexual interpretation upon the most innocent thoughts and dreams, we would develop our personalities and free our souls! This distorted and pseudo-deep psychology is typical of present-day theorists who offer their last surmise as a first discovery. No man who has practised the profound meditation which philosophic self-knowledge enjoins, will hear without a smile the Freudian psychoanalysts' doctrine that human nature is but a bundle of obscenity. Even Jung knew better.

77

Psychiatry takes itself too seriously and so overestimates the worth of its findings. If it could pick up a sense of humour, its results would be more accurate.

78

It is unreasonable to conclude that because so large a part of human activity must be attributed to the impulses of sex, the whole of human activity is attributable to that same source. Those analysts who do so have something to learn about the unconscious quest of every creature for its own spiritual self-realization.

79

The psychiatrists, being always properly qualified doctors of medicine, are expected to be more reliable in diagnoses, prognoses, and treatments than other healers. But experience shows exceptions. Others have succeeded in curing when the official psychotherapists failed. Why? It is because the unofficial ones have quite often dropped the materialistic belief that the causes of mental disease must be sought in the *physical* brain alone. The psychiatrists do not reckon with a mind having a consciousness apart from the body.

80

It is interesting to note that the author of works on Psychosynthesis, Dr. Assagioli, has dropped use of the word "spiritual" and replaced it by "transpersonal."

81

"All of my work has been directed towards myself," said Jung; "all of the books are but by-products of an intimate process of individuation."

82

Those psychoanalysts like Freud who find no Overself but only complexes in the human being are outgrown by those like Jung who do find this holy core.

83

Those who get into the hands of many psychoanalysts are likely to stay in their hands forever or until the requisite fees can no longer be afforded.

84

Psychoanalysis has harmed patients by its stirring-up of muddy waters that would have been better cleared of their dirt; by its pose as a strict science when it is only a fanciful pseudoscience; and by its narrow biased and misleading explanation of religion, which substitutes worship of the body's sex instinct for worship of the universe's higher power. Even the introversion which it so greatly excoriates as bad, is so only when it is unwilling and unable to fasten its interest on anything outside the small circle of its petty ego. Otherwise, it unfolds the capacity to intuit directly, to think metaphysically, and to meditate spiritually.

85

Hubbard's book on Dianetics had a wide circulation in this country. Despite repulsive literary style and egoistic literary arrogance, it contains information about practices which are of real worth. When I discussed it with the late Dr. Karen Horney, the leader of a more advanced, less materialistic school of psychoanalysis in New York, she thought that the danger of the patient evading the necessary work upon himself and his character by using this method as a seeming shortcut to the goal was very real. She thought that consequently this method was to be avoided. There is danger, but I do not agree that it should be completely avoided. Much of the danger could be eliminated by combining a part of the Dianetics technique with the analytic one, while avoiding the services of professionals of both schools.

86

Too much harping upon the unhappy childhood or adolescence of a person, or upon his unfortunate adult experiences, all in the name of psychoanalysis, is a mistake. The negative things in a man's past should be impersonally examined, the lessons in them carefully extracted, and then he should be done with it. It is better for the analyst to lift him up than to keep on pressing him down in this way. Similarly, the idea of writing down one's past—whether in a diary or a book—to act as a safety valve and get rid of it, is erroneous. It merely makes the past more powerful when it ought to be forgotten. A more positive attitude to the present and the future ought to be built up, and this is not to be done by dwelling on the miserable periods of the past.

87

The psychoanalysts have made it fashionable to search for a guilt complex, or to invent one if it is non-existent, and then to get rid of it as something utterly detestable, harmful, and evil. Yet insofar as it humbles its possessor, it may render a necessary and even beneficial service. Its opposite number, the smug self-righteous assurance that he is quite a fine fellow, may lead a man just as much into detestable and harmful ways.

Neurosis and its treatment

88

Highly neurotic persons are particularly eager to find a guru (or an analyst), as he or she affords an opportunity to enter into an intimate mental-emotional relationship centered round the neurotic's ego, thus feeding it still more. But the food here is "spiritual." Quite clearly philosophy, throwing the burden of self-salvation on their own shoulders, would be distasteful.

89

Those who can no longer cope with the life of today or with themselves and their experience of today are segregated and put into homes or institutions for the mentally disturbed. May it not be that there is something wrong with society itself that it has brought them to this state?

90

The neurotic person moves in a small world which is solely concerned with his own feelings and his own desires. All his thoughts are centered in his little self. How can he be released from such a prison? One way is to become interested in the lives of other people, helping them so far as he can. Another way is to become interested in understanding the World-Idea, participating consciously in its workings. His temperament will make it difficult for him to follow either of these ways. If, however, he is earnestly seeking release, the attempt to follow either of these ways will attract help from outside himself.

91

When men and women become so completely occupied with their own affairs that thought or feeling for others is entirely absent and the point of extreme obsession with self is reached, they are liable to go mad. It is certain that many of this type find their way into lunatic asylums or mental hospitals.

92

Schopenhauer was not altogether theorizing when he expressed the view that the unconscious mind retreats in the end from every effort at self-expression, because the sufferings and pains of consciousness cause it to return to its own primal and peaceful state.

93

In any madhouse one may see patients sitting for hours and staring into space, a vacuous expression on their faces. Outwardly they not only have these resemblances to the yogis but they too live in a kind of sequestered retreat, they too have in their peculiar way renounced the world and its affairs.

94

Most negative traits belong to the feelings of adolescence, most positive ones to those of real maturity. It is when the negative ones appear in adults that they become neurotic and must be treated as psychic sickness.

95

Through ignorance of the World-Idea or through disobedience to their revelators and teachers, neurotics get worse and become psychotics. They are to be found in both camps—the religious or cultist believers and the sceptical materialists.

96

Too many of these neurotics are too full of unstable egoism to have their emotional complexes soluble by any other psychological treatment than a robust and direct attack upon these complexes. A mushy sentimentality will merely prolong the life of such a complex.

97

Neurotics are moody, sometimes very attractive with their gay and brilliant charm, but sometimes repulsive with their black despairs and criticizing tantrums.

98

When anyone attaches immensely more importance to something than it really has, there is the first sign of neuroticism.

99

Some people become neurotic through too much strained activity, but others become neurotic through too little!

100

The neurotic, whose habitual reaction is entirely impulsive and quite unreasoned, may yet be intellectual or cultured or artistic. But in this matter of reaction he is too dangerously close to the animal level of evolution, with its instinctive passional response to stimulus.

101

It is a tragic fact that there are many psychoneurotic individuals and others suffering from mental disorders, who are under malign psychic influence. Whatever treatment is given such individuals, including those who are now receiving institutional care, might be more successful by having the patients take up residence at an altitude of not less than five thousand feet.

102

The electric shock and deep-freeze therapies used by several psychiatric institutions may achieve temporary success, but the price will be exacted later.

103

Where a thought of fear constantly recurs and plunges him into anxiety or even despair against all the evidence of fact and reason, he is no longer normal but is the sufferer of a phobia.

104

Sufferers from the manic phase of mental disorder are unstable in temperament and soon change their aims, policies, or goals, for none of these is clear enough.

105

In our studies, the term "the unconscious" is not used in the narrow meaning of certain arbitrarily selected innate trends, a meaning given it by the psychoanalysts, but in a broadly scientific sense, as containing in potential latency all the possibilities gained in the conscious life and all the deposits of former earth lives, and not only the personal possibilities, but also the super-personal or cosmic ones.

106

It may be that the patients who are advised by their analysts to take up painting pictures as a form of therapy benefit by the concentration involved in the work, as well as by the relaxation of transferring their thoughts for a while from their own self-affairs.

107

There are different ways of escape for those who have problems. Some of them, such as drink and sex, are frankly acknowledged to be so; others are less easily recognized as such and these include art and religion.

108

Professor Stefan de Schill, psychoanalyst: (1) A *compulsion neurosis*, of which there are several kinds, is caused by a person (technically called "a compulsive") feeling guilty over unclean thoughts. His dry washing of hands is an outer symbol of his attempt or wish to get rid of them. Or his feet swinging, fingers tapping the table, and ear-pulling are nervous habits which betray tension. (2) Any good standard work on psychiatry deals with these habit patterns, these neuroses, which annoy or irritate others.

109

In the catatonic state, the whole force of the person is turned inward and concentrated upon an idea or a picture or a happening which may be of a purely mental kind. They may or may not be aware of what is happening around them but they are unable to leave the condition at will; it must pass away of its own accord.

110

What has the person who is obsessed, insane, paranoic, or hysterical really done? He has fixed his attention on a particular thought, idea, belief, or mental picture and he will not let it go. If the thought contradicts reality, we call him insane.

111

In changing thought for the better, one of the first activities is to cleanse it of undesirable attributes, to wash them away by positive energetic willed control, immediately reacting to their appearance with a very definite mental exclamation of "No!" A mind filled with negative qualities cannot possibly be a healthy mind and is certainly unsuitable for high spiritual flights.

112

Neurotics talk about their quest but too often fail to apply its disciplinary principles, live in a perpetual muddle because they consider reasoning and planning to be anti-spiritual, and remain indecisive and unsettled because they are swaying from one emotion to another. They are easily excited, elated, or depressed. The fact is too often ignored that they have to go through a first stage in which they simply prepare themselves as grown-up human beings before trying higher flights. This is as much in their own interests as in society's, for they will then be better able to deal with others and help themselves. Surely it is more prudent to take up an ideal which is not too far off, which may be an intermediate one that seems reachable and realizable. But they must recognize this situation for what it is, practise a humble patience, and not try to put the burden of duty elsewhere. They are really looking for someone to nurse them out of their neurotic condition which, of course, means a passage from emotional adolescence to adult responsibility.

113

Too often the emotionally sick are excessively possessive and will not let go of someone.

114

The neurotic turns minor situations into great crises.

115

Freud thought that giving emotional support to distressed persons would probably come through forms of hypnosis or self-hypnosis. Today more and more use is made of methods of relaxation, imaging, suggestion, meditation, positive thinking, and kindred ways of countering stress or improving healing.

Hypnosis

116

The practice of hypnotism to help others psychologically or to heal them physically cannot be recommended indiscriminately. Just as there are dangers in the surrender of one's body and will to an invisible spirit-entity in mediumistic passivity, so there are dangers in their surrender to a visible human entity in mesmerized passivity. It should not be practised—if it is practised at all—more than is sufficient to give a needed initial impulse to start the patient's constructive energies. If he is subjected too long and too often to this controlling influence of another person while in this passive inert condition, his willpower can only get weaker and weaker until he is ruined. For if the mind has opened itself up to accept control and receive suggestions from one outside source, it will do so from other outside sources too. In the end its individuality will be destroyed and its capacity for self-protection lost.

117

Although hypnotism is useful for some nervous illnesses, its "cures" are not reliable. When carefully and conscientiously used by the right person, it may be helpful; but it is also exceedingly dangerous in the hands of the wrong one.

118

The Theosophical denunciation of hypnotism as a black art is too sweeping. Hypnotism can be good or evil. That depends partly upon the intentions with which it is practised, the depth of knowledge of the operator, and partly upon the methods used. In the field of healing it may offer useful although often merely temporary relief. The same is true of the field of psychological and moral re-education. If the hypnotist is more than that, if he is also an advanced mystic, it is possible for the alleviations which he brings about to be of a durable nature. Thus the vice of alcoholism can be and has been at times cured instantaneously. The changes are brought about by the impact of the hypnotist's aura upon the patient. When this occurs and when the hypnotist places his will and mind upon the suggestion which he gives, there is a discharge of force dynamically into the patient's aura. It is this force that brings about the change, provided the patient has been able to fall into a passive, sleepy condition. In the case of an advanced mystic, the various physical techniques which bring about this condition are not required. It is then enough if the patient has sufficient faith and is sufficiently relaxed. The mystic can then accomplish the discharge of force merely by gazing intently into the patient's eyes.(P)

119

The mild use of tobacco and the mild indulgence in alcohol are better in the end than the sudden breaking away from them under the spell of a hypnotic "cure." For in the one case the addict still has some room left for the development of self-control, whereas in the other, not only has he none but he is liable either to relapse again or else to divert his addiction into some other channel which may be not less harmful and may even be more.(P)

120

Hypnotism can bring him to a kind of peace but it will not be the real one—only a copy, as drugs also bring.

121

No one can learn the art of thorough self-control by putting his will under someone else's control and his mind in a state of helplessness. Hypnotism, mesmerism, and suggestion may be useful as momentary helps or temporary palliatives but they do not solve the problem of attaining self-liberation. They may even be permanently useful when applied by a man to himself but he who most needs their help least possesses the willpower needful to apply them.

122

Hypnosis should not be resorted to lightly, nor used ordinarily, but should be left to treat chronic cases.

123

More than half the cases reported cured by hypnotic treatment were found by one investigator to have had their symptoms temporarily lulled only, the diseased condition or bad habit returning in a worse form than before within a few weeks, a few months, or at least within one-and-a-half years. Thus the patient merely deceived himself about being cured and unwittingly allowed the disease to continue its ravages unchecked by other treatment; hence its later aggravation.

124

It is true that with hypnosis, symptoms of deeper psychological maladjustments may be banished, but the psychological difficulty will remain and may break out in a more serious form elsewhere. This is the greatest limitation on the therapeutic use of hypnosis. It is effectively applied in psychology, not as a cure, but as a bridge to the subconscious mind to locate causes of maladjustments and phobias for other types of therapy.

125

If the hypnotist's patient is given the suggestion to rely on himself rather than on the hypnotist, this should overcome the objection to hypnotism as having a weakening effect on the will.

126

The most exaggerated claims have been made on behalf of medical hypnotism. Dr. Alexander Cannon for years diagnosed ailments by using someone as a professional hypnotic subject, but the truth is that the subject will only give a diagnosis either of what the patient believes is wrong with himself, or of what someone else present believes. The subject picks up the thought in the other person's mind rather than penetrating into the true nature of the disease itself. Cannon also professed to read the past incarnations of people by the same means, and I once had amusing proof of the truth of this criticism. A lady whom I had met and who was exceedingly ambitious and conceited, who could only conceive of herself playing the most historic roles whether in the past, present, or future, once went to him for a reading. The hypnotized medium said that she had been Cleopatra. Later the lady told me this with great excitement as convincing proof of the fact that she *had* been Cleopatra. Hypnotism has enough of a case to offer for scientific study without running into farcical extremes or fantastic assertions.

127

Hypnotism is morally wrong because it is the imposition of one person's will on another person. It is also practically ineffective because its results are mostly transient and the patient relapses later into his original or even a worse state. This is because it is an attempt to cheat karma and to sidestep evolution, but the Overself of the patient will not allow that to happen. Hence hypnotism's failure, for it is an artificial attempt to do the patient's own walking for him. Every man must in the end do it for himself. The hypnotist who cures me of the drink habit leaves me just as weak-willed afterwards as I was before, nay, even more so. But if I develop my own willpower and thus cure myself of the habit I get both a permanent cure and a stronger character.

5

THE HEALING POWER
OF THE OVERSELF

Spiritual and mental healing defined

Although science has begun to note the facts of spiritual healing, it has
not really begun to explain the facts. Nor will it ever, unless it becomes
utterly humble before the great power of God.

2

The therapeutic side of meditation practices can be competently studied
only by one who both practises them from the inside as well as observes
them from the outside. The scientist and the medical physician, who can
do the latter only, are not even half-competent: they miss the essence of
the subject in missing the power at work. Their intellects may logically
theorize or imaginatively guess at it but that does not bring them into
touch with the reality of it. The very scepticism with which they usually
confront the record of these unorthodox healings and often reject their
genuineness, unfits them for such investigation. The proper openness of
mind, neither credulous nor cynical, is hard for them to establish.

3

Spiritual healing must be separated from mental healing, as the former
works by a descent of divine grace but the latter by a power-concentration
of mind. A cure in the first case will not only be permanent but also affect
the character of the patient, whereas in the second case a cure may be and
often is (especially when hypnotic methods are used) transient whilst the
character remains untouched. In this connection there are some statements
in the chapter on "Errors of the Spiritual Seeker" in my book *The Inner
Reality*.

4

A genuine spiritual healing of the physical body will always produce
spiritual results. That is, it will produce an inner change in the character of

the person healed. But when this happens it means that some kind of wrong thinking or wrong feeling is the real cause of his physical sickness. For instance, thoughts of bitterness, resentment, criticism, and condemnation strongly held and long sustained against other persons can and very often do easily produce liver trouble. So long as that kind of thinking and feeling continues, so long will the liver trouble continue. The proper way to heal it, therefore, is to get at the psychological seat of the trouble—that is, effect an inner change. Where spiritual healing treatment influences a man to give up the wrong thinking, so that it leaves him utterly, the physical effects of the change may show themselves suddenly and miraculously or slowly and gradually. Although they show themselves as a cure of a physical malady, note that it first began as a mental malady or as an emotional malady. And if the inner change is an enduring one, the following cure will be an enduring one too. This is the only type of healing which can truly be called spiritual. All other kinds of so-called spiritual healing are merely mental healing or hypnotic healing, and the cure can never be equal in quality or durability. Quite often, they have only temporary results and the sickness reappears because the inner man has been left with all his psychological neuroses uncured. Mental healing and hypnotic healing are not, strictly speaking, healing at all. They are suppression of symptoms, and at the cost of retention of the hidden causes of these symptoms.

5

In the case of mental healing there is not necessarily any change at all in the character of the patient. His angers, his hostilities, or his resentments may remain as active as before. His cure simply illustrates the power of mind over body—his own or someone else's mind. It is achieved by faith or concentration or suggestion. But in the case of spiritual healing there is an inner change along with bodily cure.

6

Why is it wrong to seek the cure of physical ailments by nonphysical remedies, and particularly by spiritual ones? To argue that the inner healing of bad character is more important—which may be granted—does not do away with the necessity of the outer healing.

7

It is not the true spiritual healing if it leaves the character and outlook untouched, unimproved. There are other kinds of healing which may relieve or cure one kind of ailment while leaving the person still open to make the karma that later brings on another kind of ailment.

8

He who sees in everything only matter and beyond it only nothing, who looks to physics and physiology for sufficient explanation of our existence and to chemical actions for sufficient explanation of our loftiest emotions, will be sceptical of mentalist principles and distrustful of spiritual healing.

9

It is often argued that psychological treatment may cure people suffering from nervous troubles or those whose sicknesses are largely the result of their own imagination, but that such treatment is useless for physically caused maladies. The only way to get at the truth about this problem is to divide psychological treatment into mental and spiritual categories. Mental treatment, which includes hypnotic treatment, is suitable only for nervous troubles, for there alone can it effect a cure; but spiritual treatment is suitable for both nervous and physical troubles because it involves a higher power than the thinking or imagining one, a truly spiritual power which is able to affect the physical body no less than the personal mentality. Mental treatment includes a large part of so-called spiritual healing, which is not genuine spiritual healing at all. Philosophy is able to make this differentiation because it understands the psyche of man and his inner constitution, because it has a deeper knowledge than scientific observers working from the outside or religious devotees working by faith alone can get.

10

Our knowledge of the laws which govern the psychological causes of sickness and the spiritual healing of disease is still incomplete and uncertain.

11

Before one talks of depending upon the Overself one must first have established a relation with it, earned a title to its grace. Otherwise, the talk is premature. Nor can such dependence ever annul the duty of utilizing all ordinary means, all human channels.

12

The possibility of healing physical ailments by spiritual means depends in the last analysis not upon the personal will of the healer but upon the divine soul of the patient. By Its grace, which is a definite force, the soul can assist both mind and body, as I have explained in Chapter 9 of my book *The Wisdom of the Overself.*

13

Those critics who deny the reality of Grace as well as those who deny the possibility of spiritual healing are tersely answered by the writer of Psalms 103:3: "Who forgiveth all thine iniquities; who healeth all thy diseases."

14

Such healing does not contradict the natural laws; it co-operates with them. Thus, to expect an old man to be turned into a young man by its aid, is unrealizable. To demand a new leg to replace an amputated one, is unreasonable.

15

The mere removal of pain, healing of lesions, elimination of tumours, or restoration of functions without any physical agent being used in the cure is itself really a miracle. But such an achievement started and completely finished within only a few hours or a few minutes is even more miraculous. It compels us to redefine the word "miracle." No longer should we regard its meaning as a suspension of natural law, a deliberate intervention by God to thwart His own creation, but rather as a natural fact arising out of still unknown laws.

16

Because I foresee that many more years of continued research are needed before I shall have any conclusions of permanent value to offer, I venture to set down here only the most elementary of my findings. Even these would have been held back for some years were it not that the pressure of our times gives them an importance and urgency that brooks no delay.

17

If only a few sufferers have left the healers' presence restored to health, this should still render it an imperative duty to find out what little we can about how or why the healing happened.

18

We are still in the process of putting together into a single inclusive pattern of Healing and Truth the oddly assorted pieces of a jigsaw puzzle. And it is only the beginning of this process!

19

Out of this world suffering, you may learn the greater lessons which Buddha learned but which Mrs. Eddy tried to evade. Life on earth is not intended to be an eternal bed of roses; it will forever be a mixture of pleasure and pain; the wheel of fate will forever keep turning up now one and then the other. True healing is primarily the healing of spiritual ignorance, never the gaining of prosperity, and only occasionally the getting of good health. It is to win an unbreakable peace and a perfect knowledge which neither death nor man can steal or impair.

20

Are we to follow the example of some holy men, both in medieval Europe and in the modern Orient, who equate the acceptance of illness with the will of God? Are we to cherish our diseases in resignation to God rather than try to cure them by spiritual means? Is such pious fatalism better than turning to spiritual healing?

21

To the extent that Christian Science instruction will make clearer to his mind and fix more deeply within it those several great truths which Christian Science shares in common with philosophy, he will benefit by it. But to the extent that he absorbs, along with them, those errors, fallacies, and confusions which are also part of Christian Science, he will not. Therefore in its study he should keep vigilance close to him and not throw away his right to use critical judgement. One fallacy is not to see that physical means may also be used by God to cure, even if it be granted that they are indirect as well as on a lower plane. They need not be rejected but merely valued for the inferior things they are. But they have their place. Another fallacy is not to see that mental means may also be used. Psychology, change of thought, is also inferior and indirect, but still has a useful place and positive value.

Healings can be done without entering the kingdom. They are achieved by the power of concentration. This leaves the ego still there. The cure is wrought then by an occult, not a spiritual, power. It is personal to the practitioner, not impersonal. Every individual practitioner who makes progress will come to the point where either his power lapses or his understanding outgrows the imposed dogmas. If he accepts this opportunity or passes this test, he may come closer to God.

The Christian Scientist adherent needs to purify his motive. His need of better health or more money may be satisfied in the proper way but must be kept in the proper place. He should not seek to exploit higher powers for lower ends. He should carefully study the meaning of Jesus' words: "Seek ye first the Kingdom of Heaven and all these things shall be added unto you."

Mental healing—its limited success

22

The body has its own laws of well-being. The man who persistently infringes them but relies on the protective shelter of spiritual healing "demonstration" to take care of his infringements is following a risky, unreasonable, and uncertain course. All observation, experience, biography, and philosophy unite to warn him that the chances of succeeding are less than those of failing.

23

Only after he has extracted and applied its lesson may he turn his back on experience and deny its reality. Only after he has learned what law of physical, emotional, or mental hygiene he has violated, and corrected the transgression, may he declare his sickness an illusion of the senses and an error of the mind. Any other course is self-deceiving.

24

The New Thought mental healing cults do not understand the difference between those occult powers (healing is one of them) performed *by* the ego deliberately and those occult powers performed *through* the ego spontaneously at the Overself's bidding. The first kind are on an inferior level and keep the practitioner still enchained within egoism. But of course, by contrast to the orthodox church teaching, this New Thought teaching is certainly broader.(P)

25

No unqualified person—that is, no unintegrated and unpurified person—has the right to audit another. Here is the error of Dianetics: it explains the disappointment of some disciples and the disillusionment of others.

26

The danger to those who seek such healing is one of falling into the materialism which exalts the body at the expense of the soul. The danger to those who practise it is one of falling into vanity, feeling more important or more powerful than others.

27

The group of powers manifesting themselves in the phenomena which have been variously named—according to the theoretical interpretation given them by various cults—as spirit healing, Christian Science, mesmeric healing, hypnotic treatment, and suggestive therapeutics, may, with one group of exceptions, conveniently be classified under the heading of "mental healing." These exceptions occur through the unconscious stimulation of physical vital force (*prana*) and usually lead to cures which are such in name only for they do not last long and are followed by a relapse into illness.

28

With the Short Path are allied all healing techniques, like Christian Science, which affirm the actual existence of God as perfect, disease-free, and all-providing. Sometimes they really do draw on the Overself's power but at other times they use a queer mixture of black magic, hypnotic suggestion, and fallacious religion.

29

If a mental healer should be interested in, or be a practitioner of, black magic, he is far more likely to do serious harm to his patients than good. It is always better to avoid meeting such people. Even the "cures" which they perform are either only temporary, or else bought at a heavily disproportionate price.

30

A teaching which seeks the chief good for human beings, but ignores robust health and freedom from pain as a necessary part of that good, is an incomplete one.

31

The old notion that mental healing is only useful to, and possible in, cases where the patient only imagines that he is sick, is outdated.

32

A doctrine which denies the body's existence while hypocritically trying to cure the body's ailments, contradicts itself. In any case, the body remains there, a hard unavoidable fact which must be accepted in the end, however much anyone believes he has thought it away.

33

The fallacy in Christian Science theory is the pretense that problems and pains, diseases and malfunctions, cancer and crime do not exist among us here in this physical world. If we turn only to pure Spirit and leave out the world in time and space and form, then, undeniably, they do not exist. But we may not leave them out of practical reckoning while we have to live in this body, much as some of us would like to. If the theory floats in mists of fatuous optimism, the art of Christian Science healing does in some cases bring very successful results. Why?

34

It is never the truly spiritual healer who temporarily feels the pain or shows the symptoms of his patient's disease, but only the physical-magnetic healer.

35

Uncritical believers in so-called metaphysical healing and in faith-cure theories are sooner or later subjected to the discipline of facts. The intensity of their pains and the gravity of their ills are intended to, and do, bring them to a truer view of actualities. Instead of blaming themselves for failure to demonstrate good health, they ought to blame these theories for having misled them. Such failure is a chance to revise imperfect beliefs, to cast out errors and start again. This surely is to the good and something to be satisfied about. The problem of bodily healing is a complicated one and often depends on more than a single factor.

36

Those who are likely to decry this proviso are always those who tell us only of the successes of mental or "spiritual" healing, but not of its failures. The comparative figures of the two sets of results are tremendously disproportionate. To open one's eyes to the flaunted successes of this system and to shut them to its aching failures, is not the way to understand it aright. To exaggerate what it has achieved and to minimize or deny what it has been unable to achieve—as is done by its ardent partisans—represents a falling away from intellectual integrity. To take a typical example, consider the famous healing sanctuary at Lourdes, France. It was established in 1860. During recent years the attendance of sick and crippled patients has been no less than six hundred thousand annually. Yet during the first seventy years of the sanctuary's existence, a total of only five thousand cures was reported. This should represent, on a conservative estimate, about one percent of successful treatments. The number of those pilgrim-patients who failed to benefit must therefore run into millions! We dwell on this example not to decry Lourdes, which is doing a blessed and benign work which everyone should respect, and certainly not to derogate its religious aspect, but to point out that the failures in every school of healing, whether materialistic, mental, or religious, must exist. That the inspiration which brought Lourdes into being was truly divine and that the most amazing cures have been achieved there in a manner only to be described as miraculous, we fully accept. But that there are limitations and disappointments inherently present in this kind of healing must also be accepted.

37

Do they not remind us of those medieval alchemists who talked glibly of transmuting brass into gold, the while their tattered sleeves and torn garments betrayed their shame-faced poverty! Facts are stern and can't be laughed off. Exaggerated expectations are inevitably disappointing. These failures are not held against such systems. No healing system, no healer, certainly not even the most orthodox, could have a record consisting only of triumphs. But no movement which boasts of its successes and ignores its failures has the right to call itself scientific. For only by studying its failures could it ever learn not only that there *are* errors mixed up with its truths, but also exactly what errors they are.

38

The mere giving of an auto-suggestion, such as "I am perfect health," which is belied by facts and made untrue by the body's condition, cannot bring about a cure. Such a fictitious statement can only bring about a fictitious result. To deny an illness' existence while refraining from denying the body's existence, is illogical.

39

In all this Christian Science teaching it is essential to note that the healer can utter these healing formulae, think these healing truths, either out of his intellect or out of his insight. In the first case his words and thoughts are merely like the map of a country. In the second case they are like an actual visit to the country. The first healer makes an unwarranted claim, does not see that his statements could be truly made only if he attained the stature and purity of Jesus. It is not enough that the patient should have faith; the healer himself must have the requisite higher consciousness. For the divine power which actually effects the healing will not come from his ordinary self but out of this higher one.

40

Since other cults holding contradictory theories are also able to claim cures, and since there is a natural healing force in the body itself, the Christian Scientists should be cautious and realize that their own theory may be only partially and not wholly correct.

41

Whereas Christian Science denies the reality of the body and hence of the body's ills, most other spiritual healing schools admit it. Whereas Christian Science nowhere speaks of man struggling upward through constant reincarnations on earth to realize his highest possibilities, its most powerful rival—the Unity school of Christianity—proclaims this doctrine.

42

Rudolf Steiner opposed psychic healing because, he said, it did not cure but merely drove the disease deeper inside, to reappear later in some other part of the body.

43

If the patient recovers, the system of healing—whether it be orthodox or unorthodox—gets the credit; but if he fails to recover, the system does not get the debit.

44

The Vedantist and Christian Scientist who are determined to exclude the idea of world-existence from their view, are nevertheless forced to yield and re-admit the exile when a simple toothache instructs them to the contrary.

45

A cautious attitude to these cures may well find them to be the result of natural healing processes; they would have happened anyway.

46

Unbiased investigation shows that there are disproportionately more cases of failure than of success by mental and religious healers. It is unfortunate for the claims made and misleading to the uncritical following that while the successes are highly advertised, the failures are buried in silence. Moreover, even among the alleged healings, not all are actual or durable ones. Thus the subject easily lends itself to deception, sometimes to imposture.

47

The therapy of spiritual healing yields results similar to those of other therapies. It has been known to cure one man of a chronic complaint yet fail to even help another man suffering from the same complaint.

48

If the published testimony to the cures by the methods of the best known of these cults is carefully and cautiously examined in the scientific manner, it will be obvious that in the first place some of the sufferers never had the particular ailment they name, but only some minor one.

49

The religious revivals which are carried on during intense excitement, with much dancing and jumping, and at which dramatic healing of the sick occurs, are too often mere displays of emotionalism. The Spirit-fire current rushes upward temporarily but soon falls down and with its return to quiescence there is the usual bodily reaction. Religious fervour abates and the cure vanishes.

50

The proportion of failures to healings is never known, and so long as the religious approach continues and a religious organization's power, wealth, and prestige are at stake, will never be known.

51

When Christian Science states profound mentalist truths it becomes elevating, but when it mixes them up with refutable conjectures, it becomes misleading. In the first case it is supported by the facts of life, whereas in the second it conflicts with them.

52

My attitude towards Christian Science–Aurobindo theory of physical immortality: continue to deny that abolition of death is possible, but admit that prolongation of physical life may well be possible. In the case of good individuals admit also its desirability.

53

The Christian Science practitioners apparently use their formulas, their statements of being, their treatments, in the form of uttered incantations. This is much like the use of mantrams in India.

54

A comparative study of the history of mental healing shows how universal and ancient are its origins; nor are its principles new.

55

Mental Moral and Spiritual Hygiene seeks to establish a proper way of living and thus prevent sickness. The healing art steps in where sickness already exists and a cure is sought.

56

Another extremely fanatical attitude of which we must beware is the belief that mental healing displaces all other systems and agencies for curing disease or keeping health; that its advocates may totally discard every branch of medicine and surgery, hygiene, and physical treatment. Sanity and balance call for the acceptance in its proper place of whatever Nature and man can contribute. With these preliminary warnings, we venture to predict that as the principles and practices of mental healing come to be better, namely more rationally understood, it will establish for itself a firm place in therapeutics which will have to be conceded—however grudgingly—by the most materialistic and most sceptical of medicos.(P)

57

We must remember that mental healing is only a single aspect of the art of healing. All the others must be brought in to make a balanced system. God has given us valuable herbs, for instance, which possess remedial virtues. We should accept the gift.

58

The error of Christian Science would appear to be that it confuses theory and wrongly applies practice. Its principles are half-right, half-wrong; its technique is the same. The injunction to "cast thy burden on Me," which it seems to apply, is misunderstood to advise neglecting practical means of healing troubles and leaving all to God. But the correct way is not to neglect them but to do them while at the same time leaving results to God and being indifferent to them.

59

Even if Christian Science and New Thought sects produce healings, they are still not truly "divine." They use some lower force—some vital force, as the Indians say. For they are all attached to the ego, which is itself a consequence of their unconscious belief in its reality. The ego has cunningly inserted itself even into these highly spiritual teachings and is still the hidden source behind both their prophets and their followers. This explains Mary B. Eddy's and so many New Thought teachers' commercialism as well as the errors which are contained in the teachings of Emmet Fox, which led to his own mental-physical breakdown and death.(P)

60

Christian Science can deny the existence of ill health only at the cost of logically denying the existence of good health also. Both are differing conditions of the same thing—the body. Christian Science calls sickness a lie. Then it should likewise call its opposite a lie. But not only does it not: it actually affirms that good health is a truth and a reality even while it denounces matter—the body—as a lie and an illusion! If, in spite of its deformed logic, Christian Science still gets healing done—as it does—this result must be attributed to the fact that the infinite Life-Power *does* take cognizance of the body's disease and does *not* deny its being there.

61

It is not only fallacious to deny the existence of a disease but also, if the attempt is made to secure healing, insincere.

62

The Christian Science attempt to deny existence to sickness as an error of mortal mind is itself an error. It is more philosophic, first, to take it as an existent fact, but to understand that the body's reality is only a limited and temporary one, and, second, to couple it with the other fact that there are healing forces and recuperative energies in the higher self of man which may dispel it.

63

If right thinking alone could sustain life and support health irrespective of every other factor, then human beings could immure themselves where sunlight, air, water, and food could not reach them and still live actively. But the only cases known to history are of a few hibernating inactive yogis. Such theorizing is self-deceptive.

64

Mary Baker Eddy, from the safe distance of the study, conveniently denied the existence of disease. Meanwhile the gods have smiled cynically as millions in Asia have picked up cholera and passed to their doom.

65

The mental peace obtained by denying facts like sickness may be welcome to the sufferer. But it may also turn out to be a false peace.

66

Although the theory of these cults is in part quite fallacious, the practice of them brings striking results at times. This is because the healing power really comes forth from the patient's own higher self, to which the cults do—although somewhat unconsciously—direct him.

One of the yoga paths is the creative use of imagination and thought for self-improvement, and so far as it embodies such a technique, Christian Science is a yoga path too. It instructs its disciples to see themselves as perfect, as the Universal Mind sees them, to concentrate on the concept of, and hold to the belief in, the divine in man. These meditations and attitudes draw forth higher resources, which may effect results where ordinary ones fail.

This thinking runs somewhat as follows. The entire universe is but an idea. Therefore the human body is also an idea. Therefore the human being, as the thinker of this idea, possesses complete power to alter, improve, and even change the body. Therefore he can abolish disease, annul sickness, restore health, and perform miraculous environmental betterments at will, provided he can suitably re-adjust and control his thoughts. All this sounds plausible and attractive, but there is a fallacy in it. And this is that the human being is the sole thinker of the World-Idea. He is not. He only participates in it along with the World Mind. His power over the body is a limited one. By his thoughts he can influence its functioning and sometimes modify its mechanism.

Healers and the spiritual path

67

Some persons have wonderful healing gifts, but they will need to keep the ego out of their use of these gifts if the quest is not to be obstructed.

68

Those who are born with healing skills, probably brought over from former births, function on different levels. The commonest is that which radiates life-force and energizes the cells of the sick person. This kind of healer must first put himself into a passive mood and then, when he feels the vibratory force of the life-force active within him, let it pass, with or without touching the patient, into the latter. The vibrations of the life-force are universal; they are not the healer's own personal property. He simply possesses a skill in letting himself be used as a channel, and it is usually concentrated in his hands. A healer like Saswitha, who says he is merely drawing the therapeutic power from his patient and redirecting it or returning it back to the patient, forgets that if this is so the patient himself gets it from the cosmic forces. It is not his own personal property.(P)

69

Jesus healed the sick, cured the diseased. Why decry the feat (when others do the same) as "merely" using an occult power, and as a deviation from the highest path of attainment, becoming an obstacle to it? For this is the criticism by Advaitic Vedantins. This criticism is unfair. If it is right to cure a man by physical means—medicine, for example—then it is right to cure him by mental means, and drawing on still deeper powers is in the same line of progression. The Advaitins grant that a physician may attain the highest truth. Is a physician like Paracelsus, using both physical and mental remedies, plus his own spiritual power, and therefore capable of helping more people more effectively, to be denied this possibility?

70

The professional in other lines can often give a reasonable assurance of the efficacy of his work, but the genuine spiritual healer cannot. For not only is his own gift involved but also both the patient's self-made destiny and his evolutionary need.

71

Apollonius tells us that Pythagoras regarded healing as "the most divine art." Why should anyone reject the views of the Greek sage, not to speak of Jesus' own confirmation by his works? Why should the Indian sages regard healing as a merely occult art, hence as a practice to be avoided?

72

Why should it be right for a spiritual master to minister to diseased minds but wrong to minister to diseased bodies? To label one as white magic and the other as black magic, or to neglect and ignore the flesh in the interest of whole-time devotion to the spirit, is unfair.

73

Too many Indian, and a few Western, gurus and cults reject the development and use of healing power. It is, they argue, an obstruction in the spiritual path because it keeps its practitioner captive to the ego, which may even become stronger through conceit. There is the historic case of Ramakrishna. He went to his prayer shrine in his temple three times to request a healing for the throat cancer which troubled him, but each time failed to utter the words. The merit of argument based on increased egotism and vanity, the danger of being sidetracked from seeking the highest goal, is admitted. But is this enough ground to ban spiritual healing completely and always? Must it be denied to all people at all times, universally, because some healers may be obstructed spiritually by its practice? The answer of common sense agrees with the example of Jesus.

74

The healing of disease was well identified with Jesus' work, with Aesculapian Greek sanctuaries, with Egyptian exorcism, with many a mystic throughout the Orient, and even with a number in the modern world, Eastern and Western. How, then, with such a religious background, can it be fair to deny divine inspiration to the man who performs healing, while allowing such inspiration to the man who only preaches?

75

Vedantic thought usually regards the *siddhis*—occult powers—as obstacles to attaining truth. Among them the healing of the body's sicknesses and the mind's disorders is included.

76

That some persons are unusual in being born with the gift of healing the sick is a historic fact. Why reject the talent or power as being unworthy of a true sage or of those who seek to become such a one? In what way is this form of serving humanity unethical, unsafe, inconsistent with the highest?

77

Remember that Jesus started his work by an act of healing a sick person.

78

The results of their use of healing powers cannot ordinarily be predicted, much less guaranteed, but must be left to the Higher Power.

79

Spiritual healing is drawing much attention but the subject is involved in much confusion. Even the healers themselves hold contradictory theories about it. Some use prayer to get their cures; others deny that prayer is of any avail. Some practise meditation alone; others combine meditation with the laying-on of hands. Some deny that there is anything more than the power of suggestion behind the healings; others find in them an evidence of God's presence. Are there any spiritual laws which will scientifically explain the healings?

80

Is the Hindu wisdom always wise? There is the warning of Patanjali's *Yoga Sutras* against the occult powers that might be acquired by yoga:

they are to be shunned because they obstruct further advance towards a higher plane. Healing is one of these listed powers. Must we accept such an attitude and reject the gift of healing, if it comes? Is good health so great an evil that disease is to be accepted dutifully? On this point a Westerner might rebel.

81

In ancient and orthodox Hinduism the profession of healer was regarded unfavourably, for the strange reason that it brought the healer and the sick together!

82

Rosa Bailly was known in France as a poetess. Quite late in life she became aware of certain radiations and found herself capable of healing sick people by using these radiations. Out of these experiences with patients she wrote a booklet entitled *La Survie du Cancer* (*Victory over Cancer*), but it is no longer in print and has never been translated. She died in the Pyrenees where she lived during this last phase of her life, devoted to healing work until she finally gave that up, saying that it exhausted her too much. What she regarded as her major contribution to the healing art was the discovery from this experience of hers that cancer has its seat "in the pithy marrow of the spine" no matter where its tumour is. She could not find a publisher for this little book in France, but it was published here in Switzerland and will not, it is said, be reprinted now that she has passed. In fact she was her own publisher. At the time of her retirement, she explained that vital energy would pass from her to the patient. It is known that some of her cures were spectacular, and even in most of the cases where she failed to save the life of the patient, she brought about a passing without suffering.

83

The confusion of thought concerning spiritual healing is tremendous. Swami Nikhilananda asserts that Ramakrishna's practice of falling into spiritual trance aggravated the cancer which finally killed him. Yet this is the very method and practice used by some healers to heal their patients, because, they believe, it releases divine energies.

84

What the healer does is to release, stimulate, or add energy to the sufferer's own natural recuperative forces.

85

The differences between healers are differences of techniques, personal fitness, and spiritual degree.

86

The power to heal the sick is a latent gift deliberately brought out by development or spontaneously released by illumination.

87

Spiritual healing is a gift which is innate in certain individuals and very difficult to acquire by others. It may, however, exist latently, and could show itself only after a certain degree of spiritual development has been attained.

88

Bernard of Clairvaux cured hundreds of the blind, deaf, and paralysed during the twelfth century simply by making the sign of the cross over the affected body part. Olcott in Ceylon, eight centuries later, cured dozens of cases of scorpion bite and even snake bite by making the sign of the pentagram over the part. Does this not show that the healing power lay in the healer himself, even more than in his method?

89

There are many puzzling cases of healers, like Saint Paul in ancient times, Saint Catherine of Siena in medieval times, and Father Matthew of Ireland in modern times, who cured the ills of many people but did not or could not cure their own. This is a paradox that is hard to resolve.

90

All healers lose their power after a time. This is to lead them to a higher level.

91

Doctors who can keep us well, long-lived, and capable of functioning properly are more needed than those who cure our diseases.

92

If words have any meaning at all, Christ's words have meant that personal sacrifice is the cost of spiritual growth. For eighteen hundred years, men of every kind—scholars, mystics, priests, laymen, ascetics, and saints—agreed on that. Then arose a new group of cults—faith-healers—which not only gave a new meaning to those words but a directly opposite meaning. Success and prosperity, they asserted, are outer signs of inner spiritual growth. The end result was that they tried to use spiritual forces solely for their own personal purposes and material benefits, instead of trying to surrender to those forces and submit to higher purposes. They denied— contrary to the experience of all religious history—that material loss and personal failure could ever be the working of such purposes.

The work of the Overself

93

My basic conclusion is that healing exists on all these different levels, which means its power comes from different sources. But this said, I feel that all healers should know their limits, their limitations, and I fear that many of them do not simply because they are carried away by their enthusiasm. Secondly, I feel that all healers would not only be none the worse for some knowledge of anatomy and physiology and the commoner maladies, but they should even attempt to acquire some of this knowledge. Otherwise many errors, many false or exaggerated claims, are made by the healers. I am not questioning their honesty; I believe most of them are honest. But I am questioning their lack of knowledge—I mean accurate knowledge and fuller knowledge. On the other hand, I criticize the medical profession for failing to enter into dialogue with the healers, for they would learn much to their own profit and to the improvement of their professional help if they adopted a humbler attitude towards the unorthodox healers.(P)

94

Before the healing processes can come into operation, the patient must be brought into a receptive state; otherwise he will unconsciously obstruct them. Faith is the first requisite.

95

Those who approach him with their wish to be healed and their faith in his power to bring it to realization, have still not approached him aright. They must also be willing to have their own contribution to the disease's existence pointed out. They must also agree to rectify wrong habits of living and thinking. If they come only for pleasant words and a successful cure, if they are not prepared to deny themselves or to discipline themselves, he cannot heal them.

96

The first and least danger which besets the possessor of occult healing power is the praise or fame it brings him from other people, who are led by it to think him greater than he really is. He feels flattered by the praise and elated by the fame, with the result that his ship runs aground on the reef of vanity. His further progress gets stopped. Few can withstand the temptation as Gandhi once withstood it. One day an old Bengali man prostrated before Mahatma Gandhi and expressed gratitude for his having cured him of chronic paralysis. The man had tried other remedies without success and finally resorted to the repeated utterance of Gandhi's name, and was completely cured. When replying, the great liberator of India showed the selfless humility of his character: "Will you oblige me by taking my photograph off your neck? It was not I but God who cured you."

97

Deep down within the heart there is a stillness which is healing, a trust in the universal laws which is unwavering, and a strength which is rock-like. But because it is so deep we need both patience and perseverance when digging for it.(P)

98

To pray for a bodily cure and nothing more is a limited and limiting procedure. Pray also to be enlightened as to *why* this sickness fell upon you. Ask also what *you* can do to remove its cause. And above all, ask for the Water of Life, as Jesus bade the woman at the well to ask.(P)

99

If he can apply this teaching *now*, if he can put his faith in and make his contact with the higher power from this very moment, if he can forget himself for an instant, he can receive healing instantaneously.(P)

100

When Jesus told the sick person, "Thy faith has brought thee recovery," he did not mean, as many now think, faith that the cure will be effected. No—he meant faith in the healing power—God. The first kind keeps the mind still centered in ego, whereas the second kind of faith lifts the mind away from ego. Another translation: "Your faith has made you well."

101

Because the Overself is not outside a man but is his own innermost nature, full faith in its presence and power is essential to experience its healing and help.

102

When the pursuit or practice of healing powers diverts him from the higher work of knowing who it is that is seeking or using them, when they no longer serve but make him their servant, he must pause and beware.

103

When he realizes how much is given by the higher power through him, and how little is really done by himself, the healer or teacher may well become careless of his fame, efface his own personality, and keep it humbly in the background. Whoever else achieves the same good results will arouse his generous joy, not his egoistic jealousy.

104

Francis Schlatter replied to a query as to the secret of his successful healings: "I am nothing, but the Father is everything. Have faith in the Father and all will be well. The Father can grow a pair of lungs just as easily as He can cure a cold."

105

The secret of exercising spiritual power is to turn towards the other and higher being which is the soul. The price of exercising it is self-abandonment. This is as true of spiritual healing as it is of spiritual initiation.

106

An honest healer can say only that his healing depends on two conditions being fulfilled: the faith of the patient and the permission of the higher powers.

107

A monk who attained great renown and reputation in Rumania for his selfless character, inspired preaching, and miraculous healing said that he asked all patients to make a confession privately to him of their wrong attitudes and wrong-doing before the work of healing could begin, as this opened the door.

108

This healing quality present in his highly developed being passes into others, although only into those who can absorb it through devotion or receive it through faith.

109

It is risky for him to forget what he primarily still is—a layman, not a medical man. He ought not attempt to occupy a position which does not belong to him.

110

Whoever wishes to experiment in healing himself or others need not be deterred by these provisos from trying to do so. He does not need to be an adept in yoga or a sage in philosophy to receive the power of grace. Technically, even a slight realization of the principle involved may suffice to bring success. For the result is not in his hands but God's. And partly because of this but partly because many physical ailments can be traced to their psychological equivalents in defective character, deep repentance is an additional factor of definite importance in such self-treatment.

111

No man in himself, his ordinary self, is a real spiritual healer in the way another man could be a medical, herbal, magnetic, homeopathic, or psychotherapeutic healer. Spiritual healing belongs only in the providence of the Overself.

112

The truth that it is not the ego which is instrumental in the higher forms of healing is made evident to every practising healer throughout his career. When Saint Augustine was dying, a sick man came to him and begged to be cured. Augustine replied that if he possessed any powers he would have used them upon himself. However, the visitor said he had been told in a dream to ask Augustine to cure him by the laying on of hands. The saint yielded and followed the instruction. The man was healed.

113

Unless a genuinely scientific and metaphysical basis is found, it will be discovered, as one famous healing cult has already discovered, that although cures are effected which cannot be doubted, many of these cures are not permanent. The principle which is the key to such healing—if it is to be real healing and not a temporary suppression of symptoms—and which overrides all others, was pointed out in an earlier book (*The Inner Reality*, also published as *Discover Yourself*). It is the surrender of the conscious will, the personal will, to a higher power. It is the giving up of ego by offering of your body-problem to the power behind all bodies. The cure is not effected and cannot be effected by the patient himself or by any professional healer who may be employed. It is done only by the Overself itself, which means that it is essentially a bestowal of grace. Now grace is an active force, not a mere intellectual thought or emotional attitude. It is the cosmic willpower, or what Indians call kundalini. This bestowal in turn requires that not merely the body alone be touched, but also the mind. Hence a cure which is genuine and permanent will always involve to some extent a mental re-adjustment, a correction of outlook, even an ethical conversion.

114

Those who do not understand the Overself's workings expect it always to manifest—if it manifests at all—in all its naked purity. If they desire healing, they think that the Overself's help can show itself only in a direct spiritual healing, for instance. The truth is that they may get the cure from a purely physical medium, like a fast, a diet, or a drug; yet that which roused them to seek this particular medium or gave it its successful result *was* the Overself.(P)

115

Jesus' primary intention was to heal the inner man, to promote a directional change in his thought and feeling, to divert him from a sinful to a righteous attitude towards life, and to convert him from spiritual indifference to spiritual enthusiasm. The healing of the body was but a by-product and took place only after these inner processes had been successfully carried out. When the higher elements in a man's character got the better of his lower ones, the victory was followed by, and symbolized in, a return of health to the sick body. It was a visible sign of the reality of the invisible healing. Jesus could not have cured the physical sicknesses if the sufferers had not previously felt his greatness, repented of their former way of life, asked forgiveness, and resolved to become righteous. The Gospels record the cases of those who were able to do this; they do not record the cases of the far larger number who could not and whose bodily maladies therefore remained uncured. Most readers erroneously believe that Jesus could heal any and every person. Nobody can do that because nobody can force faith, conversion, penitence, moral evolution, and spiritual aspiration into a stubborn man's heart. There is a further factor in Jesus' healings. They were often accompanied by the proclamation that the patient's sins were forgiven him. This means first, that the aforesaid prerequisite conditions had been established and second, that the man's Overself had intimated its gracious cancellation of the particular bad destiny which had expressed itself in the sickness. The forgiveness came through Jesus as a medium; it did not originate in him. Those who believe that Jesus personally could unburden all men's evil fate, err. He could do it only in those cases where a man's own higher self willed it. Jesus then became a medium for its grace.(P)

116

The healing does not come from the healer himself; it comes *through* him. What he does is to prepare conditions rendering it possible for this to happen. But this is no guarantee that the Overself will necessarily make use of them every time.

117

We eagerly seek to be relieved of sickness or trouble, but where relief is followed by a feeling of relationship to the Overself, we have gained something far more valuable than we originally sought.

118

When every form of available or affordable physical treatment—the unorthodox as well as the orthodox—has been exhausted without success, it is time to try spiritual healing. For the desperate it is the last hope.

119

The actual cure is so swift in time and so untechnical in method that he may be seized with the most exhilarating astonishment.

120

Genuine cures are quite possible and valid. The person responsible for it may have been used by the higher self of the sufferer as an actual instrument of spiritual healing.

121

So powerful is the force of suggestions implanted from outside that a man may be exercising the gift of healing direct from his own Soul yet he will believe, and believe firmly, that he is exercising and deriving it from the spirit of a dead man.

122

Spiritual healing cannot be successfully practised by anybody who has merely picked up its jargon and intellectually familiarized himself with its ideology. It can be successfully practised only by one who has entered into the consciousness of, and surrendered his ego to, the divine spirit within himself.

123

If, when the processes of the quest are not definitely directed towards the eradication of disease, they are still successful in contributing to such eradication, how much more successful can they be when they are quite definitely directed towards it!

124

This presence whose contact is directly felt has healing values emotionally. It frees him from frustrations and alienations.

125

"I am not a healer. Jesus is the healer. I am only the little office girl who opens the door and says, 'Come in.' "—Aimee McPherson, in explanation of her hundreds of miraculous cures

126

The spirit can operate to ameliorate bodily ills directly and internally or indirectly through an external agent or medium. The latter does not replace but only co-operates with or is used by the spirit.

127

As this Spirit-Energy passes through the man, he feels dynamized, empowered in some direction, inwardly or physically or both together.

128

He understands well enough that this power is not his own, that it must be ascribed to the Overself, and that practising humility while using it is his best protection against the sin of pride.

129

That which is heavenly is also healing.

130

The divine self cannot be aristocratically ordered by its lowly offspring to do this or that, although it may be humbly implored to do so. The ego cannot impose its will.

131

The attunement of man's mind to the Universal Mind, of his heart to the fundamental love behind things, is capable of producing various effects. One of them may be the healing of bodily ills.(P)

Seek inner peace

132

The basis of higher healing work is the *realization* of man as Mind. But the latter is a dimensionless unindividuated unconditioned entity. It is not *my* individual mind. The field of Mind is a common one whereas the field of consciousness is divided up into individual and separate holdings. This is a difference with vast implications, for whoever can cross from the second field to the first, crosses at the same time from an absurdly limited world into a supremely vital one. Consequently, genuine and permanent healing is carried on without one's conscious association and can be effected by dropping the ego-mind and with it all egoistic desires. Hence the first effort should be to ignore the disease and gain the realization. Only *after* the latter has been won should the thoughts be allowed to descend again to the disease, with the serene trust that the bodily condition may safely be left in the hands of the World-Mind for final disposal as It decides. There should not be the slightest attempt to *dictate* a cure to the higher power nor the slightest attempt to introduce personal will into the treatment. Such attempts will only defeat their purpose. The issues will partly be decided on the balance of the karmic and evolutionary factors concerned in the individual case. And yet there are cults which do not find it at all incongruous to suggest to the Infinite Mind what should thus be showered upon one, or to dictate to karma what exactly it should do! Once surrender is truly made, the desires of the self go with it and peace reigns in the inner life whether illness still reigns in the external life or not. Thus there is a false easy yielding of the will which deceives no higher power than the personal self, and there is an honest yielding which may really invoke the divine grace.(P)

133

It is a mistake, however, to turn the higher self into a mere convenience to be used chiefly for obtaining healing or getting guidance, for healing the sicknesses of the physical body, or guiding the activities of the physical ego. It should be sought for its own sake, and these other things should be sought only occasionally or incidentally, as and when needed. They should not be made habitual. In his periodic meditations, for instance, the aspirant should seek the divine source of his being because it is right, necessary, and good for him to do so and he should forget every other desire. Only after he has done that and found the source, and only on his backward journey to the day's activities, may he remember these lesser desires and utilize the serenity and power thus gained for attending to them.

134

Your assertion that Jesus primarily wished to free men of disease, or to teach them how to become so, is untenable. Whoever has entered into the consciousness of his divine soul—which Jesus had in such fullness—has his whole scale of values turned over. It is then that he sees that the physical is ephemeral by nature, whereas the reality whence it is derived is eternal by nature; that what happens inside a man's heart and head is fundamentally more important than what happens inside his body; and that the divine consciousness may and can be enjoyed even though the fleshly tenement is sick.

135

The sufferer should use whatever physical medical means are available—both orthodox and unorthodox ones. At the same time he should practise daily prayer. But he should not directly ask for the physical healing for its own sake. He should ask first for spiritual qualities and then only for the physical healing with the expressed intention of utilizing his opportunity of bodily incarnation to improve himself spiritually.

136

Healing is but a mere incident in the work of a sage. Such a one will always keep as his foremost purpose the opening of the spiritual heart of man.(P)

137

A modern mystic, the late Sister Marie of the Order of Poor Clares of Jerusalem, was told from within, "Because I love you I have given you bad health since the beginning of your life, so that you would feel how dependent you are on Me."

138

The Overself knows what you are, what you seek, and what you need.

139

"Ask not for healing, or longevity, or prosperity; ask only to be free!" exclaimed Vivekananda.

140

The Overself does have the power to heal the diseases of the body by its Grace, but whether that Grace will be thus exercised or not is unpredictable. It will do what is best for the individual in the ultimate sense, not what the ego desires. For the Divine Wisdom is back of everything every time.

141

Spiritual healing does not necessarily follow automatically upon the giving of complete faith. Nor does it necessarily follow upon the voluntary cleansing of the emotional nature. There are other factors involved in it. The place of suffering and sickness in the World-Idea is one of them. For those aspirants who will be satisfied with nothing short of achieving the Highest, the need of transcending the ego takes precedence over everything else, even over the body's healing.

142

It is impossible either to guarantee or to predict what would happen in any individual case. The difficulty is that if one tries to get at the Truth simply as a means to achieve the healing, the Truth eludes him. One has therefore to seek Truth and leave his fate to it, which will always work out for the best, materially or otherwise.

143

Continued ill health is a great trial. The very fact that an individual has been forced to endure a life of endless suffering will surely lead him to realize that worldly life yields little—if any—real satisfaction or happiness, and that it is necessary to seek it in something Higher, in the Quest of the true Spiritual Life, or in God. Somewhere, sometime, this need of his will call forth an answer.

144

People are attracted towards these cults either because they are in desperate need of physical healing or because they are in need of spiritual healing, or because they see in these doctrines an opportunity to satisfy both spiritual aspiration and material needs by a single faith and effort. They are trying to make the best of both worlds. To be able to attain the Kingdom of Heaven and to gain prosperity or cure disease along with it is certainly a most attractive benefit. But unfortunately it is also a little too good to be true. We would all like to have it, but can we have it? What did Jesus himself say about this point? He said, "Seek ye first the Kingdom of Heaven and all these things shall be added unto you." The word of greatest importance in this sentence is the word "first." If you wish to employ the help of a higher power and feeling, then you must give your first thought, your first devotion, your first reverence, your first love to that higher power and not to any lesser thing, such as material gain or even physical cure, as the price of your worship.

145

New Thought and Christian Science should correct their errors, for some of the things which they label as "negative" may not be so at all. It is divine love which sanctions losses, sicknesses, poverty, and adversities. They are not to be regarded as enemies to be shunned but rather as tutors to be heeded. Through such blows the ego may be crushed and thus allow truer thoughts to fill the emptied space. Even pleasure and prosperity may deal a man worse blows than the so-called negatives can deal him if their end effect is to close the mind's door to light.

146

All inner healing depends ultimately upon the operations of grace for its effectiveness. For grace is guided by wisdom and it is not always wise for a man to be healed quickly or even at all. In the case of certain characters, good health may be but a gate to dubious activities leading to worse ills that would befall them.

147

There are times when the Overself's grace may manifest even in the ugly form of illness! If its entry into the everyday consciousness is blocked or twisted by materialistic scepticism, animalistic obsessions, inherited complexes, or excessive extroversion, it may forcibly make its way through them. The body may then be stricken down with sickness until such time as the blockage or distortion is removed.

148

Ramana Maharshi once told us the story of a man whom he had seen when he himself was a young man. This man was crippled, could not use his legs, and had to crawl. An old man suddenly appeared before him and commanded,"Get up and walk!" The cripple was so excited that he automatically rose up and found himself able to walk properly. When he looked round to see this strange benefactor, the man had vanished. The healing was permanent. The point here is first, not whether the vision was subjective or objective, but that the healer did not even have a familiar identity, was not recognized as a Christian saint or Hindu god, and second, that the sufferer was stimulated into having enough faith to obey the command to believe he was healed already; it was not a matter of time.

149

A woman came for an interview who had exhausted all patience with her husband and announced that she was about to leave him. He was an alcoholic of the worst kind. I asked her to be patient with him, not to leave him, but to give him a further chance. Then I went into the silence for her. An hour or two after her return home, her husband made his first and last attempt at suicide. It failed and he was stopped before he could do any serious harm to his body. Then he fell into a deep sleep for a very long time. He awoke feeling better in every way but still despondent. A few weeks later the desire to drink left him completely and never returned. He was cured. "A miracle has happened," was his wife's comment in a letter.

150

Dorothy Kerin was almost instantaneously restored to health and freed from diabetes and tuberculosis. Moreover, her wasted flesh filled out and a gastric ulcer vanished within an hour. At the same time she saw a vision of Jesus, Mary, and the angels.

151

It is perfectly true that the divinity within man will shelter, feed, and clothe him materially, as it will also do spiritually, provided he looks for it, submits himself to its guidance, and obeys its promptings. But it is also true that the selfsame divinity may strip prosperity and possessions from a man's shoulders and lead him into the cold waters of destitution, and this because it has begun to make its presence felt in his life. It may do this or it may not, depending on individual circumstances and the man's degree of attachment to material possessions, but whatever it does will be wise and needful.

152

The healing power issues from an infinite source. There is no kind of disease which it may not cure; but it can do so only within the conditions imposed by the nature of the human body itself.

153

Dismayed by the failure of my physicians' last resort, I was sitting up in bed reading a passage from an old journal of John Wesley about spiritual healing. It quoted a friend as saying: "I could not move from place to place, but on crutches. In this state I continued about six years. At Bath I sent for a physician but before he came, as I sat reading the Bible, I thought, 'Asa sought to the physicians, and not to God; but God can do more for me than any physician'; soon after rising up, I found I could stand. From that time I have been perfectly well."

As soon as I finished this passage I thought it should be applied to my own case, and laid the book aside. A great mental stillness and inner indrawing came over me at the same time. I saw that all the methods hitherto used to eliminate the disease were futile precisely because they were the ego's own methods, whether physical, magical, mental, or mechanical. I had exhausted them all. So the ego had to confess its total failure and cast itself on the mercy of the higher power in humiliation and prayer. I realized that instead of thinking that *I* or my physicians were competent to cure the disease, the correct way was to disbelieve that and to look to the Overself alone for healing. I saw that the stillness was its grace, that this quietness was its power. It could best cure me, if only I would relax and let it enter. So I surrendered to it and within a few weeks was healed.

Part 2:
THE NEGATIVES

We see what appears to be evil rampant in the world, especially in this century, but it is not absolute evil. It is destined to disintegrate and vanish. How can you be so sure? Because if man grows he comes to the truth. If he does not then he loses his manhood for a time. His evil goes with him. The man who lives in the truth lives in ethereal light, beautiful peace, even if the shadows are there. He sees on deeper levels where evil cannot penetrate and where the senses of unevolved men cannot extend. If you are not able to know the great truths for yourself then believe in them.

1

THEIR NATURE

There is that in man which repeatedly works against his finer aspirations, which provides him with opposition. Upon this anvil his character is hammered out, shaped, and developed.

2

So soon as a being limits interests and welfare to its own self exclusively, so soon is it bound to come into conflict with other beings. Thus evil originates through the first being's ignorance, not through the presence of an absolute and eternal principle of evil.

3

Where there is total ignorance there is total self-love. From this proceed all negativity, sensuality, indulgence, and discord. Where there is total knowledge there is total turning to the eternal IS. From this proceed harmony, positivity, goodwill. Where hate and cruelty come to excess, there is denial of the divine principle and reversal of the twofold truth. Where attention and attraction are partly turned to the THAT WHICH IS, there is sharing of mind and will between good and evil.

4

The universal pretense of evil to be good and the occasional presence of some good in most evil create confusion or bewilderment in many minds and lead to wrong judgement in other minds. Is there any absolute way of distinguishing good from evil? The Russian Staretz Silouan, of Mount Athos, thought there was—that however good an end might seem, if the means used to attain it was bad, then it was to be rejected. It is easy for us to see that falsehood intended to lead others to act against their own welfare could be such a bad means, as also could malicious cruelty.

5

Not to see the world as it is, with all its depravity and malice, is to be a fool, even if one happens to be a saint as well. The philosopher, like the ordinary man, sees its actuality but, unlike the ordinary man, is not stained by it. Moreover, he sees also the goodness and aspiration and, more importantly, the divine World-Idea.

6

Evil is something which man encounters on his journey to Good. Evil-doing is what he expresses when still far from his destination.

7

It is true that evil forces do exist but not true that they exist on the highest level. Insight into the ultimate sees them not.

8

Evil is certainly present, plain to sight and unpleasant to experience; but it is not altogether, nor only, what it seems. It is really an appearance, and reconcilable with the benign source of good.

9

Why is history such a record of wars, oppressions, exploitations, invasions, and persecutions? Why have all the saviours, avatars, prophets, and saints succeeded only with individual men here and there, not with the mass of mankind? Is the religious dream of universal goodness nothing more than a dream? It is not a help but a self-deception to ignore the double polarity of existence, the yin-and-yang in the universe, the shadow-self in man. Only outside of religion, in the philosophic realm of ultimate being, the Unique, the Real, where the entire world itself is cast out, can we talk of friction-free consciousness, and only in the deepest meditation can we share it. Although the experience is a temporary one, the peace in it so passes the understanding that "the kingdom of heaven" is its fit name. Here indeed is the Good raised to its highest degree. Here is a demonstration that human evil is but privation of good.

10

What may be true on the ultimate level—the non-existence of evil, the reality of the Good, the True, the Beautiful—becomes false on the level of duality. Here the twofold powers, the opposites, do exist, do hold the world in their sway. To deny relative evil here is to confuse different planes of being.(P)

11

The man who would deliberately harm his fellows for his own ends is a sinner.

12

Evil arises only when an entity goes astray into the delusions of separateness and materialism, and thence into conflict with other entities. There is no ultimate and eternal principle of evil, but there are forces of evil, unseen entities who have gone so far astray and are so powerful in themselves that they work against goodness, truth, and justice. But by their very nature such entities are doomed to eventual destruction, and even their work of opposition is utilized for good in the end and becomes the resistance against which evolution tests its own achievements, the grindstone against which it sharpens man's intelligence, the mirror in which it shows him his flaws.(P)

13

The lower nature is incurably hostile to the higher one. It prefers its fleeting joys with their attendant miseries, its ugly sins with their painful consequences, because this spells life to it.(P)

14

Everything and everyone has a negative side. One could fill up a lifetime looking for and finding it. One could go on grumbling, criticizing, ranting, and hating. But there is also the positive and opposite side. The philosophical attitude seeks deeper, keeps calmer, for it finds equilibrium on another plane.

15

The descent from faith in Holy Spirit to faith in unholy spirits happens to those who are either too weak to remain at such a high altitude or too incapable of rising from a sensate view of existence.

16

Evil can take every form, even that of the guru, the quest, and the learner.

17

Some years ago someone asked me, "What about absolute evil?" The answer is this: with Confucius we say that sin is due to ignorance, and with Pythagoras that evil is due to the absence of good. Ignorance leads to selfishness, and extreme ignorance leads to extreme selfishness, which in turn leads to extreme evil. Now, all these are relative conditions and pass away in time as the person learns his lessons through the series of experiences and corrects his mistakes during the reincarnations. There cannot be an absolute evil because there is only one Absolute Power, one God, one Supreme Being; and it is this which inspires the highest goodness known to man when he discovers its presence, through the Overself, in his heart. In that sense only I said there was an absolute good. The pairs of opposites exist only in the finite, relative, and limited world. There is no opposite to the Supreme Power in the timeless and infinite world, no Satan with whom God is in everlasting conflict. But, on its own level, Mind knows neither good nor bad. There is only IS-ness.

18

It seems that there is evil in the world, but why? What bad men have done is to let their evil grow like a noxious weed too large and their good too little, whereas good men have cultivated a high proportion of good-ness. There is no absolute evil. It is truer to talk of absolute good for that is there first. Why? Because God is there first. Men came later and broke the divine laws little by little. They created their own evil consequences. Or for different reasons they harm others and have later to suffer for it.

19

When the good is absent the evil is present. The cynic who denies the existence of the good, the dreamer who denies the existence of the evil—each ignores the other half of life as evidenced in history and in the world around him.

20

A cultivated man of taste and feeling can find much that is beautiful in nature and art; and if he is also a moral idealist, he will find much that is good and virtuous in human life and experience. But it would be in-complete to stop there and ignore the fact that there is also around us much that is base, dark, and even evil. The two sides put together form a complete observation. But it is only the mystics and the philosophers who can see—because it requires a deeper penetration than the intellect and the senses can give—that the dark side deals with the world of appearances, a world which is fleeting and ephemeral, whereas the good side and the beautiful side is merely a hint of that other world closer to Reality.

21

Evil is a very real problem in this world of time and space. Evil forces exist and must be fought with all our strength. Nevertheless the Power out of which all things and all entities come is a beneficent one. Love is its radiation. There is no evil and no pain in it. They begin only on the lower levels of separation and differentiation.

22

Philosophy does not agree with the doctrine that man can sink into oblivion permanently. If man's fundamental nature, however hidden it be, is essentially immaterial and of the same stuff as divinity, where can he sink back to except to that self-same divinity? The mystery of evil is perhaps the profoundest of all but it cannot be understood through surface views. Evil is closely connected with suffering and the latter in its turn with karma, which again is itself an expression of the fundamental self. It is all an educative process from which nobody can escape—not even Satan himself were there such a personal devil, which philosophy does not admit, al-though there are evil spirits, evil beings, and evil men. *All* will be saved because when seen from the timeless viewpoint they *are* already saved. The great mass of humanity are moving in the right direction, despite appearances to the contrary, and they shall enter the kingdom of heaven one day. *Do not doubt that*; the guarantee is that they are in their hidden selves already divine.

23

No man is beyond redemption for no man is utterly evil.

24

The problem of evil must be considered in the light of various factors. One of these is standpoint; one man's evil is another man's good. Another is karma; the individual has enough latitude to go to the dogs but has to suffer from the consequences of his acts. Then there is the question of rebirth. It seems impossible for human beings to be reborn as animals but Nature has made some provision for it. Then the ethical value of suffering must be considered. But most important of all are the questions of the nature of God, His relation to the universe and to humanity, and the purpose, if any, which is being worked out.

25

When a man commits an act of violence and destruction against other men, he is denounced and punished as a criminal. But when Nature commits such an act and maims or kills a mass of people, God is not denounced. Instead, poet and priest search for some excuse, find some hidden good intention, for God's reputation for goodness must be saved.

26

If the forces of evolution or laws of nature, as the expression of the World-Mind, have evoked the World-Idea and with it the possibilities of evil, we must unflinchingly accept the logical conclusion. This is that the World-Mind certainly permits the presence of Evil, allows and does not hinder its actuality. Nevertheless, we should always couple with this admission the equal and attendant truth that there is a higher outcome from the working of evil, a nobler purpose in its actuality. Through the operations of the law of recompense and the pressures of divine evolution it is transmuted into good. Evil has nowhere else to turn in the end except to turn itself into good!

27

To accept God as the source of this universe but to reject God as the source of those things contained in the universe which we dislike, is to deny God. Because we humans dislike evil and suffering, we separate them from God. But when we do that we separate ourselves from God.

28

The good and the bad are all part of the world-picture, although their proportions vary as the time-wheel turns around.

29

It is the function of such opposing forces, environments, or persons to *compel* him to negotiate them properly, or suffer the consequences.

30

It would be a totally unobservant or totally theoretic person who denied the presence of evil, but it would be an ill-informed one who did not perceive that its life and power are circumscribed.

31

I hope I shall not be misunderstood for saying that I saw clearly how the physical expression of evil is a necessary prerequisite to the spiritual redemption from evil. For what the sinner *does* is after all only an outcome of what he thinks. If the doing of wrong actions will, by the higher law of recompense, bring him ultimately the physical punitive consequences of those actions, they will also bring him—and again ultimately—the thought that the two are inseparably connected together. This is a step—admittedly only a first step—toward that repentance and that purification which make redemption possible.

32

The notion that the God-Power is engaged in a desperate struggle with an evil power, that God calls on man to give his help and that the outcome of this warfare depends to any extent on such help—this notion is a ridiculous one.

33

My experience of life and observation of others have taught me that there is no situation in which you will find good alone present without some concomitant evil. To look for undiluted good is utopian, unrealistic, and self-deceptive.

34

The awful fact of innate evil, the hideous mystery of innate sin, must be recognized and faced. *We* cannot make bad men into good men; but Nature, Life, with millions of years at her disposal, can.

35

Evil arises where the good is still undeveloped from its latency, but sometimes it is the distortion of the good.

36

We will understand this problem better when we understand that the presence of good and evil in the universe does not signify a division of power but a division of thought.

37

Thought is the cause; thought is the cure.

38

Satan can pretend to be an Angel of Light. There are adepts in evil who hide their real aim behind an outward show of altruistic purpose.

39

These secret purposes disguise themselves in a convenient form, and if no other is convenient they will even use some open purpose which stands in total opposition to them. They emerge in the most unlikely and un-looked-for places.

40

The evil in human relations springs from the ignorance in human beings. As each one brings the principle of truth into his own conscious-ness, he brings it into his relation with others as a result. The love which accompanies it denies birth to cruelty, anger, and lust or dissolves any which already exist.

41

Although it is perfectly true that divine goodness is at the heart of things, it is no less true that demonic evil is on the surface of things. The followers of simple cults which stubbornly try to see only the goodness and not the evil, which deny things as they are and indulge wishful think-ing, have themselves and their leaders to blame when disaster awakens them to the errors in the map they are following. They would do better to arouse themselves, while there is yet time, to keep a soundly balanced attitude, neither falling over to one side or the other overmuch, yet always remembering that superphysical experience between the incarnations is disproportionately good and free from evil, by contrast with physical plane experience.

42

Let us not insult human reason by denying human evil.

43

In any universal arrangement or personal situation, there is either gross disorder, with its consequent turmoil trouble and suffering, or there is real order, with its harmonious co-operation with the divine will working outward from the divine centre—be it man's heart or the sun's rays.

44

The great ills (miscalled evils) of bodily life, such as disease and poverty, are often forced upon him by an implacable fate. But it would be a delu-sion to class them always with the great evils of mental life, such as hate and cruelty. For their control is frequently beyond his power, and their course may have to be endured, whereas sinful thoughts and their resultant deeds are not independent of his control and may be avoided.

45

When right principles, theories, or concepts are taken up by the wrong persons, they become wrong themselves—because misused, falsified, perverted.

46

Suffering is not always an evil. It is often educative. All evil is then seen to spring from separativeness, which is a stage inevitable to all creatures as they follow the line of unfoldment. Evil therefore is the adverse element in Nature. Man can conquer it in his mind by conquering separativeness and realizing the All as himself. At the same time he discovers that the whole creation is really a mental one, hence *like* but not *the same as* a dream; and if he keeps awake to the *Static* Reality whilst in the midst of the earthly dream, the whole world becomes merely a school for educating consciousness. Then suffering, evil, and the like are transient aspects leaving permanent results.

47

The wedding of heaven and earth can never be brought about, since the Perfect and the Imperfect are incompatibles. But they can be brought into some sort of equilibrium, into better balance, so that life in the world would not be as bad as it is.

48

Those who ignorantly believe that God needs their help to ensure his triumph over evil in this world, have yet to learn that this triumph has been eternally accomplished already. The human being who can affect this situation either by helping or hindering does not exist.

49

It is a disturbing concept which holds that man's goodness seldom becomes actualized without the presence of, and struggle against, man's evil.

50

If men engaged themselves more in asking not "What is good and what is evil?" but rather "What is the Highest Good?" the first question would get itself answered automatically and peace would then follow anyway.

51

When the evil in man is washed out, he will find in all its goodness the original stuff of which he is made—beneficent to all, a joy to himself.

52

But because we affirm that the powers of evil will destroy themselves in the end, this must not be mistaken to mean that we may all sit down in smug complacency. We ought not to make this an excuse for inaction. On the contrary, it should inspire us to stronger efforts to preserve the noblest things in life from their attack.

53

Burke may have over-weighted his judgement by applying it to all cases, but there is still plenty of substance in it when he declared: "All that is necessary for the triumph of evil is that good men do nothing."

54

The night's darkness shelters the evil forces, the sun's brightness tells us where the divine ones are centralized.

2

THEIR ROOTS IN EGO

The wonder of the human soul which, even surrounded by the depravity and folly of today, can still aspire nobly and think loftily, would be quite puzzling did we not know the dual nature of the human entity and the divine nature of the laws which govern it.

2

So long as separate egos exist—separate from the cosmic ego in their own view, that is—so long will their ignorance produce what we call evil.

3

The ego, let loose upon the world, uninstructed and unbridled, cannot in the final reckoning benefit the world. To talk of service, without wisdom or character, may squander its goodwill in egoistic mire.

4

The evolution of each ego, of each entity conscious of a personal "I," passes through three stages through immense periods of time. In the first and earliest stage, it unfolds its distinct physical selfhood, acquires more and more consciousness of the personal "I," and hence divides and isolates itself from other egos. It seeks to differentiate itself from them. It feels the need to assert itself and its interests. This leads inevitably to antagonism towards them. Its movement is towards externality, a movement which must inevitably end in its taking the surface or appearance of things for reality, that is, in materialism. Here it is acquisitive. In its second and intermediate stage, it unfolds its mental selfhood and hence adds cunning to its separative and grasping tendencies, with intellect expanding to its extremest point. Here it is inquisitive. But midway in this stage, its descent comes to an end with a turning point where it halts, turns around, and begins to travel backward to its original source. In the third and last stage, the return towards its divine source continues. Its movement is now toward internality and—through meditation, investigation, and reflection—it ultimately achieves knowledge of its true being: its source, the Overself. And as all egos arise out of the Overself, the end of such a movement is one and the same for all—a common centre. Conflicts between them cease; mutual understanding, cooperation, and compassion spread. Hence, this stage is unitive.

The central point of the entire evolution is about where we now stand. Human attitudes and relations have reached their extreme degree of selfishness, separateness, struggle, and division, have experienced the resulting exhaustion of an unheard-of world crisis, but are beginning to reorient themselves towards an acknowledgment of the fundamental unity of the whole race. Thus, war reaches its most violent and terrible phase in the second stage and then abruptly begins to vanish from human life altogether. The separatist outlook must cease. Most of our troubles have arisen because we have continued it beyond the point where it was either useful or needful.

The unequal state of evolution of all these egos, when thrown together into a conglomerate group on a single planet, is also responsible for the conflicts which have marked mankind's own history. They stand on different steps of the ladder all the way from savagery to maturity. The backward ego naturally attacks or preys on the advanced one. Thus, the purely self-regarding ego, which was once an essential pattern of the evolutionary scheme—a necessary goal in the movement of life—becomes with time a discordant ingredient of that scheme, an obstructive impediment to that movement. If humanity is to travel upward and fulfil its higher destiny, it can do so only by enlarging its area of interest and extending its field of consciousness. It must, in short, seek to realize the Overself on the one hand, to feel its oneness on the other.

5

The ego's misapprehension of its own nature and misuse of its own capacities, create one form of evil. There are other forms.

6

We need not deny the presence of evil in the world in order to deny its permanence. It is here, but it is only a transient thing. Moreover, it exists not as a personified power like Satan, nor as a subtle unseen opponent of everything divine, but only as a condition of ignorance in the human mind and as a passing phase of its evolution. In short, it is merely a way of human thinking and it will disappear when deeper thinking reveals the why and wherefore of things. It lasts only as long as the dominance of the ego lasts.

7

The prehistoric animals are now totally gone and the only monster to be found on earth today is MAN. His history is splashed with war and hate and crime. There would appear to be little of the angel in him so far.

8

To the extent that man exercises his creative powers he copies, in his limited way, the World-Mind. But to the extent that he uses them to bring misery, injury, and perversity to others, or to himself, he copies the opposing force.

9

Ultimately he must find fault with himself when he seeks to trace the cause of most of his troubles. But this will require him to bring great moral courage to the examination of his life's course. For the personal ego is an inveterate alibi-hunter. If he is to overcome its insidious suggestions, its slippery arguments, he must see himself in the worst light.

10

It is not necessary that he should be conscious of his virtues, but it is necessary that he should be conscious of his faults.

11

The ego's interference shows itself in practical life no less than in mystical life. Under its influence, people create a false and favourable mental picture of a situation or of a person. They then expect one or the other to yield results that by their very nature could not be yielded. This leads to disappointment and unhappiness within themselves. Or the same people create a false but unfavourable picture and then severely criticize another for faults which do not exist outside the picture itself. This leads to disharmony and friction with others. From this simple instance we may see that the elimination of egotistic interference—a goal that philosophic discipline sets for itself—is not merely a theoretical affair for dreamers or hermits with nothing else to do, but is a practical affair promising great practical benefits for everyone who has to live or work in the world. The charge that philosophy is useless can only be made by those who have failed to inform themselves sufficiently about it.

12

Our only enemies are those inside ourselves. They are our weaknesses and vices, our lower passions and intellectual deformities. It is better to fight them than to fight other men.

13

When the last word of the last argument against the realization of the principles has been uttered, it will be found that all the obstacles lie inside and not outside us. There are mountains of selfishness, ignorance, and inertia in the human heart, but—as Jesus pointed out—faith can remove them.

14

All history—recent, medieval, ancient, Occidental, and Oriental—tells us that we do not have to look very deep into the hearts of men to find the presence of tigers, demons, savages, and brutes.

15

The struggles and conflicts, within men and between them, come from the ego's presence.

16

The philosopher has to look very far into human history and very deep into human nature for the ultimate causes of human errors.

17

The ego is behind each point of resistance in a man which holds him down from advancing further on this quest.

18

What lies at the root of all these errors in conduct and defects in character? It is the failure to understand that he is more than his body. It is, in one word, materialism.(P)

19

It is a man's own internal defects which often conspire against him and which show their faces in many of the external troubles that beset him. Yet it is hard for him to accept this truth because his whole life-habit is to look outwards, to construct defensive alibis rather than to engage in censorious self-inquisition. Sheikh al Khuttali, a Sufi adept, addressing a disciple who complained at his circumstances, said: "O my son, be assured that there is a cause for every decree of Providence. Whatever good or evil God creates, do not in any place or circumstance quarrel with his action or be aggrieved in thy heart." Therefore, the aspirant who is really earnest about the quest should develop the attitude that his personal misfortunes, troubles, and disappointments must be traced back to his own weaknesses, defects, faults, deficiencies, and indisciplines. Let him not blame them on other persons or on fate. In this way he will make the quickest progress whereas by self-defending or self-justifying or self-pitying apportionment of blame to causes outside himself, he will delay or prevent it. For the one means clinging to the ego, the other means giving it up. Nothing is to be gained by such flattering self-deception while much may be lost by it. He must bring himself to admit frankly that he himself is the primary cause of most of his ills, as well as the secondary cause of some of the ills of others. He must recognize that the emotions of resentment, anger, self-pity, or despondency are often engendered by a wounded ego. Instead of reviling fate at each unfortunate event, he should analyse his moral and mental make-up and look for the weaknesses which led to it. He will gain more in the end by mercilessly accusing his own stubbornness in pursuing wrong courses than by taking shelter in alibis that censure other people. Like a stone in a shoe which he stubbornly refuses to remove, the fault still remains in his character when he stubbornly insists on blaming things or condemning persons for its consequences. In this event the chance to eliminate it is lost, and the same dire consequences may repeat themselves in his life again.

The faith of the lower ego in itself and the strength with which it clings to its own standpoint are almost terrifying to contemplate. The aspirant is often unconscious of its selfishness. But if he can desert its standpoint, he shall then be in a position to perceive how large an element it has contributed in the making of his own troubles, how heavy is its responsibility for unpleasant events which he has hitherto ascribed to outside sources. He shall see that his miserable fate derives largely from his own miserable faults. He is naturally unwilling to open his eyes to his own deficiencies and faults, his little weaknesses and large maladjustments. So suffering comes to open his eyes for him, to shock and shame him into belated awareness and eventual amendment. But quite apart from its unfortunate results in personal fortunes, whenever the aspirant persists in taking the lower ego's side and justifying its action, he merely displays a stupid resolve to hinder his own spiritual advancement. Behind a self-deceiving facade of pretexts, excuses, alibis, and rationalizations, the ego is forever seeking to gratify its unworthy feelings or to defend them. On the same principle as the pseudo-patriotism which prompted the Italians to follow Mussolini blindly throughout his Ethiopian adventure to its final disaster, the principle of "My country! right or wrong," he follows the ego through all its operations just as blindly and as perversely, justifying its standpoints merely because they happen to be his own. But the higher Self accepts no rivals. The aspirant must choose between denying his ego's aggressiveness or asserting it. The distance to be mentally travelled between these two steps is so long and so painful that it is understandable why few will ever finish it. It is only the exceptional student who will frankly admit his faults and earnestly work to correct them. It is only he whose self-criticizing detachment can gain the upper hand, who can also gain philosophy's highest prize.(P)

20

To live in intellect and passion alone, unguided and unvivified by higher ideals, is to be unregenerate.

21

How often in history there is a record of fierce, blind, and fanatic hatred directed against those of marked difference in race, caste, religion, class, custom, or habit. With time and strength it explodes into persecution, violence, or war. The root of this evil may be fear, suspicion, envy, greed, or unbalance; but all these find their roots in the ego, and can only be radically removed by transcending egoism.

22

The root of all the trouble is not man's wickedness or animality or cunning greedy mind. It is his very I-ness, for all those other evils grow out of it. It is his own ego. Here is the extraordinary and baffling self-contradiction of the human situation. It is man's individual existence which brings him suffering and yet it is this very existence which he holds as dear as life to him!(P)

23

Either man does not hear the interior message or else he does not want to hear it. That which causes him to be so deaf may be mere heedlessness, but it is more likely to be worldly desire and personal conceit.

24

What are the blockages which prevent the soul's light, grace, peace, love, and healing from reaching us? There are many different kinds, but they are resolvable into the following: first, all negative; second, all egoistic; and third, all aggressive. By "aggressive" I mean that we are intruding our personality and imposing our ideas all the time. If we would stop this endless aggression and be inwardly still for a while, we would be able to hear and receive what the Soul has to say and to give us.(P)

25

These are some of the negative traits of erring human character—undesirable for their own sake, as well as for the sake of their bad effects—hatred, irritability, jealousy, maliciousness, excessive criticism and suspicion, destructiveness and cruelty.

26

It is not that they lack intelligence, but that they let their intelligence be guided by their baser qualities.

27

When the results are pleasant for the moment, we like to deceive ourselves. We like to put a pretty mask on an ugly passion, for instance, or wear a magnificent cloak around a wretchedly selfish act. But karma cannot so easily be deceived and works out its own results with time. And these depend not only on the appearance of what we are and do but also on the real character and hidden nature behind it.

28

So what are depressions and sadnesses but the ego pitying itself, shedding silent tears over itself, loving itself, looking at itself and enwrapped in itself? What is a happy calm but a killing of such egoism?(P)

29

The complacence with which men view themselves, the satisfaction with which they fit into their ego, acts as a barrier to the influx of spiritual influence and understanding.

30

Identically the same facts will be used by different groups parties and persons to support widely or quite divergently varying conclusions! The ego, with its prejudices, passions, selfish motives, or desires, is the real cause of these differences.

31

Everything is used by the ego to affirm itself. Even the aspirations and practices and experiences of a quester are used to his own deception and to its profit.

32

Few persons have either the capacity or the wish to stand back sufficiently far from themselves to see what it is they are really doing and where it is they are really going. We play different roles in the cosmic drama at different levels, and this is true of all men. We all have to rise from the animal to the human, from the human to the divine. The ego is there, but consciousness can either use it as free being or get stuck in it and be used by it. When consciousness is free that means it is free of all the negatives too and especially free of all those identifications with undesirable conditions of the ego and unworthy manifestations of it.

33

Wide travels among all kinds have shown me more and more that the endless wars and strifes between races, nations, classes, tribes, and individual persons must be met on two levels if they are to be brought to any end. It is not sufficient to meet them on the level of their outward visible causes; that has to be done, of course, but it is even more important to get out of the seething cauldron of hates and wraths, resentments and egotisms and greeds, for here are the unseen causes of the visible ones. This calls for a leap: the recognition that one's real enemy is not so much the person outside as the person inside oneself.

34

The inner life is the root of the outer one. What is created there, is eventually expressed here.

35

Out of the immense and varied past, in previous births man has transmitted to him and accumulated in him the tendencies which today obscure his inner light and drive him toward evil acts.

36

Post-war clash, hatred, greed, and tension are rife, between nations or between different groups in a single nation. At the bottom of it all lies a selfishness which always places its own gain above justice or above mercy and sometimes even seeks that gain at the unwarrantable expense of others. The ego-worship which filled the Nazi with his "I" was only a monstrously swollen form of the same idolatry as it existed in other people all over the world. Instead of trying to curtail their inflated ego, deluded groups and leaders yield to it and enlarge it still more. The meaning of spirituality has ceased to register with millions of such people.

37

Where the ego rules in the business world, it is trying to get more than it gives. This is an offense against the law of justice, an attempt to get what is not its fair due. The dark karma of such an attempt may be seen in the strife and conflict and clash of interests and lack of peaceful harmony which sound as discords in politico-economic relationships today.

38

The ego hates another and sorrows over its troubles: these are negative feelings.

39

Despite all the tall talk about love and charity, service and selflessness, it still remains that most people serve others only because consciously or unconsciously they are serving their own interest.

40

The problems raised in connection with my radio talk on "Is Hitler a Mystic?" are very pertinent and interesting, but I do not suppose that any tribunal would take my theories into account seriously. Indeed it could not afford to do so. Once it entered into the metaphysical and psychic aspects of crime it would find itself in a deep abyss. For instance there is the Catholic Christian doctrine that sin is the consequence of yielding to the inner promptings of Satan. My own view is that, speaking generally and with due allowance for special cases, the practical responsibility for a man's crime must lie within himself—even though he be a spiritualist medium who has been led step by step to perform crimes from which he would have shrunk at the beginning of his downward path.

41

There are some who are so insane as to proclaim evil to be their good and Satan to be their worshipped God. But most men have to justify evil by disguising it as good. They do so either consciously or unconsciously, either to others or to themselves, or to both.

42

They never hear the voice of conscience, never feel any sense of what is right or wrong. The only moral code which exists for them is that of success or failure. Anything that assists them to get what they want is ethically good; anything that hinders them from doing so is ethically evil!

43

How can men be saved who are not aware that they need salvation, not awake to their predicament, not able to come away from the distraction of personal affairs or the stupefaction of sensual pleasure?

44

Those who are enemies to their own real good, and so to their own selves, will necessarily be enemies to one another.

45

Man unhelped by the divine, depending on his own human efforts, must fail.

46

If a man could keep himself out of his thinking and feeling, he would more easily arrive at truth. If he could believe his personal views to be nothing, but truth everything, he would sooner receive its grace.

Special tests for questers

47

Because of what he is and what he seeks to do, the quester has special trials, special experiences and temptations, apart from the ordinary ones which accompany all human activities.(P)

48

Elaborate traps are set at intervals along his road, made up of a combination of his own weaknesses with persons or events related to them. He must be wary of relapsing into complacency, must be prepared for tests and temptations in a variety of forms.(P)

49

It is tantalizingly hard to effect the passage from the lower to the higher state. For between them lies an intermediate zone of consciousness which possesses an ensnaring quality and in which the ego makes its last desperate effort to keep him captive. Hence this zone is the source of attractive psychic experiences, of spiritual self-aggrandizements, of so-called messianic personal claims and redemptive missions, of great truths cunningly coalesced into great deceptions.(P)

50

A man may travel quite a distance on the way towards this goal of self-conquest and then, as success begins to appear on the horizon, may fail and fall from it in the last few tests. His very success may begin to generate vanity, pride, self-importance, ambition, and arrogance. In this way his ego is once more stimulated instead of being subjugated. Thus he steps aside from the path although he has already gone so far along it.

51

Certain negative tendencies of his character, by now controlled and largely suppressed but still lying latent in the subconscious, may rush up to the surface at intervals if impulsiveness is present. When he is taken off his guard, they appear in speech or even action until he recovers himself. The damage is done and although he returns to normal freedom from these faults, the consequences may remain and make him suffer for a disproportionate period. The farther he advances, the more important is the lapse.

52

Deep down in the lowest layers of the subconscious nature there lurk evil tendencies and evil memories belonging to the far past and not yet wholly wiped out by the spiritual rebirth. It is these tendencies which rise to the surface layers and challenge us at crucial moments when we seek initiation into the Higher Self or when we seek acceptance from a Master. In their totality they have been named by the Western Rosicrucians as the "dweller on the threshold." No man can be taken possession of by his Higher Self or enter into a permanent relation with a Master unless and until he develops within himself sufficient calm and sufficient strength to meet and overcome these arisen tendencies, whose character is marked by extreme sensuality or extreme cunning or extreme brutality, or even by a combination of two or three of these.

53

They are crude remnants and ugly reminders of the savage violence which he has inherited from pre-human reincarnations.

54

His failure follows inevitably from his attempt to serve two masters. The ego is strong and cunning and clamant. The Overself is silent and patient and remote. In every battle the dice are loaded in the ego's favour. In every battle high principle runs counter to innate prejudice.(P)

55

If the ego cannot trap him through his vices it will try to do so through his virtues. When he has made enough progress to warrant it, he will be led cunningly and insensibly into spiritual pride. Too quickly and too mistakenly he will believe himself to be set apart from other men by his attainments. When this belief is strong and sustained, that is, when his malady of conceit calls for a necessary cure, a pit will be dug unconsciously for him by other men and his own ego will lead him straight into it. Out of the suffering which will follow this downfall, he will have a chance to grow humbler.(P)

56

The risk is greater because a human emissary of the adverse element in Nature will automatically appear at critical moments and consciously or unconsciously seek hypnotically or passively to lead him astray as he or she has gone astray. Our own world-wide experience, embracing the written reports and spoken confidences of thousands of individual cases of mystical, yogic, and occult seekers, both Oriental and Occidental, has gravely taught the need of this warning.(P)

57

Whoever seeks to tread a path such as the one shown here will sooner or later find that these forces set themselves in opposition to his interior journey. His way will be blocked by external circumstances that entangle him in hopeless struggles or heart-breaking oppressions and enslavements, or by psychical attacks which seek to sweep him off his spiritual feet and destroy his higher aspirations. Persons in his immediate environment may be moved by these invisible forces to work against him, causing uprisings of hatred and misunderstanding; one-time friends may turn into treacherous enemies more virulent than the poison of a cobra. Public critics will appear and endeavour to nullify whatever good he is doing for humanity, or to prevent its continuance. The single aim and object of all these attempts will be to prevent his alignment with the Overself, to render mental quiet impossible, or to keep his heart and mind crushed down to earth and earthly things. He must needs suffer these things. Their power, scope, and duration may be diminished, however.(P)

58

The path is beset not only by the pitfalls arising out of one's own human failings, but at critical times by unconscious or conscious evil beings in human form who seek to destroy faith through falsehoods and to undermine reliance on true guidance through sidetracks and traps.(P)

59

The advancing mystic has to undergo a very real temptation at certain points of his career—a temptation not unlike that of Jesus by Satan to great worldly honours or that of Buddha by Mara to great sensual indulgence. It may come through the crafty instigations of his enemies or through the innocent flatteries of his friends. He must beware especially of those whose excessive faith would exalt him to the role of a master, or perchance even glorify him as a new messiah! He must be on guard against being seduced by the attractions of power or the disguises of sensuality.

60

He may have to suffer the hostility of unseen malignant force besetting the path at certain stages, especially at advanced stages.

61

H.P. Blavatsky (in a private talk with W.Q. Judge): "You force yourself into a Master's presence and you take the consequences of the immense forces around him playing on yourself. If you are weak in character anywhere, the Black Ones will use the disturbance by directing the forces engendered to that spot and may compass your ruin. It is so always. Pass the boundary that hedges in the occult realm, and quick forces, new ones, dreadful ones, must be met. Then if you are not strong you may become a wreck for that life. This is the danger. This is one reason why Masters do not appear and do not act directly very often, but nearly always by intermediate degrees."

62

As that esteemed Indian yogi and philosopher, the late Sri Aurobindo, more than once mentioned, those who are working for the survival of Truth in a truthless world thereby become targets for powerful forces of hatred wrath and falsehood. Whoever publicly bears a deeply spiritual message to humanity, has to suffer from evil's opposition.(P)

63

These are warped minds who, fumbling on the lower levels of human existence, spit venom and spill hatred over the man who declares the existence of higher ones.

64

These hostile manifestations invariably make their appearance after the teacher has made an appearance anywhere. Light must inevitably cast a shadow. Yet on the credit side they served a useful purpose. They help him and they help his probationers. They remind him that he must not stake a claim on any part of this earth's surface or in any human heart. They test the intuition and keenness of the probationers. When these have survived all the tests, he may accept them and begin their real inner work together; thereafter God himself cannot prize them apart from their teacher, for then they know with whom they are dealing.

65

The course of life brings encounters with those who are either inspired by, or symbolically represent, the adverse powers which at times beset it.

66

Subconscious evil creeps out of its cage in moments of temptation.

67

A Kabbalist adept: "The neophyte who enters the portals becomes at once a victim of the malicious attention of Shaitans (demons) who plague him with a multitude of temptations and work on his mind. Rare is he who does not succumb."

68

Tests can appear in very ordinary, quite prosaic situations.

69

The things which hamper the student's progress are varied, and although they may bring despondency and discouragement, impatience and rebellion, they need not and should not be permitted to bring the loss of all hope. Difficulties there must be, but they need not make us cowards. The times of swift progress are generally followed by times of slow moving; success alternates with failure as day with night. He must go on with the faith and trust that obstacles are not for all time, that fluctuations on the path are inevitable, and that his own inner divine possibilities are the best guarantee of ultimate attainment. The trials of the path, as indeed the trials of life itself, are inescapable. He should endure the tribulations with the inner conviction that a brighter world awaits him; hope and faith will lead him to it.(P)

3

THEIR PRESENCE IN THE WORLD

If we look at what has happened in the world during the past hundred years, and what is still happening today, the exhibition of the negatives in human character is discouraging: so many weaknesses and cruelties, animalities and jealousies, pettinesses and stupidities.

2

Animal man has been violently on the rampage in our times, robbing, hating, attacking, destroying, and killing. Spiritual man has remained weakly in the background. Reasoning man has oscillated between the two poles, sometimes sensitive to higher ideals in the guidance of his thinking, more often selfishly blind to any other welfare than his own.

3

All sincere well-wishers of humanity are today distressed in heart and doubt-ridden in mind. Baffled and bewildered, they stand before the complex spectacle of this disordered age. Doubt is a figure always pictured by the ancient world with a bandage across her eyes. This is the exact condition of our age.

4

Whoever looks around at the world of the past half century, at its negativity, its folly and insanity, its horrors, may say that it is a wicked world, that man is incorrigibly evil. It would be fairer to introduce a note of balance and refer to the existence of Yin and Yang in life, in the universe, and consequently in human character.

5

It is the work of evolution in our time to bring to the surface of thought and action the most ferocious instincts and darkest bestiality which many men still hide beneath their civilized exterior. But such an outbreak of evil is destined eventually to modify evil itself, to tame those instincts and subside the bestiality. The night is darkest just before dawn.

6

The evil things we have seen and still see all around us in contemporary humanity have come to the surface only to be carried off again. The decadence of human society and the degeneration of the human race which shadow contemporary history, are signs of the scum arising out of the human subconscious. But they arise only to be cleared away. Out of this clearance there will later come an awakening to the Good, an appreciation of the True. In this sense their darkness is an inverted precursor of the light, the worse which makes a way for the better. It is a token that the cycle of materialism will eventually turn on itself and yield to a cycle of spirituality.

7

If the world's present state is so ugly and menacing, we ought not to blame it as a failure on the part of God but rather on the part of man.

8

The monstrous cruelty and baleful influences which have shown their detestable faces in world history from time to time, are reminders of how far man has yet to go in fulfilment of the World-Idea.

9

In large regions of the earth it seems as though moral darkness has enveloped mankind. Although a fair appraisal requires us to examine how far this swing of the pendulum against established religion represents rebellion against its superstition and imposture and how far it represents a real loss of conscience and deterioration of character, there is still enough residue of evil to instigate apprehension as to the future course and results of this situation.

10

Anyone who has travelled this wide earth knows that there are greedy men who are like ferocious tigers, and smooth-tongued women who are as dangerous as devouring serpents. The evil of such people lies not so much in the character which they reveal as in the character which they hide. It is the suave dissembler who reproduces the words of goodness without its heart and who cynically divorces creed from conduct that we must fear, rather than the man who has "scoundrel" stamped all over his face and actions. We are not apt to be on our guard against a silky voice, saintly manner, and smiling lips, but when these things hide a devil's heart of dark intentions, we are in peril of being undone.

11

It is true that the respectable often hides the rotten.

12

Whether they call it evil and sin with the Christians, or ignorance and immaturity with the Hindus, or insufficiency of the good with the Platonic thinker, or weakness and failure, or the blindness of materialism, the presence of deplorable or horrible or criminal tendencies need not be denied. They are in the world, but then, other better nobler and purer tendencies are also there.

13

There are savage creatures, moral monsters, and insane animals who look like men but have only partially entered into the human species in their passage up from lower ones. Having human faces and limbs, digestive and sense organs, is not enough to render them worthy of human classification.

14

If there is so much more interest in the spiritual truth, there is also much more interest in its sinister reversions and perversions, in black magic, satanic forces, the misuse of drugs and the abuse of sex, witchcraft, sorcery, influencing others through mental means for selfish ends, and worship of the powers of darkness. Young naïve and unbalanced persons seeking occult thrills and excitements, or recklessly curious about (to them) psychical novelties, are brought into foul malignant circles where their character is degraded and their understanding twisted.

15

The sinister spread of black magic, witchcraft, sexual perversion, and drug addiction in our own time is menacing. Some of their votaries are consciously worshipping demonic powers, evil as such, others only because they have been misled into the belief that it is the Good.(P)

16

We find that the character of these black magicians contains much of cruelty and hatred. To inflict suffering on others gives them pleasure: and this is not necessarily a reference to those who have studied what is technically known as "black magic." It may also refer to cold-blooded scientists and politicians, misguided idealists and statesmen, obsessed drug addicts and one-sided vivisectors.

17

The world today, more fiercely than ever, is a battleground for this ancient conflict between Right and Wrong.

18

Various kinds and degrees of madness have appeared in the world in various expressions—in the forms of immorality, in the frictions of politics, and in the teachings of religion.

19

If there is infinite love in or behind the world, there is also infinite suffering in the world, as Buddha noted.

20

The evil forces have stirred up evil events and provocative crises, and striven to get the masses to react to them in an evil way.

21

If you could trace out the intricate ramifications of the effects of all your actions, you would find that the good ones were eventually shadowed by evil, and the evil ones brightened by good. This idea may seem strange when first heard of, and may require some analysis to make it seem plausible. But if you ponder on it, you will begin to understand why modern European thinkers like Schopenhauer and Spengler and modern Hindu seers like Atmananda and Vivekananda reject the belief that the world's evil is growing less as much as they reject the assertion that it is growing more. If we compare the general moral level of different centuries, some sort of a balance between the good and evil can be seen. If we are to look for any striking advance in the good, we shall have to look for it not in the masses but in single individuals who are seeking and nearing the Overself. This is because our planet is like a class at school where the average standard remains not too widely different. The progress and deterioration which appear at times do not alter this fact, since they appear within these maximum and minimum levels and shift about from one part of the planet to another. There is no room here for undue optimism but neither is there any for undue pessimism. The savage of low degree may be taught the tricks of science until he can shoot from atomic artillery instead of from stringed bows, but he still remains a savage. Recent history has shown this plainly and revealed civilization as a fact in technics only and as a myth in morals.

22

Coming events cast their good or evil configuration beforehand upon calm, sensitive souls. That the unseen hand of destiny is unfolding the vivid scenes of a unique drama is evident to them. That the contemporary currents of world-throbbing happenings are but presages indicating that a radical shift-over in human existence is upon us is also clear to them. In geological history, earthquakes are a means adopted by Nature to restore a disturbed equilibrium. In human history, wartime world-upheaval is both karma's way of attaining equilibrium in an unbalanced society and evolution's way of making another spurt forward.

23

The opposition has its role to play in this world-crisis. Even while obeying its own evil nature, it is frightening half of mankind with its menaces and undermining their confidence in keeping alive for a reasonable period.

24

These are the forces which foment hatred and disrupt society, which deny truth and garble fact.

25

We are victims of a civilization which does not know where it is going, trivial in purpose and corrupt in character.

26

Strife or hate, dissension or violence rears its fearsome face in every quarter of the globe, like some hydra-headed dinosauric monster.

27

We dwell in chaos and violence, in a world that knows no peace without and feels none within.

28

The lunacy which has poured into the political demagogues and their followings, the pseudo-artists and their audience, has spread into the religio-mystics and their believers.

29

The evil which is present in the world may show a new, exaggerated, and deceitful form but in itself is no new thing. On the contrary, it is an ancient thing. Plato predicted that if one of the gods came to this earth, he would not be allowed to live. His ethical ideals would be rejected in practice. His physical presence would be removed in murder.

30

The universal despair which has crept over the world—a world which has watched the savings of many years dwindle or disappear within a year or two, which has found its jobs become daily less secure—induces people to draw a slender comfort from that hope which is supposed to spring eternal in the human breast. The hope formulates in the possibility of hearing that Fortune's wheel will now turn for them. Perchance the fates will relent tomorrow, relentless though they have been in the past. The old stand-bys such as religion and a good bank-balance are going or have already gone. Can one blame them if, in their anxiety, they summon planetary support to allay their fears?

31

We are struggling into a finer epoch. But because we are and have been struggling blindly, the course of events has and had to get worse before getting better.

32

From one point of view, the atomic bomb has created wholly new problems. From another point of view, it has only pushed to the front for urgent dealing quite old ones. Both are correct.

33

The second world war now belongs to the past. Yet nobody feels that peace has come, everybody fears what the future might bring. None of us is living happily ever after.

34

Evil men and dangerous forces thrive today as they did in Nazi days.

35

It is the danger and tragedy of our generation that just at the time when man's power to injure his fellows has reached its peak, the religious checks and controls of hurtful propensities have fallen to their lowest influence.

36

Internal disquiet and external disorder characterize our times.

37

Inside himself, the Good the True and the Beautiful may seem to be the governing forces; but outside himself, in the world of toiling and fighting men, the Bad the False and the Ugly may seem dominant.

38

Mankind has proved itself unworthy to handle powers of atomic destructiveness and unable to manage its affairs without stupidity or its relations without evil-doing.

39

Life today is filled with too many cares or uncertainties for anyone in any part of the world to enjoy complete happiness.

40

Although our practical duty involves resistance to evil, it should be clear that such resistance is itself an evil, but it is the lesser of two evils and a necessary result of the imperfect side of human nature today. It plays the same part in each individual's life that a police force plays in the social life. The presence of the policeman is an indication of the presence of the criminal. With the development of human character, criminal tendencies would disappear and with them police forces. But we cannot anticipate that time so far as the immediate present is concerned, although we ought to deal with the crime in the most enlightened way possible.

41

The malevolent energies and destructive forces which have been abroad in our time tell us how strong is the evil that lies mixed with the good in humanity's heart.

42

He need not have a low opinion of the human race to conclude that there is sufficient evil in it—whether petty or serious—to make a sloppy sentimental idealization of its character just silly and perilous.

43

The upsurge of interest in Eastern religion and Western cults is welcome, and may help a turn to the Good; but it has its negative side in a matching interest in Evil with a capital E.

44

These evils, sufferings, and calamities exist for all, the good and the bad; such is the human lot.

45

Whether in politics or in society, there is widespread double-talk, publicly upheld untruth, and differing views expressed.

46

Boehme's illumination opened his eyes to the depth and extent of the evil in man. He became very sad over it. Today nobody needs to become illumined in order to see the same thing.

47

If some men wish to withdraw from the world, disgusted with its repeated brutalities and malignancies, need we wonder?

48

Because the universe is a manifestation of the Divine, it must be divinely guided. Therefore its history must be divinely controlled. What has happened in human world affairs so recently and so dramatically is not outside the divine will. What is happening today is just as much inside it.

49

The degenerative process which replaced the universal-mindedness of Goethe by the fanatic narrowness of Goebbels, the calm wisdom of the earlier man by the obscene insanity of the later one, is a subject for reflection.

50

The good and the evil in man are such long-associated partners that co-operation of the good alone between men is impossible. At some point of their contact, in some way, the reptilian evil will creep in and make its unpleasant discordant presence felt. Hence universal brotherhood is only a beautiful dream, to be shattered upon awakening to the ugly facts.

51

The lives of so many good men in our time have moved inexorably to disaster, like the gloomy story of a Greek tragedy, that the helpless but friendly onlooker may well wonder where God is.

52

A period so filled with confusion and so rife with evil, drives thoughtless people to more sensuality and materialism but thoughtful ones to more aspiration and higher values.

53

The real enemies of mankind today—as in the recent past—are doctrines which have issued from the womb of hate and greed, suspicion and violence, and grown only to spread hate and greed, suspicion and violence. For the inevitable harm of such thinking is as self-destructive as it is socially destructive.

54

If they could penetrate, by some mystical insight, the awful horrors and repulsive episodes which mar modern history, they would find something unimaginably grand, beautiful, and wise behind it all, unseen and undreamt by the human agents responsible for this misery.

55

It is unjustified escapism. Postwar sensualism is as much a form of escapism as postwar ashramism.

56

Folly and evil play the most powerful parts on the contemporary world stage.

57

If we look at the large panorama of twentieth century history, with its tortures and devastations, its epidemics and destructions, its famines and depopulations, above all, its menace of horrors yet to come, we can see how trivial a thing in fate's eyes is personal life, how unimportant in them is personal emotion. What does fate, God, Nature, care about the little histories, the little loves, the little griefs of pullulating humans, who must appear in those same eyes as hardly more noteworthy than pullulating ants! There are millions—nay, billions—of these men and women who are so like each other in their basic natures and desires, that it does not make any difference to the planetary Mind or the protoplasmic Force whether some of them die or survive, mate or frustrate, are ecstatically happy or dully miserable, stay perfectly whole or limp hideously maimed.

58

The fact is that the world finds itself today very nearly spiritually bankrupt.

59

Snobbishness is only misplaced reverence. Any good that is misplaced easily becomes an evil. The older nations were permeated with this evil far too much.

60

The world approaches insane chaos and convulsion at most, perilous conditions at least.

61

The fault lies not only with the criminal but also with the society which created the conditions which tempted him to enter criminality.

62

There is such insecurity and instability, so much demoralization and so much discontent.

63

Are human life and human destiny ruled by mere chance or by iron law? If by chance, then our race is wholly at the mercy of evil men, but if by law, then we may hope to see the pattern of ultimate good eventually show itself in its history as these men and all men are steered back to righteous courses by suffering and intuition, by revelation and reflection.

64

The fact that human character as a whole seems not to have improved in our time does not mean that it will fail to improve in the future. Human virtue is only in its infancy and will one day attain its maturity. Human goodness in essence is indestructible because the divine soul in man is indestructible.

65

There is in the very midst of humanity today, albeit hidden and awaiting its hour of manifestation, that which is the very opposite of what has already manifested itself through the evil channels. There is divine pity as against barbarous cruelty, sublime wisdom as against materialistic ignorance, altruistic service as against aggressive selfishness, and exalted reverence against hard atheism. There is the recall to a forgotten God. There is redemptive grace. There is a hand outstretched in mercy to the worst sinner, and in consolation to the worst sufferer. Those who are mystically sensitive feel its presence even now, however intermittently.

Materialism

66

Too many people hold, whether consciously or unconsciously, the materialistic belief that they are here on earth to satisfy their material desires only, and that they have no higher responsibility.

67

This is no time for smooth words that hide the true state of affairs, no time for shallow optimism that screens the precipice along whose edge we are walking. Humanity passed through the five-year agony of life-and-death conflict against Nazi attempts at world domination because it earlier hugged the delusion either that the danger did not exist or that it was very slight even if it did exist. It cannot afford to repeat that error. The peril in which it now stands from materialism—whether avowed, open, or disguised, supported by out-of-date science, or molded from out-of-date religion—is just as grave in its own way because of its terrifying spiritual and physical consequences.

68

The materialistic view of man, which would regard his life-functioning as a set of physical processes only, which would condemn him to an absolute lack of spiritual awareness, must die or man himself will die with it.

69

Materialism leads to a faulty interpretation of historic events and a one-sided interpretation of personal ones.

70

Most of the modern civilizations which are based on materialism and take no account of the spiritual nature of man are building towers of Babel which, when they have reached a certain height, will topple down. The greater the height, the larger the number of broken pieces. The creativity of these civilizations is illusory; they seem to be productive, but they are really destructive, for since they do not conform to the World-Idea the karma they are making must inevitably bring all this about.

71

The gods of quiet virtue and spiritual wisdom have had fewer votaries than at most other parallel periods of our history, while the grinning demons of brazen pleasure and materialistic pursuits have been far busier. Folly holds the field. Despite all the scientific backwardness and primitive character attributed to them, there was always a place in most of the civilizations of antiquity—and there still is in the Orient—for the sage or the prophet. In the West there does not seem to be one for him today—on the contrary, he is too often met with unjust suspicions and hopeless misunderstanding and so can do nothing else than crawl into his shell. This accusing fact that our society has no place for him, sets no importance on him and perceives no value in him, is of itself enough to damn it for having strayed so far from its higher purpose. There is something seriously wrong with a civilization which thinks that the effort to come into Overself-consciousness is an abnormal and even an insane one.

72

It is a stupid and narrow outlook which equates the desire for material progress with the pursuit of materialism.

73

We have passed out of the centuries of superstitious belief in fossilized creeds only to pass into the centuries of superstitious belief in credalized fossils—such as the materialistic conception of Man, the crude notion that might can ultimately conquer right, the ignorant acceptance of a belief in the inferiority of all Oriental knowledge.

74

Whether we take the industrialized machine-ridden civilization of Europe or that of the United States, in the end they are setting up the same goals—the creation of a slavery to technology which can only end in nervous breakdown and physical illness.

75

When a people is concerned only with material things, and when their desires are wholly confined to them, it is proper to call them materialists.

Unbalanced technological development

76

To regard all material improvements as a move away from spirituality, to assert that science and the industries based on it are absolutely evil, is unfair and untrue.

77

The grim needs of war pushed technological advance ahead at an amazing speed. This advance may be used either to make us more materialistic or to make us less so. In itself it is neutral.

78

There is a line of connection which can be traced from the appearance of gentle Jesus to the terrors of the Inquisition. There is another line which can be traced from the work of pioneer scientists like Galileo and Bacon to the work of atomic scientists like Einstein and Oppenheimer. If Jesus' gospel was a message from God, science was a different kind of revelation from God. Both Inquisitional tortures and Hiroshima's horrors are evidences of what men have done to the fine things entrusted to them. It is for the men themselves to undo their misdeeds and not wait for a Saviour to do it. The responsibility is theirs.

79

It was the prevalence of superstition in all departments of human life, activity, belief, and thought which brought about the needed counterculture of the exact sciences. But under the various superstitions there was not seldom some measure of covert fact and hidden truth. Science has itself become, because of its one-sided, self-made limitation, and through refusal to depart from materialistic views, a sort of superstition. Technical skill, verified experiment, and laboratory research are necessary and valuable, but their presence ought not to be used as an excuse for abandoning everything else which ought to be considered. Hence we witness today such evils as the pollution of nature and the poisoning of human nutriment. There is no other way out now than to compensate for the missing elements, to broaden culture in a basic way—a coexistence previously believed to be impossible.

80

Man looked into the mysteries of the atom when he was too selfish to use it rightly, too ignorant of the higher laws to use it wisely—that is, when he was unworthy and unready. He is in such danger today that many regret he ever did so. But he could not help it, could not have done otherwise. The mind wants to know; this is its essential nature: it was inevitable that what began as simple childish curiosity should end as rigorous scientific investigation. Nothing could stop this process in the past. This was the warning of Greek, European, and American history. It is now the warning of Chinese, Southeast Asian, and Indian history, where seemingly static civilizations become more dynamic.

81

When science serves politics only, and both are unguided by knowledge of the higher laws governing mankind, then both, in this age of nuclear weapons, put mankind in danger of nuclear annihilation.

82

Where the nineteenth-century Westerner displaced religion by science, the twentieth-century Westerner is increasingly being faced, through the unexpected results of nuclear science, with having to refind interest in religion, recover the truth in religious teaching, and regain the peace in religious experience.

83

The scientists conceived the atomic bomb, the heads of government financed it, and the military used it. This was the triple combination which brought humanity to its present plight. Admittedly, they did this with the best intentions and under the stress of seeming outer necessity. But the fact still remains that it was they who created the danger for all of us and it is they who now seem unable to free us from it.

84

It is necessary for man to be reminded of his comparative nothingness when his intellect swells into dangerous arrogance. With the triumphs of atomic research and the gadgets of mechanical civilization, he has reached such a point. He will not have to wait long to see that the failure to balance them with moral and spiritual advance will bring its own punishment.

85

The scientist who foresees a happy abundant future for mankind (because of technological advance) while so many of his colleagues are preparing the weapons to wipe out the species itself, is either insane or incapable of non-specialized thinking.

86

If the scientific gropers-in-the-dark were allowed fully to explore, and their political masters to exploit, the atom until all its energy were released, our Earth would either blow up into pieces and all mankind with it, or else have its atmosphere so poisoned by radioactivity as to make any life within it impossible. But it is not in the World-Mind's World-Idea that this shall be allowed. The so-called progress of man in this direction will be arrested. He will be allowed to injure himself, since he insists on playing with these dangerous forces, but not to destroy himself.

87

This one event has dominated the intelligent human mind in the mid-twentieth century more than any other. This release of the atom's energy has forced a rethinking of the human position in politics, society, health, and economics.

88

The social, economic, and political problems which have developed with the development of science, and its use in industry, have reached their ultimate in the hydrogen bomb. This is the Frankenstein monster which will destroy its master, if he does not soon renounce all nuclear weapons.

89

The worth to mankind of an invention or a discovery depends on the uses made of it. If these are warlike and destructive to an appalling degree, then it might have been better for mankind to have continued in ignorance.

90

The world has moved too far from the quest of religious values to the quest of earthly ones; it is passing too quickly from faith in the myth to faith in the machine.

91

Many have been forced to stop and think about the failure of science to improve man despite its success in improving his tools. For the nineteenth-century naïveté about "progress" which had believed one would inevitably lead to the other, has been exposed for the foolish thing it is.

92

Progression forwards, which is what we have witnessed in this scientific age, is not the same as progress.

93

The end of all one-sided growth is usually catastrophic. This is true of the outer world of science as of the inner world of man himself. If the wonderful achievements of the scientist in controlling physical energies have now become highly dangerous to man, this is simply because they are unbalanced by equal knowledge of his own nature and equal achievement in controlling it.

94

The greater the pressure produced by this machine age, the greater is the revolt against it. Foolish materialists call this revolt escapism. Whether it appears as a turning to the arts or to mysticism, it is the cry of the human soul seeking to remember again that it *is* a soul.

95

If every invention which has benefited the human species has also introduced evils or disadvantages not present before, too often that has been due to human misuse or greed, materialism or ignorance.

96

I know there is some belief that not only has human capacity been extended by modern scientific knowledge but also that human character has been improved by modern civilization and culture. I doubt that this is so.

97

As modern technological civilization increased in power, the size of its problems increased too.

98

Even without a war the mere belief that they have to go on improving their nuclear knowledge by experiments and nuclear weapons by tests is leading to a disastrous result—the poisoning of the entire human race and the damaging of its organs, or its children's organs, and the deforming of its next generations.

99

Of what use are all these vaunted conquests over Nature if they are all to be lost again in a vast man-made calamity?

100

Control of mind by electronic machines is being actively sought by researchers without conscience, devoid of ethics, sorcerers using twentieth-century science.

101

Man's success in using his knowledge of the working of the external world can come only if it is linked with the knowledge of the working of his own psycho-physical mechanism and function. For if the first leads him into self-destruction, as it is now doing, the second can control and safeguard him against such an ill destiny.

102

To believe that the old past was quite barbaric, that the new present is quite civilized, as do those who pin all their faith to the "progress" brought about by science, shows definite ignorance of the past and lack of insight into the present. Moreover it also shows a dangerous lack of humility, dangerous because the first need of humanity is to be humble, is to confess its failure and admit its weakness.

103

Technological triumph, if held in equilibrium by spiritual intuition, can lead to a glorious civilization, but without such intuition, it can lead to mankind's destruction.

104

It is not enough for our civilization to express the discoveries arising out of scientific knowledge. It must also express the ethics arising out of spiritual knowledge.

Hatred and violent revolution

105

The forces of evil which are unloosed upon the world attain their maximum potency with the attainment of maximum hatred. Hence revolution based on hatred is not foolish; it is criminal.

106

Movements or men spreading hate or promoting violence to achieve a religious, political, or social aim fall into an ancient error—that the release of evil passions can increase and not hurt the general welfare.

107

I prefer evolution to revolution in political affairs. All revolutions are born of violence, hatred, and assassination whilst the attempt to establish and maintain them leads to oppression and despotism until their karma is exhausted. Evolution moves more slowly but also moves more peacefully, more bloodlessly.

108

Those who seek reform are too often too impatient: so they resort to revolution or violence. The price then may be exceedingly heavy. Even where the reform has been successfully brought about by such means, the success was due chiefly to other factors.

109

The vengeful hate-filled hysteria with which black leaders, leftist revolutionaries, and political fanatics try to arouse their young followers can only destroy them spiritually.

110

Agitators work up passions and hatreds and lead mobs to commit violent acts. It is thus that the first Alexandrian Library in ancient Egypt was destroyed.

111

Those youngsters who call hysterically for proletarian revolution, fill their minds with hate at the same time. This is as destructive to themselves as it is hurtful to others. If social injustices are repaired in the wrong spirit, new injustices replace the old ones. "Seek ye first the Kingdom of Heaven, and all these things shall be added unto you." That is, seek first the revolution *in man* himself, and then your quest of social justice will be aided by higher forces.

112

Those who demand liberty in order to destroy liberty itself are often in the noisy minority which claims that any attempt to protect liberty is an attack on "civil liberties"!

113

If those who denounce the world so strongly would then go on to renounce it, their attacks would be more convincing. The fact that most of them continue to stay in it, to live among all its evils (and attractions), is sufficient answer to their criticisms.

114

The mistake is to be so affected by the evils as not to see the good, so eager to destroy what is wrong that the right is destroyed along with it.

115

They are not evil in the fundamental sense of the word, all these men who commit crimes to further what they believe to be a righteous cause: they are mistaken.

Totalitarianism, Communism

116

It is significant that Communist leaders like Lenin despised all schools of spiritual thought, denounced religion, and scorned metaphysical reflection. This is now the nominal inheritance of half the world, most particularly the so-called workers' class.

117

If social justice means that every man, however deprived his background, should have a chance to develop himself and to better his standards of living, then it is certainly a good thing. But if it means the forced regimentation of everyone, the compulsory equalization of everything, the denial of individuality and the destruction of freedom, then it is surely a bad thing.

118

If we only pause to consider that half the entire human race has fallen under the enforced leadership and tyrannical domination of those who would limit man to his ego and reality to matter, we may see how urgently necessary is an arrest to this downward trend. The world is in a state of spiritual crisis.

119

Where the physical body is cherished as the sole reality and made the sole basis for social and political reform, where hate-driven men advocate physical violence as the sole means of effecting progress, be sure of the presence of evil forces, dangers to society, ignorant opponents of truth, and enemies of the Light.(P)

120

It is very meaningful that the filthy abuse which Lenin put into his writings against the idealist metaphysicians like Berkeley is no longer able to detain Soviet psychologists and philosophers in the utter blindness which he left them as part of his spiritual legacy. More and more they begin to question the nature of consciousness as well as its relationship to the external world, more and more they investigate borderland experiences like telepathy and hypnotism. On the question of consciousness' relationship to the brain they are now arguing quite widely, but, for obvious reasons, they remain unable to come to definitive conclusions on which all could agree. They are not satisfied with the completely materialistic answer and yet dare not venture into the purely mentalistic one. Meanwhile they go on debating, and so long as this continues, it is spiritually much healthier than their state of thirty years ago. Problems are being stated and solutions are being discussed. If the Leninist inheritance overshadows it all, that cannot be helped in a totalitarian Communist country. At the present stage of history the truth must be left out in such a land, but it cannot be left out forever. Out of all their mental and verbal activity, the

Russians will have to draw a little nearer to it intellectually. What is happening on a deeper plane is outside their knowledge.

121

No materialistic organization of society can prevent the appearance and development of spirituality in the individual, but it can create the conditions which will obstruct the appearance or hinder the development of spirituality.

122

The intellect, uncontrolled by intuition and unguided by revelation, has spawned the two great masters of our time—Science holding the atom bomb and Communism holding revolution. Science, which in the last century promised so much, gave us the terrible problem of atomic war instead. Its ardent advocates pointed at it only yesterday as the road to our salvation. Today it has become the road to our destruction. This is not to say that it was a false light, but that we mistook its proper place and claimed too much for its human possibilities. We let it run away with us and with our religion. We lost ourselves and our bearings. It made us regard Nature as self-operative in a solely mechanical way. It left life on earth without spiritual meaning, without moral purpose. Communism is the other heaven-promising panacea which has helped to make this earth a little hell. There can be no worthwhile future for humanity if it accepts the leadership of men, such as Communists, who regard conscience as a disease. The Communist insensibility in practice to human suffering accords ill with its vaunted idealism in theory. Communism's twisted ethic of wild hatred, its hard cruel face, its blind slavish obedience to a brutal organization which cares more for itself than for the workers it was supposed to save, its insane preachments against religion and denial of life beyond matter, have brought enough suffering to make its claims sound absurdly exaggerated. But the intellectual movement which produced Science and the social movement which produced Communism will not continue unchecked. They are approaching the utmost limit possible. The violent materialism for which they are responsible will culminate in the next Armageddon, which will not only end them, but also end the epoch itself.

123

Excerpt from an article in a Czech magazine on contemporary Czech literature: "Those ideals which were formerly given to the world by prophets of religion, headed by Jesus the Nazarene, are now practically applied by scientific socialists beginning with Karl Marx." Such is the plausible self-deception into which so many intellectuals have fallen. This quotation shows a grave lack of understanding of religion, of the prophets, and especially of Jesus. The distance between the Nazarene and the author of the first Communist Manifesto is not merely horizontal, it is vertical. The two men stand on different levels, belong to different worlds.

124

The presence of hatred as one of its animating ingredients is a moral disadvantage to any social movement. This is one reason why modern Communism is built on an unsure foundation.

125

The organized politico-economic substitutes for organized religion have hardly proved any better when put into active life rather than mere theory. They have introduced much hate, misery, oppression, persecution, superstition, and war, like the other.

126

In connection with the Cultural Revolution of the 1960s, Mao Tsetung wrote that the working classes would from then on take over leadership in all activities. That is to say, the least fitted by natural mental development, experience, and acquired education would dictate what was to be taught in philosophical and similar reflections about life, man, and history, if indeed such subjects would not be dropped altogether as unpractical, hence useless. The Peking Institute of Philosophy, a leading one in China, stopped publishing its journal *Philosophical Research* in 1966.

127

The fundamental mistake which is responsible for the harm and evil and misery caused when these teachings of economic equality are put into harsh practice, is to do so in separation from the teachings concerning man's spiritual life and spiritual needs. If the two were joined together then the fanaticism, delusion, and brutality of such practice would eliminate itself.

128

It is inevitable that a group which espouses belief in atheistic materialism will also espouse belief in the use of force and violence to establish itself and its views. If there will be no peace, it is because they do not really want it.

129

The most frenzied exponents of materialistic values today are those who have developed enough intellect to lose their faith in the hypocrisies of conventional religion but who have lost their true intuition along with their false belief. Such are the leaders and advocates of communism everywhere. Thus the good in their development is offset by the evil. The result is spiritual chaos and social turmoil for the masses who follow them. Since both the religious and their rebels have contributed to this situation, there is no remedy save in a clearer insight on the part of both.

130

It is impossible to reconcile the criminal ethics and materialistic ideology of Communism with the lofty ethics and mystical ideology of philosophy. There is no communication and every disparity between them.

131

The itch to meddle in other people's affairs and to mind their business for them is an ancient one. It was rightly reprimanded by the *Bhagavad Gita* in India and by the *Tao Teh Ching* in China. It reaches its extreme degree in tyrannies like the German Nazi and the Russian Communist, where state interference in the people's lives, culture, religion, and freedom becomes intolerable.

132

The Evil Spectre of Communism (Essay)

Abundant living will belong to the twenty-first rather than the twentieth century. Years must pass before even Europe alone can restore its shattered economy. For a number of years there will be immense and tragic shortages of food, clothing, and other necessities. The era of abundance is, therefore, not an immediate possibility. The postwar years are necessarily filled with privation for many millions of people.

Now this may be done and these problems may be solved by peaceful discussions and mutual agreement, which is the philosophic way, or by bitter strife and physical violence, which has been the common way. The first seeks the general welfare whereas the second seeks a partisan victory. The advantages of the philosophic way of speeded up evolutionary change are manifold in the economic sphere. The afflicted world's need is not more hatred but less, not more warfare but more co-operation. Philosophy is opposed to all doctrines of class hatred. It believes that the situation today requires an integral multi-class outlook. Its opposition to the old-fashioned materialistic propaganda for abrupt social change is not to its egalitarian aims but to the preaching of hatred as a personal ethic and the advocacy of violence as an instrument of attainment. For both hatred and violence are the voices of the beast in man. An age sickened by the horrors of scientific warfare ought not need to witness the further horrors of scientific revolution. But it is hard to persuade them that reconstruction is a saner and safer path to take than revolution, the ballot-box wiser than bloodshed, and that our duty is not to imitate the terrorists but to build peacefully a better order suited to sensible kindly and decent human beings. It cannot accept hatred as an inspiration to social betterment. For it knows that we cannot gather grapes off thistles nor human happiness off the tree of hatred. The history of mankind has shown what psychology always knew, that the hater will start looking for new human objects of his hatred, new enemies, as soon as the existing ones have been, in his horrible modern terminology, "liquidated." The ugly passion of hatred, having been developed and nurtured, will still exist and still seek an outlet as soon as it can persuade the mind to interpret conditions in its favour.

This is why the Buddha said: "Hatred ceaseth not by hatred. It ceaseth by compassion." If philosophy advocates the peaceful way of quickened evolution and dynamic progressivism as against the violent way of abrupt revolution, it is because it knows that the moral evils which are introduced by brutality—not to speak of the physical ones which inevitably follow from it—constitute too high a price for the benefits received. For if the latter tend to disappear, the former tend to become stabilized. A great social change which stimulated hatred, passion, selfishness, and material-ism would negate the ultimate purpose which lies behind all social evolu-tion—the spiritualization of human character. A better society, to be based on goodwill and co-operation, cannot be reached by arousing ha-tred and selfishness. The defense that ends justify means is a self-deceptive one. It is for the votaries of philosophy to follow the right path and to abstain from brutal or bloody methods, especially as we know that whilst conditions create them, there will always be others who are naturally inclined towards the transplanted barbarism of Communism.

Russia is today the homeland of Communism. Her achievements, sacri-fices, and struggles during World War II, unexpected as they were and so valuable in giving other nations a respite of time to eliminate their own unpreparedness for the Nazi aggressions, forcibly brought Russia's thought and fate to the whole world's attention. By reason of her exceptional geographical position, with one foot in Europe and another in Asia, Russia would have been a suitable mediator between the cultures of both conti-nents and an especially suitable interpreter of Asiatic wisdom to European minds, had she not been formerly so cut off from the rest of Europe by her intellectual and industrial backwardness, her difficult language and her deliberate exclusion of foreigners. The course of recent history, and es-pecially wartime history, delusively appeared to be bringing these hin-drances to an end. Given entirely different leadership, there might have been within the Slavonic republic the impending gestation of a new spiritual-practice culture, of a spiritually aspiring economic order. Russia and Germany constitute the two largest national populations in Europe. If the old Slav mysticism and the vanished German idealism could have been reincarnated in new non-materialistic, uncorrupt, and undistorted forms, there would have been hope for Europe. But the criminal leadership which existed actually destroyed this chance. This was all the more regrettable because, before the revolution of 1917, the Russians were particularly reputed to be a religious and mystical people whilst their literature was known to reflect these attributes. However, the explanation is easy. Russia was then a land of peasant communities with very few towns. Because their daily work keeps them in constant touch with nature, the peasant classes everywhere in the world have more religious emotion and mystical feeling than the others. But because they are also the most illiterate, the least educated, the most economically depressed and least travelled of all classes, their religion is more virulently intolerant and stupidly superstitious and their mysticism more medievally anti-rational and emotionally unbalanced than are those of other classes. All these undesirable features were prominent in pre-revolutionary Russia. The type of mysticism which can best flourish today and best meet the modern need can arise and develop only in more advanced countries, where the agricultural and industrial classes are more evenly distributed.

What is happening inside the Russian soul must interest us because it is important to us. The direction taken there is deciding the fate of other peoples as well as that of the Russians. They are a remarkable people, a bridge between Asia and Europe, and it would have been fitting that out of their tremendous sufferings and sacrifices there should emerge a happier country. Everything had depended on how far the Russians could overcome their greatest defect—fanatical lack of balance. Had they done this quickly enough, they could have risen to the grand height of a spiritual-material civilization. But, because they failed, because they listened too long to the evil voice of Communism, we have the danger of a third world war.

We should feel sorry for the Russian masses, who are blind dupes of their leaders, where the real evil resides. The inspiration of Russian leadership has been brutal hatred and camouflaged materialism, as well as the selfish preservation of their own power. But the law of compensation makes the masses responsible for their surrender and obedience to such criminal leadership. Their years of sacrifice in blood and comfort profit them nothing. They are sacrifices made in an evil cause. Those whose whole attitude is quarrelsome and carping and hating and irresponsible can contribute only unscrupulous criticism and hysterical destruction towards life. They are eager to obstruct and even destroy, but never to create, to co-operate, or to build. The Communist leaders, as distinct from their blind dupes, are the poisonous scorpions of society.

Their fanatic hostility to all spiritual enlightenment is inspired by the same dark forces that inspired the fanatic hostility of Nazism. The second world war was the epochal struggle between the unseen powers of evil working through mesmerized Germans and barbarized Japanese and the unseen powers of good instilling ideals of decency into other peoples. This inner war between good and evil goes on at all times; the military world war was but a dramatic outward representation of it. That—the real war—is not ended. We must beware of those who never went to Germany and never wore a swastika on a brown shirt, but who nevertheless imbibed the Nazi spirit and wore the swastika in their hearts. They have reappeared in Russia. Those unseen spirits which animated, prompted, and inspired the Nazi leaders are now performing the same office for the Communist leaders. It would have been better for Europe if the Communists and their twins, the Nazis with their slippery morality, had never existed. It is an unendurable thought; nevertheless, the truth must be faced that we shall have peace only by having war. The dangers to which humanity was exposed did not all vanish with the Nazis' defeat. Those unseen powers still exist. What they could not achieve through a straightforward conflict, they will desperately try to achieve through a confused one. This indeed is the next phase of experience through which we are about to pass and which we shall have to endure.

Nevertheless the presence of an evil tyranny in both Russia and Germany ought not to blind us to the vital difference between their forms of government. In Russia, Stalin's dictatorial control was expounded and accepted theoretically as a purely temporary measure on the road to full democratic freedom, whereas in Germany Hitler's dictatorial control was expounded and accepted as an ultimate ideal in itself. The dangers to which Nazism exposed the human race were immeasurably larger than those to which Communism exposes it. For no matter how brutal, how violent, and how materialistic Communism became, it always remained in theory an anguished and desperate attempt—however ugly in form—to win justice for the underprivileged and to compel the social whole to accept responsibility for their unavoidable sufferings. But the ultimate trend of the Nazification of Europe could only be the animalization of Europeans. All that gives dignity and worth to human beings, all their ethics and rationality, all their art and idealism would have disappeared under Nazi reign within a generation or two. The disfigured form of man would thenceforth bear a close resemblance to the worst kind of beast, albeit a cunning one, whose God was Hatred. If we must compare the two evil systems, Bolshevism had this superiority at most, that it arose under the inspiration of great hope, whereas Nazism arose under that of great despair and revenge.

But alas, just as the arising of Nazism earlier forced the world unwillingly into a struggle to the death, so the leaders of Communism are now forcing the world into the same kind of struggle. The human race is being made to chalk out a boundary line and to take sides in preparation for the inevitable.

The responsibility for this degeneration does not lie with those who still believe in the ideals of freedom and truth, but with those who reject these ideals. The guilt does not lie with those who seek to defend themselves against the aggressions of an evil doctrine, it lies with those who spread this doctrine by every means, including the most criminal means.

It is better, indeed, that the face of Communism should be seen for what it is, with all its malignant cruelty and materialistic criminality, than that the world should continue in complacent blindness to the danger in which it stands. Ever since the war ended we have tried to make peace or effect compromises with this dark force, but to no avail. It does not want peace because it does not believe in peace. It is committed to the doctrine that it must fight for the soul of humanity—which soul it seeks to enslave for its own evil purposes.

The frightful shape which the next war would necessarily take may make us wonder whether it would be better for humanity to save its body at least, by appeasing the powers of evil or by surrendering to them. But is it only for the body's sake that we are upon this earth? If there were no higher purpose to life than preserving the body, such appeasement and such surrender might be worthwhile. But we know that there is such a purpose, that we are here for soul development even more than for any other kind. If appeasement and surrender are the only price at which we can purchase peace, then the still small voice within answers, "War is still better—even if costlier."

The effort is one thing, whilst its effect is another. We must estimate the Bolshevik achievement by its practical results rather than by its theoretical claims. We must keep close to earth in these matters and test the printed page by the human scene. And if we do this without paying uncritical homage to the dynamism it has shown, we find that Bolshevism has dragged men's souls in mire and their bodies in prison—for Russia became nothing else—and the economic lot of the peasant and the workman is no better, and generally is far worse, than it is in most capitalistic countries. Russia suffered the painful consequences of her own barbarities and fanaticisms, and she has pruned her communistic ideas of some of their extremism. She found by experience that it was an error to withdraw the profit motive entirely. Human nature being psychologically what it is, sufficient financial inducement had to be given to evolve personal efficiency and enterprise and to encourage new inventions. She found that any economic order which ignored the inequalities of capacity and qualifications, talents and minds among its members, could only be a half-success and must be a half-failure. Men require the energizing motive of more pay for more work or higher pay for higher type of work. Men must have rewards for extra labour or extra talent, which means they must own possessions and get privileges in unequal degrees. Any economic scheme must frankly face and accept this psychological fact, otherwise it would set up a perpetual friction between the individual and the state. Russian Communism was compelled, by initial failures in obtaining adequate production, to give more remuneration to skilled workers and to institute hierarchic organization in factories. Moreover, the ever-present need of stimulating general human evolution requires the offering of rewards to draw out the varied possibilities lying latent within man, the holding-up of baits to make him realize the fuller stature of his being.

The crude kind of socialism which would erect the state into a tyrannous dictator, create an order of bureaucratic parasites, and organize every detail of the mental and physical existence of its unfortunate victims, is intolerable to intelligent people who rightly wish to exercise their personal initiative, to develop their creative abilities, to attain self-responsibility, to achieve economic independence, and to think for themselves. Only those who possess slave-mentalities can fail to be opposed by temperament to any totalitarian form which would compel every man to walk in standardized step with all other men, which would dictate how he should think, live, talk, work, rest, and marry, and which would reduce all society to a dead monotony of uniformity. Such a system is the kind which can suit only a people which has made materialism its religion. On the other hand, a system which would allow room for diverse forms of living, which would encourage and not stifle individual initiative, and which would lead men to liberation and not to enslavement is the kind which is based on the right comprehension of existence. Man cannot live by Marxism alone. A system which deprived its citizens of their personal initiative and individual enterprise would thereby deprive society of valuable gifts. The delight of creative self-expression and personal initiative ought to be encouraged and not chilled, as it is under Communism. It is better for a man—and consequently for the nation—that he should farm his own little piece of land in economic and individual freedom than that he should be a mere labouring "hand" under State employ on a mammoth agricultural enterprise. The notion that slavery becomes innocuous when it is slavery under a bureaucratic State instead of under a particular master is a notion to be repudiated. The worthwhile values which have been so far derived from a free system should not be sacrificed, even though the system itself may have to be brought up-to-date. It must defend itself against the hard dogmas which would destroy individuality. Nobody who loves liberty can be happy if he is numbered, regimented, dragged about, and enslaved by a cold, unfeeling, abstract entity called the State. The intellectual mistake of destroying personal freedom in order to achieve the ends, alone renders Communism unacceptable to the philosophic mind. The emotional mistake of effecting such destruction violently and brutally renders it still more unacceptable.

He who loves freedom to follow a spiritual path and values independence of mental outlook will not care to be rigorously controlled at every step of his work and for every hour of his intellectual life by any bureaucratic regime. When, for instance, writers, artists, and clergymen have to serve the State first and truth, beauty, or God afterwards, they can do so only at the cost of forfeiting the authentic inspiration which these ideals provide. They must be free or the community will get not their best but their worst work. The extinction of intellectual and spiritual liberty, the destruction of personal self-respect, and the disregard of the sacredness of individual life are definite evils. Philosophy is opposed to totalitarianism in all its forms because it believes in the necessity of preserving human dignity, human freedom, and human individuality, within proper limits. Unless there is respect for such aspirations, spiritual growth will be hampered. To a totalitarian order, things are more important than men, frontiers than the people behind them, and the State than its citizens. But to a true philosophy, men in their final essence are creatures with divine possibilities, human dignity is sacred, inviolable, and human individuality is to be sacrificed only at God's behest. This development is one of the last things that a totalitarian state can wish or permit. Therefore, the practice of true religion, mysticism, and philosophy, which leads to the development of man's spiritual individuality, could only end in collision between the seeker and such a state. Consequently, the latter could afford to sanction the existence only of a false, nationalistic, materialistic, pseudo-spiritual teaching or, in the end, prohibit it altogether. Fatalism has crept into economic thinking in the most vicious and distorted form, the form of Communism. According to this doctrine, history's course is predetermined: the capitalistic phase of society cannot avoid being followed by the chaotic phase of its own dissolution, and that, in its turn, cannot avoid being followed by the Communistic form of a rigid reorganization. This is a materialistic caricature of the doctrine of fatalism, which in its true form as karma has so far entered only into the *spiritual* thinking of the West. This Marxian view, that is to say, the short-sighted view, is too simple to be true. Life is more complex than that. It is true that Demos is astir and seeks at the least to better his lot and at the most a paradise on earth. When a man passes through a long period of unemployment or earns too little for adequate support of his family, he begins to feel despairingly that society has no use for him. This bitterness weakens his ethical sense and renders him liable to fall into the illusion that any social change, even a violent one, is necessarily a change for the better. If, instead of making proper efforts to remove the deficiencies and eliminate shortcomings, we merely seek for plausible pretexts to justify them, then we ought not to be astonished when disaster comes. Those who feel that economic reform is the most urgent duty facing humanity have usually opposed the mystical movement. They have done so on the grounds that it diverts attention from the real (that is, the economic) issues, that it enfeebles the urge towards social improvement and individual ambition, and that it leads to sleepy, dreamy complacency. Karl Marx's criticism of religion, that it had become a mere appendix of bourgeois thought, had some truth in it for his own times. But today many religious leaders have been aroused to the danger and are sincerely striving to bring the social order into line with religious ethics. They are no longer falsifying religious ethics by striving to bring them into line with the social order.

Yet the solution Communists offer is philosophically unsatisfactory for it is born out of crude materialism, based on venomous class hatred, and stiffened by bureaucratic tyranny. Their ultimate aim, however, is a good one only insofar as it is the elimination of capitalism's defects, such as avoidable unemployment, extreme poverty, and social injustices, but their means and methods are very bad. There is only one real capitalist—Nature—one real proprietor of the earth and all that therein is, and consequently all the children of earth are its rightful heirs. We usually forget that we have no ethical right to possess what we have not toiled for. This is overlooked by society as a whole and we, as individuals, take shelter beneath the common sin. For sin it is, albeit only one of omission. Those, however, who have cast aside the conventional view can see it for what it is. That which this earth produces is for all. Every man has his birthright in what it stores or gives forth, although not an equal birthright to every other man's. This, surely, is Nature's view, although man in his ignorance has developed other ideas upon the matter and so brought great misery upon his fellows and great nemesis upon himself. The world is for our temporary use and does not constitute our eternal property. Whoever thinks otherwise—whether it be a single individual or a community of individuals called a "nation"—and excludes all others from consideration, whoever thinks he has a full right to eat whilst others have a full right to starve, whoever cannot identify himself with the suffering people of his own or another country, will be tutored by pain and instructed by loss. We are all stewards, not proprietors, and own nothing in reality. This was pithily expressed by a highly advanced Indian mystic of well-deserved repute. He was the Jain Mahatma Shantivijaya who lived on Mount Abu until he died during the War. When one of his devotees, a rich landlord, came to him and complained of having been robbed of some jewels, the yogi observed, "Perhaps Nature regards you also as a thief. Perhaps she thinks you have no more right to appropriate such a large piece of land than you think the other man has to your jewels?" The same idea was beautifully expressed in a verse by my revered Irish friend, the late A.E. [George W. Russell]: "How would they think on, with what shame, all that fierce talk of thine and mine, if the true Master made His claim, the World He fashioned so divine. What could they answer did He say, 'When did I give my world away?'"

But there is a great distance from such abstract reflections to the concrete realities of contemporary social and economic life. The whole structure of laws and rights is based on these realities. And this is as it should be, for humanity, at its present stage of evolution, can best express itself and serve itself in that way. The anarchist would ignore them because he is one-sided and the Communist would violate them because he is unscrupulous. Philosophy does not object to any effort to remold society for the common welfare, but welcomes it.

No amount of academic sophistry can justify a system which permits the few to have more food than they can eat and forces the many to have less food than they need to eat. No amount of legal enactment can justify the ownership of a hundred thousand acres of land merely because five hundred years earlier some ancestor seized it. These ancient wrongs must be redressed. Both altruistic sentiment and political strategy—no less than karmic adjustment—demand such a revision, although the attempt to do so by violent means would introduce far worse wrongs.

In this momentous task, we have to prepare a blueprint—not of the ideal State which we would like to see arise, but of the actual State which can arise under the given circumstances. This means that we must follow a middle path. Any other way will be either too realistic or too idealistic and will lead to failure. For we must find not only what is theoretically right but also what is practically possible.

We cannot and we ought not do away wildly, abruptly, and violently with our social environment. Without it we would be savages. Those vanished men of the past had to learn arduously how to live on earth, how to adapt themselves to it. Think of what it would mean to be born into a world where no houses existed, no land was cultivated, no roads had been cut, no books were available, no shops could be found, no tools had been made, no machines invented, no knowledge and no art were known! All these and infinitely more exist today and constitute our surroundings, our civilization; but they did not spring up in a single night. They are the inheritance which we owe to a long trailing line of Egyptian, Asiatic, and European ancestors living and working and dying for countless centuries. They are our own racial past. We cannot dismiss this legacy without descending anew to the most barbarous existence. There are grave defects in this environment, it is true, but the young rebel who wishes to tear everything down in order to remove these defects, will also remove treasures bought at a price which will take the toil of millions through centuries to pay again. The past efforts of man appear in our present environment. Let us use it, but use it wisely. It is here to serve us. We need not be afraid to improve and alter it. Unbalanced hot-heads who say that such improvement and such alteration is only possible through complete destruction of what is the present order so that what may be shall rise on its ruins, have misread history.

But there is a right as well as a wrong way of doing this. The only proper way is by persuasion, by the persuasion and education of social conscience and by the uplift of social morality to loftier standards. Such reforms can be brought about only in an atmosphere of goodwill and calmness, not in an atmosphere of hatred and brutality. Man must choose which God he will serve, the God of hatred or the God of love, for he cannot serve both. He must effect these changes not by brutality or by blood, but by the gentler persuasions of reason and goodwill, slower though they necessarily are. Wisdom prefers to see needed reforms and overdue changes brought in by peaceful and not violent means, by the acknowledgment of their ethical need rather than by submission to materialistic values.

Orthodox Communism is a typical nineteenth-century product. The doctrine arose out of a completely materialistic view of history. It was formulated in an age when the mechanistic conception of life had captured the thinking world. It led naturally to an ethic of hatred and violence. It excluded all consideration of the higher destiny of men. Consequently it is emotionally unbalanced and intellectually unsatisfactory. The evil lies less in the doctrine itself, which is a confused mixture of nonsense and wisdom, of justice and crime, than in its human leaders. They are men without a conscience and maniacs entrenched in the seats of power. They trade on this confusion of doctrine to suborn the masses who lack the capacity to understand the inner source of Communism and its inability to redeem its promises. They achieve for themselves positions of power because they mercilessly push aside and trample all who are hapless enough to stand in their way.

He who thinks in terms of class hatred and class murder reveals himself as being naturally neurotic or malignant. As such he is unfit to lead people into a better condition than before and can only lead them into a worse one. The average Communist is unfit to lead a people or govern a nation. He is an extraordinary compound of keen critical thinking and irrational obsessions and class prejudices; consequently his thinking is distorted and unbalanced. He lives in a private Marxist world of his own, which he stupidly imagines to be a real world. But the greatest defect in himself and the greatest danger to others is the powerful hatred which actuates him and which has made him in fact a pathological case. He has become semi-insane because he cannot escape from it.

Both the Nazi and Bolshevik revolutions failed to bring a better society, a happier healthier and more honourable world for the underdog, because they failed to recognize that the only way this could be achieved was by leaders of disinterested character and superior quality descending to the service of the lower classes. The reconstruction of the world's social and economic order cannot succeed if it comes from the mentally ungrown and ethically immature masses themselves. This has been clearly demonstrated by the melancholy history and comparative failure of the brutal Russian and German attempts. It could not be achieved by leaders of inferior character and merit rising from the ranks of the masses. The right way of social-economic progress is from the top downwards and not from the bottom upwards. The fruits of wisdom cannot come from below. But this does not mean they come from the aristocracy of blood; they can come only from aristocracy of mind and character. The masses will be best served by the man who disdains their approbation and waves aside their applause. For intellectual awakening of a people does not begin as an awakening of the masses; it begins as an awakening of the educated classes and proceeds downwards to the people. The masses must naturally follow more intelligent leaders, assimilate the ideas which are earlier embraced by their betters but which are gradually filtered down and thus rendered more acceptable. For it is not the ignorant blind toilers who can perceive the crowning principle of right reconstruction; they can perceive only their immediate needs, not their ultimate ones. Therefore the creation of a new order must not come from below but from above. It must come from the intellectual cream, the spiritual elite of society—from those who can reflect philosophically and serve selflessly and act calmly. They stand on the mountain peak, as it were, and see clearly what ought to be done whereas the masses are herded on the plains and can only run hither or thither as their emotions drive them.

The Communists cannot be regarded as sane, normal people; they are mentally in a psychopathic condition. Consequently they leave themselves open to submoral influences, and that they fully absorb these influences we may judge from the fact that they do indeed come to believe that the end justifies any means, however evil. It is a sophistry common alike to criminal gangsters and to totalitarian dictators that the sacrifice of ethical restraints and the aggressive use of brutal methods are quite justified by the achievement of success in their aims. Such callous belief, however, has a hundred times been proven worthless by history. Any totalitarian or revolutionary regime which, dead to humanitarian impulses, would brutally bring death and suffering and misery to millions now alive in order to bring prosperity and comfort and power to future and fortunate millions yet unborn, which would deny pity and peace to those in its midst in order to bestow them on those who are remote and unseen, is trying to purchase a possibility at such a tragically high present cost that it is not worth having. This is why philosophy says that the same change which, when naturally evolved tomorrow will be right and successful, may be arbitrary, premature, and disastrous today if it can be got only by violence and brutality on a vast scale.

The terrible human cost of these totalitarian and brutalitarian changes is at least equally as important as the economic cost. The resulting success or failure of these changes must be measured by broken hearts and broken bodies as much as by flaunting figures and astronomical statistics. To say that what the world needs today is *only* a new economic system is as fanatical and unbalanced as to say that it needs only a new dietetic outlook. It does need both these things, and needs them brought into reciprocal balance as well, but it certainly needs something else even more—a new spiritual outlook. The moment we have the understanding or courage to lift our public, economic, political, and social difficulties to the higher levels of religious, mystical, or philosophic insight and thus meet them with full consciousness, that moment they will all be solved. After all, the best laws people can obey are not the dried parchments of written statutes but the living ethical forces of justice, goodwill, truth, and service. A country which has such a real ethical foundation will get all the social economic and political reforms it needs as and when it needs them; no murderous revolution will be necessary whenever change must be made to adapt itself to new conditions. Back of the state laws there will then always be unwritten laws shaping them automatically and naturally.

The regimentation of the masses on a solely materialistic basis would enslave them in a different and, to some misguided people, more bearable form than the capitalistic order has already; but still it would enslave them. Any system which forcibly regimented the masses in order to guarantee their basic necessities could doubtless succeed in doing so. But if it would fill their stomachs it might still leave their souls empty.

When the inner life of mankind suffers from acute starvation it becomes inevitable, under the law that governs thought, that his outer life will, in time, also suffer acute starvation. There is this difference: that whereas the inner hunger, being spiritual, is unconscious, the outer hunger, being physical, is conscious. If civilization is dying it is dying because it has no vision, no ideals, no spiritual life. It is not dying because of the War; the War merely accelerated the process which started in prewar days. The storm is upon us and there is no shelter from it.

War

133
War is a leveller which spreads suffering with a wide swathe. It is also a teacher which pulls men up sharply and forces them to look at their lives and, even more important, at themselves.

134
War is the *normal* state of wild beasts. If human beings engage in it too, that is because they have not got rid of the tiger and wolf within themselves.

135
Although war itself is full of horrors it must not be forgotten that it has an obverse side. In some ways it acts like the old-fashioned surgical operation of blood-letting. All the moral scum in humanity's character rises to the surface, concentrated mostly amongst the totalitarian gangsters, but it rises only that it may be seen for what it is and cleared off. The sufferings of mankind have an educative value and tend to adjust the sins and excesses of mankind. It is the ultimate tendency of evil forces to destroy themselves from within as well as to suffer destruction from without through the mysterious operation of karma. Materialism reaches its final culmination in the social and personal crises generated by war. By displaying its own horrible results before humanity's very eyes, it is, by reaction, awakening many sleeping mentalities to the need of a spiritual outlook.

136
In a world which has the conflict of opposites as part of its inherent nature, peace is an illusory goal. Nor in reality is there even such a thing as neutrality and nonalignment.

137
If brute force really ruled this world then the Romans would still be ruling the Britons, and the Huns who sacked Rome would still be ruling that beautiful city. The Persian troops would still be masters of Egypt and Alexander's troops would still be the masters of Persia. But brute force is a success only in the beginning and a failure always in the end.

138
It is true that some wars seem to have achieved a creative result, but how much more painlessly, bloodlessly, could not the same result have been achieved by nonviolent methods. It might have required a longer time, more patience, but the cruelty and horror and loss of war would have been avoided.

139

We may watch the democratic nations trying to prevent open conflict with the totalitarian ones, but all they are succeeding in doing is merely to put off the inevitable clash from one year to another. They cannot succeed because it is in the nature of things that between good and evil there must be conflict. The evil ever seeks to destroy the good, and the good must defend itself ever. It could not happen otherwise.

140

The fears which war engenders and the deprivations which it causes are painful. Yet for those who are too attached to outward things they are often necessary teachers. Out of the fears, great heroism has been learned; out of the deprivations, great unselfishness; but those who respond to such lessons are too few, the influence of the lessons themselves too ephemeral.

141

When it is said that war is a purifying agent, it is not meant that our morals are purified; on the contrary, war notoriously makes them temporarily worse. By enthroning passion and displacing reason, by generating wild fears and brutal hatreds, the very smoke of war tends to smother those civilized self-disciplines which make for decent living during the normal times of peace.

142

This is a world of struggle. The word "peace" has only a relative meaning. The notion that a society, a civilization, or an individual can exist in a continuously inert state is an illusory one. As soon as one kind of war ends, another kind of war begins. A peace of endless stagnation is impossible. The last kind of peace is that wherein the forces which must inevitably contend against each other are properly balanced.

143

A great war brings humanity to an emotional crisis. Such a crisis shakes it out of complacency and indifference toward religious values.

144

War, with its frightful threat to life and possessions, its dreadful menace to personal relations, forces mankind to revise long-established attitudes for better or worse. If it opens one door to atheism, it also opens another door to religion and still another to mysticism.

145

We live in a state of perpetual war. Back and forth go the ghostly armies of construction and destruction. Sometimes one and sometimes the other holds the field in triumph.

146

It is easy for those who are addicted to the worship of force and violence to misread history and fall into partial or complete error. They do not understand why an individual or a nation must become and stay strong from within if victories are not to turn into whips which one day lash back at the victor.

147

The Roman Eagle flew high into the sky of power but in the end fell ingloriously to earth. The Indian Lotus flourished long before yet lives today still. Why? A civilization based on higher laws will always survive where one based on violence will not.

148

The crushing of finer moral qualities like mercy, pity, calmness, and forgiveness, which war brings about, helps to inaugurate a more materialistic period after the war.

149

War always brings about the brutalization of most of the men who fight in it and yet, paradoxically, the spiritualization of a minority.

150

The memory of slain relatives and the sight of crippled ones teaches terrible lessons. Only the fanatic or the ruthless will refuse to absorb these lessons and will see in those very sufferings a stimulant to revenge, an inducement to plot for further war.

151

Although war ennobles many people by providing them with larger motives and wider outlooks through the union of all individuals in a common aim, although it forces them to make personal aims secondary and subordinate to the common welfare, it still brutalizes them. It arouses bestial passions and forms evil characters. It is still an evil and destructive enterprise which takes away more than it gives, lowers more than it elevates.

152

The bitter lessons of war may be learned aright but they may also be soon forgotten.

153

What man, what country can feel safe so long as thermonuclear weapons remain in existence? But if they are banned what of the lesser horrors which War Departments have developed—germs, gases, rays, and other obscene nightmarish things?

154

If Atlantis went to its grave under the impulse of violent eruptions that rocked the world, the Atlantean use of atomic power for warlike purposes lay behind the eruptions themselves.

155

If men had better character and more intuition they would not and could not accept such horrors, even in the name of self-defense.

156

War disrupts customs, dissolves morality, and destroys art. It alters fate and reveals the good and the bad in human character. It is the severest test both of a man and a nation. It shocks religion, blacks out mysticism, but confirms philosophy.

When the usefulness of a tradition is at an end both men and events attack and disintegrate it. The longer the war went on, the less did it become probable that the old order of thought could be restored after it.

Causes of war

157

If war comes, the blame must fall not only outwardly on the men and policies which provoke it, but also inwardly on the passions and greeds and egoisms which influence leaders and led alike.

158

When there is more of hate than of goodwill between two nations, and for a sufficient time, it is inevitable under the law of compensation that physical war will break out between them.

159

War, being ultimately the expression of the mind's errors and the heart's passions, can only be stopped by getting at it in the places where it starts: in the mind and the heart themselves. Its cause being primarily internal it cannot be cured by an external remedy. This means that neither organized religion nor organized politics can save the world from the ruin that awaits it. We may wish them well in their attempts but we cannot help seeing facts which all history causes us to see. The guns and bombs, the gases and tanks of modern war are only the symbols of man's inner disorder. The reality behind them is his ignorance of spiritual laws, his blindness to the fact that all war is a consequence and not a cause. All the national days of prayer and the eminent ecclesiastics who led them have failed to stop two world wars in our time. And they failed because they were trying to escape from a consequence whilst leaving the cause untouched.

160

The sufferings that World War II brought to so many have deeply shocked us but the significance of those sufferings must also be examined from a fresh standpoint. In all the theories offered to a bewildered world concerning its own woes, there is much anxiety and alarm at the symptoms but little search for the causes. If people accept a deceptive world-view as the Germans did and as the Russians do, or a defective one as so many others did and do, they must also accept the troubles and disasters which go with it.

161

We must push the spade of enquiry deep down into the earth that surrounds the roots of this problem of wars and riots, aggressions and crimes, rather than be content with a mere surface view. The evils that menace our existence will then be found to grow out of two roots: ignorant egoism and unchecked emotion. The one is unnecessary, the other unreasonable.

162

Each of the world wars which afflicted mankind was the inevitable self-earned effect of causes previously set going. The unerring law of karma brings whatever good or evil recompense is deserved. The debit account of wrong done is allowed to run on until the end of the page and then it has to be totalled and the balance entered to adjust the total. The great famines, like the great wars, which afflicted and still afflict mankind, constitute part of this adjustment, part of the payment which mankind is forced to make by the higher governing law of karma. Their causes are as plural as the causes of the wars, although on the deepest level there is only the same single cause of human ignorance leading to human wrong-doing. One of them is the refusal of mankind to utilize the earth's grain harvests for its own direct use, diverting them instead to the use of animals deliberately bred for slaughter and then eating the grain indirectly in the form of those animals' corpses. Such a way of supporting life is both utterly unnecessary and utterly cruel. The life of innocent creatures cannot be taken upon such baseless grounds with impunity. Retribution has hit mankind again and again in the past, with the weapons of hunger, disease, and war, and it is hitting them again in the present. No reorganization of agricultural methods on more efficient and more productive lines, no re-arrangement of trading relations, no governmental subsidies in cash, tractors, seeds, fertilizers, pesticides, or equipment will save mankind from suffering famines and enduring starvation if it does not face the real challenge and meet it. A radical change of life is demanded from it, a repentant change of heart is the only way to win back Nature's smile. It must stop this unjustified murder of helpless living beings, murdered merely because they are lower in the scale of evolution. It must accept the perfectly sufficient diet of grains, cereals, vegetables, pulses, fruits, nuts, and dairy produce which will enable it to live with less suffering and more health, less punishment and more conscience, than a meat diet permits.

163

Life brings man what he needs, which is sometimes what he desires but at other times what he fears. The modern world badly needed a shake-up, and got one. However, it received only what it deserved. The war descended on it in accordance with karmic law. When nation arose against nation, it was only an end-expression of the innate selfishness which had been actuating them. We must expect such situations, for they are the natural and inevitable consequence of all that has happened before. Unless the war has brought a vivid realization of the truth of the law of compensation, it has not brought any spiritual progress. But it is too much at this time to expect the modern world to understand the cause of its tribulations. What valuable ethical and psychological significances, what striking illustrations of the inexorable law of retribution, could be drawn from the war!

164

The evolutionary pressure upon humanity is not to give up its fratricidal warfare, although it will eventuate in that, but to give up the aggressive selfishness in which such warfare has its roots.

165

If the nations cannot settle their differences peacefully it is because the ego in them is too strong, the passions too violent, and the antagonisms too blind. The differences must be faced on deeper than physical levels, and the refusal to do this on the grounds that such are idealistic and not practical results in superficial and not true considerations and results.

166

How hard it is to get people to draw accurate conclusions from their experience one can read from the annals of history. Again and again the people of one nation race or religion who have been subjected to persecution by a different one, have failed to behave justly and tolerantly when the turning wheel of destiny put them later into power.

167

The gusts of hate or anger or greed which blow men off their mental balance, blow them eventually to war.

168

In spite of the spiritual messages which have been given to mankind by the great prophets, the savagery of war still continues to show the strength of the animal in man.

169

If their compassion for helpless animals is so small that they will not give up eating flesh, by what right do they call upon God to show compassion toward them and stop war?

170

The world war was not only the consequence of the desecration of the Egyptian graves, of course. It was much more a consequence of the evil thoughts and feelings which exist in men's hearts and of the spiritual ignorance which exists in their minds. The desecration was itself only one of the symptoms of that ignorance.

171

Evil desires and unjust acts were the seed: the horrors of war were the fruit. The awful retribution which fell upon whole nations was impelled and guided by the power behind the eternal and immutable law of consequences. Up to a certain point, it could have been modified and even prevented, but beyond this point nothing could annul its appointed course.

172

Let us blame none but ourselves. This holocaust was needed in order to bring humanity fully to its senses, to purge its materialistic atheism of its pride, and to show it how hollow and hypocritical was its facade of civilization.

173

When we penetrate these social, economic, political, educational, and national problems to rock bottom we find that they are really ethical problems.

174

Virgil, the Roman, dreamt of universal peace. Many today entertain the same dream but at the same time they are contradicted by piled-up evidences of the violence in human nature, the strife engendered by blind self-interest, the killing instinct that is a heritage from the animal.

175

So long as egos come into conflict with one another, so long will nations do the same. We are to expect the brutal carnage and concentrated massacre of war until and unless we are impelled to renounce it at last as a method of removing affronts to justice.

World War II, Nazism, Fascism, Hitler

176

For those whose inward eyes were sufficiently open to see what was happening behind the scenes and beneath the surface of things, World War II was a war not only on the military and political planes but also against those powerful evil spirits whom the apostle Paul called "The rulers of darkness" practising "spiritual wickedness in high places." That is to say, it was also a war against a demonistic incursion into human affairs unparalleled in human history. We were not merely fighting deluded Germans. We were also fighting unseen evil powers.

177

When the New Year of 1919 dawned, Europe particularly and mankind almost everywhere believed that what had been lived through was the most dreadful war in all history. When, however, a score of years later a second war was spelled in letters of red fire across the frightened face of this planet, the whole world was lost in bewilderment. Governments and nations stood aghast at the spectacle of the failure of their own baffled and bewildered struggles to escape from the spider's web of terrors into which they had fallen. They gazed perplexed upon an amazing scene such as the past had never known. A period precisely like unto it was looked for in vain through all the known records of time.

A surface view of the war informs us that mankind was sacrificed on the blood-stained altar of one man's insensate ambition in Europe and of one clique's militaristic passion in Asia. A philosophic view, however, informs us that this is only partly true. There was very much more behind the war than this simplification suggests. Activating all the other factors and rising from the uncharted depths of human consciousness, there was a cruel psychic attack upon humanity itself, upon all its best hopes and finest prospects, upon everything that had raised it from kinship with the teeth-bared beasts to companionship with sacred intuitions and holy thoughts. And to bring this attack to the completest possible triumph, it was directed against both the bodies and minds of men, against their whole being. . . . [several lines were deleted here in the notebook—Ed.]

The second is the opposition which it encounters from invisible creatures who dwell in a supernatural sphere of utter darkness, who do not belong to its kingdom but who have psychic points of contact with it and ranges of influence over it. This sphere constitutes an element in Nature which is averse to man's upward movement and hostile to his higher characteristics. We do not have to go back to the great religions of antiquity for testimony to its real existence; the recorded experiences of scientific psychical researchers of modernity can provide that too.

It was more difficult for most people to understand correctly what was at stake in the war and what indeed were the forces aligned behind it when the struggle first started than after it had passed progressively through some of its earlier phases. Not till Hitler had overrun nearly all of Europe was it quite clear to everyone except the emotionally foolish or the selfishly biased that the aims which inspired him were such that humanity's whole future was at stake. Those who said World War II was a continuation of World War I were partly mistaken. It was so in a military sense only but not in any other sense. Those who chose to see this as a war between rival exploiting Imperialisms only were blinded by their own emotional complexes. All this terrible holocaust of suffering did not occur in the defense of Euro-American life and liberty alone; it also occurred in the defense of the life and liberty of generations to come throughout the five continents. All were taking part in events of the profoundest historical character.

Why did the dark forces choose our own generation for the launching of their attack? Why did they not choose the seventeenth, eighteenth, or nineteenth centuries? First, never before could such an operation be so effective in result, for never before could a single movement reach so many human souls on a planet-wide scale and at the same moment in time. Hitherto, only a limited area or a particular race could be its objective; now all areas and all races are within its scope. Second, never before was a choice of roads so fateful in its ultimate results. The directions travelled now, the turn given to the stream of events during these few momentous years, the decisions taken by mankind's leaders in this stupendous crisis, will govern the fate and shape the social, spiritual, economic, cultural, political, and personal history of the whole world for many centuries to come.

These reasons combined to make the dark forces attach supreme importance to choosing that time for their attack.

178

Many believed, even up to a decade ago, that humanity was ready for its next important step forward. But the Nazis showed that millions were equally ready for its next important step backward. Hence we must not overestimate the power and scope of the idealism that so fortunately proved triumphant in the end.

179

It was not merely the fate of this or that country which was at stake; it was the fate of all mankind. Only an inadequate comprehension of its background and an imperfect perception of its consequences could limit its significance to anything less than a universal one.

180

Humanity escaped from the most fearful danger, the most awful evil of its modern history. The gospel of hate failed to capture it, but only just failed.

181

There is really another unseen and vicious struggle beneath the visible one, a desperate aggression against the soul of humanity itself of which the war became an outward symbol.

182

War came with the thundering gallop of the Four Horsemen. Its deafening tumult all but drowned the whispers that came from the higher regions of man's own heart. It threatened to engulf humanity and to vanquish its soul. No earlier war has had such profound effects on human lives just as no earlier war has touched so many human lives. Millions of men and women have been forcibly dislodged from their own homes and even their own countries and have had to fit themselves in with strangers or with foreigners. Hitler has heaped sorrow after sorrow upon this unfortunate generation to so stupendous a degree that history cannot parallel the record. Yet, the end of this miserable tragedy has been a victory of the forces of light over those of darkness. Thus, we who live today have lived to see the dramatic vindication of the moral law.

183

They suffered and fought so bravely in the hope that evil might not dominate the world.

184

It was not only a war to save what is physically most precious—our lives and homes—but still more a war to save what is spiritually most precious—our ethical values. For it is true to say that no man could be a hardened Nazi with any sincerity and yet possess an ethical outlook on life.

185

The era of Nazism meant the crucifixion of love in the Nazis themselves.

186

The issue is whether they wish to take their place with the evolutionary forces or against them. The Nazis did the latter and lost.

187

We may frankly admit that those who opposed and fought Hitler were not entirely disinterested in their motives and that they made many mistakes out of selfishness in the past. But this must not blind us to the fact that later the commission of several of those mistakes was frankly acknowledged and an attempt made to atone for them even though under the duress of danger and loss.

188

Mussolini told the Italian troops whom he sent to fight in Russia: "We shall triumph because history teaches that peoples which represent the ideas of the past must give way before peoples which represent the ideas of the future." What he said of history was true but what he predicted of Fascism was false. It was false because there is no future for the glorification of brute force, elevated though it be to the pedestal of a philosophic doctrine, in a century which is getting sick and tired of war and which is growing more enlightened and more rational.

189

Kersten relates that at his first meeting with the Gestapo chief, he found a copy of the *Koran* on Himmler's night table, and that the holy book of the Moslems accompanied the dread little man on all his travels.

190

Hitler came into power at Berlin in the very same month and the very same year that Roosevelt came into power at Washington. The timing was both symbolic and karmic.

191

We have fought this war against military aggression. But we have yet to realize that it has also been fought against mental aggression. The Nazis invaded first the minds of their own people and later those of the people of the countries they occupied. The Japanese Fascists did precisely the same. For some years before the war the Japanese Government prohibited the possession of short-wave radio sets. Consequently the Japanese people were unable to listen in to foreign broadcasts, were unable to hear any expositions of the democratic standpoint and were inoculated solely with the same kind of totalitarian poisonous falsehood with which the Nazi government inoculated the Germans. This planned object of casting the mind of the entire Japanese nation into the desired mould even took the extreme measure, so curious to the occidental observer, of a "thought control" police, with its extraordinary mission of jailing anyone for thinking the wrong thoughts!

192

If we consider the recent history of the Far East, we shall see the same inexorable force of karma at work. It is known in certain circles that following the historic events of the 1850s when the Japanese were forced by foreign warships to open their ports to foreign commerce, a secret council of the most powerful noble families decided to revenge themselves on the Westerners as soon as they were in a position to do so. To bring this about they resolved on a twofold program. The first part was economic, the second was military. It was at this council too that the plan of sending capable young men to the West to master its industrial commercial military and naval secrets was first formulated and at once implemented. The economic part of this program eventually was completed, and an amazed world witnessed Japan's industrial and commercial triumph in successfully placing goods—which a century ago she had not even heard of—at ridiculously low prices in markets and bazaars throughout the five continents. The second part of this superlatively ambitious program which came to a climax with the war sought first to drive the whites out of their Asiatic possessions and then to place all Asia including Siberia, China, and India within a mammoth Japanese empire. The Japanese war lords bear the onus of having brilliantly conceived and patiently executed this master plan for domination of the nations. The "Tanaka Memorial," with its infamous doctrine of conquest through "blood and iron," is evidence of such a blueprint for conquest when each succeeding stage of the plan was brought to a successful conclusion. What is the inner meaning of the spirit which actuated this secret council and the successes which followed it? The obvious reply to this question is that Japan was hysterically driven by a subconscious intellectual and physical inferiority-complex to seek revenge. This is correct but it lies upon the surface of history and does not touch the depths. For still more was Japan raised up in Asia by the same karmic forces which raised up Hitler in Europe.

193

The history of the melancholy capitulation to German arms or to German terrorism or to German bribery of the smaller countries, one by one, during World War II is a history of the disaster of suicidal disunity. Standing shoulder to shoulder, speaking and fighting simultaneously, they could have put up a vigorous resistance—sufficient to have brought worthwhile external aid in time. Further, the tragedy of France's quick catastrophic fall before the onslaught of Hitler's legions was twofold. On the mental side it was a tragedy of shameful treachery in high places, of divided counsels and clashing leadership, of corrupt politicians and conservative generals, and finally of national inability to rise above narrow interests. Even the military defeat of France was largely a stage-managed affair. A few highly placed French Nazis as good as betrayed their country to the German Nazis. Their intentions were good but their understanding was bad. The consequences of these defects appeared in the half hearted-ness with which she wasted the valuable opening weeks of the war, those weeks when Hitler was attacking Poland, and in the suicidal spirit of indifference and lack of conviction which permeated the army. On the physical side it was a tragedy of out-of-date technique and inferior equip-ment, of inability to understand that men could no longer hold out against machines. The Old Staff, wedded to the Maginot line as they were, did not perceive how rapidly it had become antiquated strategy. For armoured motorized divisions and blitzkrieg tactics had largely destroyed the value of line and position fighting. The plane, the tank, and the parachute, massed in synchronized attack, were the symbols of modern warfare—but the significance of this symbolism was only half-understood. The fact is that France was defeated from within even before she was attacked from without. Finally, during that fateful September of 1939, there was the pathetic spectacle of Polish generals—twentieth-century men with nine-teenth-century minds—honestly and sincerely attempting to oppose Nazi tank offensives with cavalry charges!

194

Mussolini was acquainted as a young man with the Buddhist mystical doctrines and did a little reading on them, but he flatly said in the end he did not want them because they were enervating to his ego. When Rosita Forbes, the well-known traveller, once asked Mussolini, "Do you believe in God?" he answered, "No, I do not believe in any power other than my own. If I did I should be smashed." He was interested, for the avowed object of developing his personal force, in the study and practice of Tan-trika yoga. This is a system of yoga which originated in Bengal but is now prevalent chiefly in Tibet. It easily becomes an instrument to serve per-sonal ambitions.

195

The evil forces working through mediums are cunning enough not to show their true ultimate aims all at once. These become clear to the observer only by successive stages, only gradually. Whoever has critically studied the ways of evil spirits will know that they first lure their medi-umistic victims or gullible public along the path of self-injury or even self-destruction by winning their confidence with a series of successful predic-tions or favourable interventions. When this confidence has been well established, these dark forces then reveal their real intent by persuading their victims, through gigantic lies or false predictions, to commit a final act in which everything is staked on a single throw. The unhappy dupes invariably lose this last throw and are then overwhelmed by shattering disaster. This occurred in Hitler's case with his sudden attack on Russia in 1941. He then stated his belief that Moscow would be reached within six to seven weeks. But his soldiers never reached Moscow. His invisible guides had indeed betrayed him. How true are Shakespeare's words from *Macbeth*, Act 1, Scene 3: "But 'tis strange:/ And oftentimes, to win us to our harm,/ The instruments of darkness tell us truths,/ Win us with honest trifles, to betray us/ In deepest consequence."(P)

196

Hitler was a man who had been born with a natural faith in selfishly used occultism. On the one hand, his hypnotic forces were of a superlative order whilst on the other, he had completely surrendered himself to the direction of intuitive influences; next, he was a clairvoyant visionary and dynamic worker who both saw the coming of and sought to materialize a new epoch for mankind.

We may regard the appearance of a Hitler sitting on his Bavarian peak and menacingly surveying the European scene as a phenomenon as evil as a tiger looking for prey. We do so because he appears such a strange inversion of all that is elevated in human character. Millions still regard him as a devil incarnate because he wounded their best feelings or behaved towards them in monstrous ogre-like fashion or stretched them on the rack of mental or physical torture or shattered their domestic comfort or brought horrible sufferings down upon them. He is loathed as a base and brutal megalomaniac who wielded his power by creating fear, exploiting prejudice, and falsifying facts.

197

It was a part of Hitler's evil mission to draw the Germans into a trap of moral self-destruction. The bait was worldly aggrandizement based on an unscientific and arrogant racial exclusiveness, narrower and crueler than any the world has ever seen. Such a bait was eagerly swallowed. All the Satanic strength of the Nazis was concentrated on its accomplishment. The result was ruin and chaos, complete and final, for the entire German people. And over the dismal scene that was the prostrate body of a once-proud nation lay the shadow of that ruthless colossus with feet of clay— Hitler!

It may be nowadays a platitude to declare that the Germans have failed to recognize any higher moral law than "Might is right," yet it is the sad truth. The first tragedy of the Germans is their failure to learn from experience. How to revive their moral faculties which have been deadened by blind obedience to evil leaders is another problem. The Nazis with their savage mentality and terrible might, have lost their high priest, Hitler. But they have lost neither their vindictiveness nor their arrogance. They are unteachable. Every thoughtful person must feel uneasy about mankind's future. He will remember that late in 1944, when the Russian army had already invaded German soil, Hitler's Chief of Staff, General Guderian, told a gathering of cheering adolescent youths, "We shall wage war again even if we are defeated." He will remember too that when Rudolf Hess told his British captors, "If we are beaten this time, we shall fight a third war and win," he was not only speaking for himself but also for millions of young Nazis.

198

Nazism, for all its humbug, pretense, and imposture, was essentially the dangerous incarnation of a totally evil force, dedicated to serve the criminal instincts and lustful appetites of its adherents. It was an attempt to lead the masses into spiritual perdition. Its massed power found a perfect focal point in the mediumship of Hitler and his traffic with unclean spirits. There is no doubt he had given his active consent in full consciousness at every stage of his career to the evil forces which were swaying him. He could not be held irresponsible for them to any degree whatsoever. The terrible forces of malevolent design and fierce hatred operated through him and all his Nazi plotters. Hitler's insane lust to degrade the human mind and destroy its ideals was, to those who were clairvoyant enough to pierce the psychic veil, nothing less than the outcome on the physical plane of these violent attempts by diabolic forces to possess us for their own evil purposes. The dark forces which ensouled the Nazi leaders strove to promote animosity, bitterness, jealousy, and greed, and to inflame the most bestial elements of mankind. Attacking the human soul from another angle, Nazi theory and practice drastically curtailed or totally denied the free exercise of the human entity's highest rights—to think, to speak, to choose between right and wrong, and to worship God. The spiritual dangers to mankind which resided in a Nazi victory are awful to contemplate. Never before had its inner life been so satanically invaded. From the very first, the guiding hands of the Powers of Darkness were in evidence when the use of ruthless force became the Nazi rule, because the way of brutal compulsion belongs to the unseen destroyers, the adverse element in creation.

But the long battle between the instruments of Light and Darkness is not at an end. The dark powers have sought to prevent the emergence of a more enlightened era. They have tried to do this through the virulent and violent German Nazis but failed. They will try to do it again. The realignment of the Nazi-minded and their antagonists will now take place in a lesser form inside many countries. The forces of evil did not sound their retreat with the downfall of Hitler. The anti-Nazi powers are gathering great strength but they will have to face a fresh alignment of these opponents. The struggle will next be so fundamental and against such irredeemable vicious enemies then as it was during the war itself.

199

Hitler talked of setting up a United States of Europe, an idea which he borrowed from Napoleon. But whereas Napoleon wanted to unite Europe in peace, prosperity, and intellectual progress, Hitler wanted to unite it in misery, enslavement, and intellectual retrogression. Napoleon sought out the intelligentsia wherever his armies went but Hitler imprisoned, tortured, or killed them wherever his Gestapo could catch them. Napoleon in his heart fought for the extension of democracy whereas Hitler in his materialism fought for the extension of Germany's boundaries. Napoleon's troops marched to the tune of an international ideal of freedom from medieval fetters whereas Hitler marched to the tune of national greed. He spread his brown horror of carnage and corruption all over Europe, whilst Liberty lay dying in a dungeon. He saw truth indeed but only to distort and pervert it. He talked like a sage of "the nothingness and insignificance of the individual human being," but whereas the sage uses this truth to point the way to individual liberation, Hitler used it to point the way to individual enslavement. His self-proclaimed inspiration was spurious, his sociological insight was chimerical, and only he himself knew how much his reiterated pacifism was a fraudulent camouflage. It is true that he first animated the German people into a feverish activity, but instead of directing their prodigious efforts toward worthy ends which could have made millions happier, he directed them toward ignoble ones and made more millions more wretched than any other dominant group had ever done in history. Hitler's talk of a new order meant in his own mind an order under which Germany enslaved feudalistically but exploited modernistically every other nation.

200

Hitler's private conversations, even more than his public declarations, amply reveal that he clearly realized that. He not only saw much of this but, in his brutal and ignorant way, tried to construct this new order by deliberate planned effort. He set waves in motion. "The Nazi movement has finally closed the Feudal Age forever," he once declared privately. "All these tremendous changes are inevitable and it is National Socialism alone which understands their significance and works actively for a new era. Our task is to remake the world on modern and unprecedented lines. We alone possess the vast imagination and creative willpower to get out of the common somnolence of living in the antiquated past and attempt it successfully." Amid all his obvious charlatanry, Hitler was something of a clairvoyant. But his mental eyes being diseased, he could see only distorted visions. Consequently, he not only caricatured, degraded, and falsified ideas which were originally sound, but instead of understanding that the greatly needed historical upheaval was to be brought about for the universal benefit of all mankind, he could understand only that it was to be brought about for the exclusive benefit of the Germans. Hence his evil visions led in the end to miserable failure where they might have led to the success that attends the perception of dynamic historical inner necessity, and his idealism became so grossly limited and distorted that its artificial achievements constituted a curse and not a blessing for mankind. What, at a time when contemporary history was so drastically at work, could have become a movement for ending world enslavement, what the time-spirit demanded for the uplift of all men, Hitler was willing to concede only for the selfish aggrandizement of a particular group of men. This is why he achieved the gigantic success that he did and why it was followed later by equally gigantic failure. He could have rendered an incomparable service to the world but instead rendered an incomparable disservice to it. For the new age he tried to usher in was immeasurably worse than the old one. Nazi victory would have spiritually put the evolutionary clock back for centuries. It would have meant a spiritual defeat, a moral degeneration, and an intellectual black-out.

201

Childhood, adolescence, and the threshold of adulthood represent the most impressionable periods of the human being's life. The possibilities of uplifting moral character, improving thinking power, and unfolding mystical intuition during such periods are much more than most people believe. Hitler fully realized this truth and turned it to suit his own devilish purposes with such startling success as to vindicate its immense importance. He falsified science and mutilated history, but his greatest harm was to poison the minds of the younger generation with that most dangerous of all infections—hatred. He cunningly taught millions of young boys and girls to think daily and solely of the righteousness of his cause until they came to believe in it with the strong faith that an earlier generation gave to God.

202

There is a historical connection between the Jews, Egypt, India, and ultimately Atlantis which carries a story that curiously repeats itself. What Hitler did to the Jews was done under purely psychic guidance, for he was an excellent spiritistic medium and knew it. He almost daily took a half hour or so to go into semi-trance and get his guidance, inspiration, and spirit-communications.

203

The Director General of Archeology of India visited Germany shortly before the war. He told me there were twenty-seven university chairs of Sanskrit in Germany prior to the Nazi regime. Under Hitler they did next to nothing for there were hardly any students to use them!

204

The growth of totalitarian beliefs before that fateful September day in 1939 when the first bombs broke upon Europe again, however much and however rightly it is to be deplored, is not to be dismissed as an historical accident. Powerful causes must have lain behind it. The philosophically minded have to probe beneath the surface and find why totalitarianism succeeded in having for a time the fatal appeal which it did. And—leaving aside such success as it gained through wielding the bloody clubs of brutal violence and barbarian terror, as well as its offering of a speedy solution of harassing economic difficulties—among these reasons we shall find that it represented a half-formed substitute in the popular mind for the religion which it had lost. We shall never understand the meaning of totalitarianism's appeal unless we begin to understand that it was not only the outcome of a few evil men's crooked personal ambitions, but also the outcome of a falsely directed religious instinct.

205

At the very outset a contemplation of Hitler's significance is faced by an intricate interweaving of separate questions such as the psychological character and philosophic place of his personality, the function of war, the play of historic, economic, and political forces, and so on. He stood in such an intimate relation with his age that valuable lessons may be drawn from its study.

What was Hitler? We all know about the rapid and remarkable progress of this ex-corporal in a Bavarian regiment to the citadel of continental power, but what was his psychological and philosophical significance? It would be a mistake to regard him as an arrogant if ignorant man who, by starting the Nazi party at Munich, merely sought to complete the logical chain and conclude the chauvinistic work initiated by his predecessors and contemplated by the unteachable Army High Command. He sought to achieve something tremendously larger, something of which the mere expansion of Germany was but a part, although a most important part.

Instrumental puppets of Destiny like him are pushed forward at the appointed time on the stage of historical events, allowed to play their parts, and then are doomed to disappear. Hence although Hitler gained the temporary empire that he sought, spread from the Arctic to the Aegean seas as it was, it fell rapidly from his grasp when the inevitable karmic reaction came into play. When the tides of karma turned against him, he met first with frustration and then with failure. And the destruction of effete forms does not take so long a time as the construction of new ones. Therefore we could confidently have looked forward to an early end of that chaotic period. The doom of the terror-filled Nazi regime was preordained. The other agencies that were to complete this historical drama were being groomed for the dramatic epilogue.

Because the thoughts of millions of people were concentrated against him; because thought is a potent power which tends sooner or later to objectify itself; because all these millions were thinking destructively and antagonistically against him; because such a tremendous volume of intensely one-pointed thought has never before been known in world history; because all this power, which clutched him and his people like an octopus, was bound to materialize eventually; a complete defeat for Hitler's military and civilian armies and a complete collapse of Hitler himself were inevitable, even though his crooked cross had been bombastically carried right through the entire continent of Europe. Those who knew the occult powers of thought and the inner workings of karma knew also that nothing was surer than the nemesis which would fall inexorably upon this barbarous man and his gang, for their vast violation of moral laws. He sowed and therefore unfailingly reaped the worst destiny which any man of the twentieth century has yet made. Even during his lifetime his own arrogance turned eventually to anxiety and that again to despair. And when his pilgrimage to perdition was at an end with his career, he had to undergo a preliminary purgation in the only hell that there is, the hell of the awful dream of forcibly receiving the suppressed hatreds of his victims, the terrible post-death nightmare of re-witnessing their agonized experiences from their standpoint. It were a dozen times better for Hitler and his misguided helpmates to have died early than to have lived long. For the evil destiny they made for themselves during those extra years of life will be nothing more than so much extra suffering they will have to endure.

206

Hitler sat upon his Bavarian peak and cunningly meditated in his diseased vanity how to sit upon all Europe itself and gain the chauvinistic glory he thirsted for. He finally translated his dream into visibility, but only to find in the end that he had sat upon a volcano in which all the peoples of Europe burst forth in the mightiest revenge-seeking upheaval history has ever known.

Many people became so depressed by Hitler's early and easy recurring victories as to believe that he would win the war, and they became so deceived by his High Command's facade of ruthless efficiency as to believe that he was utterly invincible. Apart from other factors of internal weakness, they often overlooked one which was of immense importance: the mental one. They did not notice the invisible deterioration of the nerve of the German people, the hidden breaking of morale, and the spread of social neurosis. Underneath even the egoistic bombast of the Nazi Party members themselves, there gradually grew up a psychosis of fear, a malady of jittery nerves, and a palsy of flagging will. The German mind generally became more and more filled with confusions and anxieties, with inability to defeat growing doubts. The passage from these concealed cracks to a sudden and open national nervous breakdown, as the realization of useless suffering and needless loss became clearer, was therefore only a matter of time.

207

Hitler successfully dealt out iconoclastic blows not only at the conventional political religions and military ideology of his time but also at the conventional theories of economics of his time. A Germany ruined first by defeat and then by inflation, a Germany filled with the misery of six million registered unemployed and their families was turned by him into a Germany everywhere busily at work, filled with new activity, throbbing with new enterprise. What though this was done as a preparation for war? It could have been done—just as easily—if Hitler had been less evil-minded, as a preparation for peace, and the factories which made guns and tanks could have made harmless useful goods instead. But the fact is that the factories ceased to remain empty, the workers ceased to remain idle, and the wheels of industry began to go round again. Aside from what he stole from the Jews, this was done without importing fresh capital from abroad. But greatly to increase the productive capacity of the country without first greatly increasing the capital of the country was an impossible feat according to the orthodox doctrines of economics. This historic accomplishment exposed the foolishness of those stupid and selfish doctrines which had made money, the physical token of exchange, into the one and only symbol of wealth, which had tried to perpetuate the antiquities and heartlessness of capitalism. Our social and economic ills must be healed. Yet they cannot be healed by the old medicines any more than by the new poisons of Hitler.

208

The war was a test which showed humanity (and those who observe it) just where it stood. It showed up the hidden evil as well as the hidden good, revealed the lurking weakness and the unused strength. If true religion had prevailed in Germany, the Nazis with their selfishness, aggressiveness, and trickery could not have prevailed also. But this test was an extreme one. We need not fear that fresh Hitlers, more Mussolinis, are always going to arise. They will not. Dictators and their dictations are but transient instruments of the world-changes which mark the last years of a dying age. The world did not encourage the initial monstrous acts of Hitler, but neither did it oppose them. This was evidence of its own inner weakness. It is true, Hitler led his people finally to humiliation and ruin but that does not absolve the world of having contributed to the possibility of the Hitleristic regime. He was our tutor, raised to cause suffering to himself, his people, and ourselves, that the world might learn the futility of materialism, greed, envy, and selfishness.

209

Hitler confused statecraft with stagecraft. Hence, his love of taking the limelight with a new sensation every now and then before the war! But with the turn of the tide of events in his enemies' favour, Hitler was singularly silent. His speeches became rare and even then were filled with feeble evasions of the true and terrible situation into which he had led those who so blindly followed him. For nothing was so formidable as its facts. He twisted arguments and tortured words—but there were its facts staring everybody in the face. His judgements became faulty, his new ventures ill-fated, even his fresh conquest of territory proved in the end to be a fresh burden he had to bear. Hitler's procrastination in attacking England immediately after Dunkirk was the beginning of that series of colossal mistakes which he was led to commit and which themselves led first to a process of crumbling and then to his downfall. Like all his lesser prototypes, he was ruined by his own ambitions. Thus Hitler, the arch-destroyer, has himself been destroyed.

210

In becoming the unparalleled monster which he did become, Hitler was a traitor to the human race. For he sank back to the cruelty, passion, and rage of the wild-animal kingdom but added to them the mental profits of his sojourn in the human kingdom, all its perverted thinking power, without however showing those finer qualities which even animals possess. Those who talked with him were often appalled by the hatred and vindictiveness which punctuated his coarse criticisms. Such swift and strong passions had to find an outlet and this was provided by the cruel, aggressive, and brutal acts which marked his rule. He was a votary of violence. In the field of international diplomacy, his brutality was marked by crafty artfulness. It took some time before the contrast between his suave, disarming speeches and his violent, ferocious deeds became evident. He dwelt in an atmosphere of pure evil, and hatred was the natural air he breathed. When it came to expressing it, he wielded a really wicked tongue. He not only flayed the skin off those who stood in his path but thereafter proceeded to disembowel them. The hate-poisoned atmosphere which he created throughout Europe, both amongst his sympathizers and his victims, was his worst legacy.

211

Why did the Nazis quickly proceed to clamp down all freedom of speech and to shoot or shut up in concentration prisons all the intelligentsia? It is simply because truth can afford to encourage criticism, whereas falsehood fears it. Nazi Germany proved the irony of human suggestibility, that there, where truth was most absent, the people were led to believe it was most present. The Nazis invented pretexts for invasion as they invented history for propaganda. They did this because it was useful to them. Their followers, however, honestly believed both pretexts and history because the hypnotic power of suggestion had influenced them. If we remember the mentally dark and morally savage state of Europe during the long stretch of centuries between the time of Justinian and the twelfth century, that period which has been well named the Dark Ages, we can picture something of the New Order which Hitler wanted to inaugurate. Had he triumphed there would have been no further philosophy for a generation. From national falsehoods to international deceptions, his work of instilling darkness into men's minds went on unimpeded. The ideal of a government with clean hands and clear conscience was not only utterly alien to him, but also utterly despised by him. He raised brigandage to the status of statesmanship! His faithful satellites and partners in treachery busied themselves feverishly to explain away the deceptions and duplicities which lurked behind Hitler's words. First the German nation believed his fabrications, then large numbers in other nations believed them. It illustrated how those who begin by disdaining reason, end by accepting absurdity. Most people have only dimmed spiritual lights but here we have the awful case of men with wholly extinguished lights, without retaining the slightest trace of reverence for spiritual values.

212

Impulsive immature youth could not fail to see that farcical outworn ideas were still being imposed on the people. It was natural that in countries where the economic structure was quickly disintegrating and where emotions are always strong they should fall victim to the impassioned voice of iconoclastic demagogues like Hitler. He disregarded the old idols which had lost their charm and began to construct new but not better ones, for their hollowness was hidden behind cheap gaudy tinsel. He invested these materialistic and militaristic gods with the glamour of messianic religiosity and thus satisfied both the political and inner yearnings of the young at a single stroke. Today's call is for inspired leaders and inspired teachers; today's need is of institutions that will serve rather than exploit, and concepts that will ennoble rather than degrade. The new currents of life need new molds in which to flow, new institutions through which to reveal themselves. The task ahead of them is vitally important and extremely difficult but also tremendously inspiring.

213

Hitler is to be seen not as he was first hailed, that is, as the re-creator of his country, but as the unconscious instrument of Nemesis, as a vulgar channel for inescapable historic forces. Above all human dictators rises the unnoticed figure of *their* dictator—karma! Even this vile unspeakable Hitler was a punitive instrument in the hands of mankind's karma, a sadistic agent of planetary self-earned fate.

214

Did Hitler, as some assert, sit in communion with spirit-forces before he gave those electrifying speeches in the stadium at Nuremburg? And was the building erected for this purpose a copy of the Temple of the Sphinx? What is the evidence for these assertions? That Hitler was a medium and that he did sit for periods in this kind of trance is known.

215

Since ancient times the swastika, turning clockwise, symbolizes universal creation, but turning anti-clockwise, it symbolizes universal destruction.

216

After Hitler rose from being the Madman of Munich to a dizzier success as the Barbarian of Berlin, he did not fail frequently to refer to himself in his public speeches as being the instrument of a God-ordained mission, the holy co-worker with Divine Providence. "I can only thank God Almighty for giving me the strength and knowledge to do what had to be done," he told the Reichstag in the midst of the war. He spoke of the mission which Providence had entrusted to him. But in the end his mission turned out to be nothing more than an insane desire to exploit the bodies of all non-Germans and enslave the minds of all Germans. He talked in public of relying on the Almighty God but actually in private relied on the Almighty Gestapo. He spoke, too, of the New Order he was creating which would unify Europe. But in the last scenes it turned out to be merely the old tyranny in new disguise. In his book *Mein Kampf* Hitler preened himself on being an astute psychologist. So far as the appeal to all that is basest and worst in men was concerned this is undoubtedly true. But so far as the understanding of all that makes up the pattern of human existence was concerned it is undoubtedly false. In the end he showed himself to be the worst psychologist history has yet known. He was astute enough to hit on the urgent need of mankind for dynamic leadership, its acute yearning for a Moses to bring it out of the confusion in which it found itself. But being himself mentally unbalanced he could and did lead it into only more and not less mental confusion, more and not less physical misery.

Effects of World War II

217

Even amid the wartime turmoil there were some who found their way—however intermittently and fragmentarily—to the deep peace of the spiritual life. To have achieved this during such a period is a good augury, for consider what these individuals will be able to achieve in the somewhat more leisurely and quieter postwar period. Within the atmosphere of inner peace, they will be able to continue their progress into the knowledge of the profounder realities of life.

218

Although the war aroused a number of people to mystical seeking, it was unfavourable to mystical practice. It broke into the privacy of the individual's life, introduced the communal pattern of living, and in many cases destroyed one's chance for a long period of getting any solitude at all, and—even much more—of that precious creative silence which is indispensable for the mystical life.

219

It was hard to study metaphysics during the era of bursting bombs, almost impossible to practise meditation during the din of a six-year war. The call then was to action in the service of menaced humanity, to prayer in the deepening of personal faith, and to endurance of ideals amid a planet's trembling and rocking.

220

The war, with its abnormal excitement, physical hardship, and enormous suffering—and especially its loss of privacy—made meditation difficult, unattractive, and, to most people, even impossible. It can be said therefore that the art of meditation was one of the inevitable casualties of the war. Although the tumult, violence, and extroversion of the time made it more needed than ever before, unfortunately the opportunities and conditions for its practice became more difficult than ever before. The general shake-up of wartime broke the even lives of many aspirants. Many, if not most, were forced into entirely new and often uncongenial environments with apparently uncongenial companions. They may have deplored the inability to make any spiritual progress under such conditions, but they were wrong. Progress is not solely a matter of having the time and solitude, the freedom and quietude for study and meditation. Nor is it dependent solely on forming contacts with like-minded people. Other factors are also concerned. Indeed, insofar as it showed them how the unfamiliar so-called materialistic half of the world lived, insofar as it drew them out of complacent attitudes and smug intellectual ruts, insofar as it shattered ignorance of realities—however hard or ugly—that form important parts of human experience but which had previously been fled from, the change was not a useless one.

221

Throughout the stress of the war period the human mind was tuned to a pitch of constant anxiety and the human body was often subject to pain or hardship. Nerves need to be healed. External peace must be matched by internal peace. The time for a wide-scale establishing of meditation, whose liberating practice brings peace and whose right pursuit weaves a necklace of noble thoughts around the neck, is at hand.

222

Only a small percentage of the mystically minded could escape the influence of the war. Most could not adopt the ivory tower attitude but had to look problems straight in the face.

223

Only after the guns of war are silenced do most men and women have the leisure in which to receive the instruction and appraise the worth of philosophy.

224

Many people found no compensating good at all in the tragedy of World War II. Most Europeans lost more or less of their possessions, such as money, property, relatives, home, security, even life itself. What was this but a compulsory self-mortification, a forced renunciation of the world, an involuntary detachment from earthly things? The ascetics, would-be saints, and God-seekers of all lands and times have practised a precisely similar renunciation but they did it voluntarily. They gave up the external life in the hope of finding a better one internally. Millions of people during the war who tried to cling to their earthly things and life, as well as the few who did not, were forcibly detached from both. This created the feeling of being tired of living, of the hopelessness of seeking satisfaction in transitory existence, and of the instability of all external situations. Such a drastic experience forced them to *think*, to wonder at the meaning of it all, and thus, to a microscopic extent, to *seek after Truth*. And what is one here on this planet for if not for this same purpose? It is humanity's school.

225

Let us not submit to the feeling of utter despair which would paralyse all efforts at self-improvement or at world-improvement. The recent wars have given birth to much pondering by many persons about the meaning of life, although most of it is as yet inarticulate. If they could see the meaning of the events which have crashed into life during recent years, they would see that the evolutionary trend is carrying them away from crass materialism and unbalanced externality.

226

The war was a cause of bringing people to the quest of the Overself and its serene blessedness. The aftermath of uncertain peace is bringing more. For they find so much present insecurity of life and possessions, so much uncertainty of future, that they turn to the Quest for peace.

227

Where they will not make a beginning to go out of their negative side, out of their lower nature, life itself is forcing them out of it. Where they will not let others educate them into a larger understanding, the violence of events is starting to teach it.

228

The metaphysical basis of altruistic proposals is, in part, sound enough. It teaches that we must clearly negate the illusions of individual existence if we would arrive at the truth of individual existence. The greatest of those illusions is that, in the external world, an individual stands separate, apart and alone. He does not. He cannot. Hence when the war compelled entire nations and entire classes within a nation to co-operate in many different ways in order to win it, this dire necessity showed them the virtue and value of co-operation. It made every individual realize that he was not merely a separate individual alone but also a member of an interdependent community. That is to say, the individual began to work for the common welfare because it was essential to his own welfare, too. At first he did it involuntarily and unavoidably, but he did it. And through the actual experience of doing so, a few individuals began to appreciate the ideal itself. But they were only the few: for the many, when the war ended, the outer stimulus to such an attitude also ended. So the altruistic ideal quickly sank below the horizon again.

229

We are not suggesting that anyone should embrace the fatalism so characteristic of the Orient; we are suggesting only that one should arrive at a more balanced view of life. The lack of it forced soldiers and civilians alike to learn through the sufferings of experiences what they could have learned through the calmness of reflection. The perilous situations of war-time brought about a vein of fatalism in many minds to whom it was hitherto unknown. It made them realize for the first time how small is the circle of freedom in which the human will operates. Those who so arrogantly defended the extreme freedom of the human will in the past are losing their following, as the opposite idea of extreme fatalism creeps into the Western hemisphere from Asia.

230

This belief in an inevitable destiny had largely gone from the modern mind, until the activities of Hitler and the atomic menace began to put it back there.

231

It is as misleading an oversimplification to assert that the war has made men more spiritual as it is to assert that it has made them more materialistic.

232

Those who hold the thought that the postwar world can continue to hold the materialistic outlook of the prewar one without destroying itself hold an illusion. It would be pleasant for many to be able to do so comfortably, but that assuredly is not happening and those who look forward to it are merely cultivating self-deception.

233

After the shattering of great cities and the uprooting of agonized millions, smug unthought-out ideas began to disappear along with smug unthought-out lives. Disillusionment crept into the air. With the hoarse tumultuous roar of ack-ack guns, the need of a new conception of human existence sounded in human consciousness.

234

The war and preparations for it aroused everyone to the need of re-adjustment to the new problems which it raised. Such a re-adjustment cannot be effected by escapist meditation alone nor by blind action alone nor by merely intellectual reasoning alone. What is needed to meet these problems successfully is a combination of all the three. This is one of the foremost lessons of the war.

235

Such a historical crisis gave millions of people the chance to make a fresh start in moral life.

236

The coming of peace will affect different sections and divergent groups variously. Some will turn more than ever towards scepticism in thought and sensualism in conduct. Others will take the greatest interest in political reforms and economic changes and regard these as all-important for society and the individual. A third section will become aware of their spiritual poverty, feeling an inner void which, do what they will, cannot be evaded and which they will have to fill by religious revival or mystical practices.

237

Those who thought that the gamble with death which war brought to almost the entire younger generation, called them to snatch hastily at brief, trivial frivolities, or even entitled them to cast moral restraints impatiently aside, naturally outnumbered those who were brought by the same tragic gamble to a more serious and spiritual outlook and a more disciplined and elevated conduct. It is the easier way to forget danger in feverish but transient pleasure, the harder one to remember it in stern, ennobling self-dedication.

238

Although these widespread wartime changes are leading to greater individualization, this is not an affirmation that the break-up of family life is at all desirable. The moral dangers which such a dislocation would lead to have already been revealed in the war's effect on many young people. Family life is an indispensable social safeguard, the most valuable medium for promoting right moral attitudes amongst those who are passing through the stages of childhood and adolescence. A true individualization of the human entity will not destroy but rather conserve all that is best in the family spirit.

239

More and more people are striving to realize the divine presence within themselves. But although markedly larger than was the case before the war, their number is still all too few.

240

Thus, out of the pain and death of war, one section of humanity has learnt to cherish the finer values of life and to nurture those attributes which distinguish them from the animals, whereas another section has become more selfish, more destructive, and more sensual. The limited degree of free will which both possess has been used for advancement by the one and for debasement by the other.

241

The stupendous trials of this war and the perplexing chaos of this period have demonstrated the need of inner support as the placid relaxations of peace had never done. Those who have found such support for the first time, who have wrested such profit from their misfortunes, who have alleviated their earthly grief by newly learned lessons of religious, mystical, or philosophical import, represent those who have responded to the new evolutionary influence of our transitional age.

242

If it will lead to anything it will lead to a greatly altered world. The religious and cultural problems which follow in its wake cannot be dealt with in the old way. Men feel the need and utter the demand for a rational realistic revision of religion and a broadening of science and outlook which will be iconoclastic in scope.

243

The war has passed over our heads and left us with three groups of religious attitudes: people who believe in the reign of higher laws, people who disbelieve in it, and (the largest group) people who half-believe in it.

244

The evolutionary forces are against those who would cling to the comfortable prewar egotisms and materialisms. Inability to draw correct lessons from recent experience still being widespread, they may try their utmost to do so but will only gather fresh miseries for their trouble. They must either move their thinking with the new times and their morality with the new ideals or endure the consequences.

245

The war produced two different reactions among people. Either it uplifted them or it degraded them.

246

The terrific shocks which nations and individuals received during the war aroused them to the imperative need of finding new ways of life. The breakdown of old supports was most marked. What people would not do voluntarily was expedited by the painful hammer-blows of calamitous karma into urgent birth.

247

A large class has emerged from the war which has had its lower nature strengthened by the grim experience. It does not care for serious truths or noble ideals.

248

Some men have begun to think about life. They want to know its meaning and to trace out its purpose. The world upheaval, war, and crisis have forced them into situations which showed up their ignorance of both.

249

The world wars have hardened hearts, brutalized natures, and externalized interests. That is, they have made people more materialistic. But on the other hand they have also brought Orient and Occident into closer touch, so that the cultures of both have widened. Our spiritual knowledge has been enlarged and aesthetic life has been refined.

250

The prewar structure of society, being built on the sands of a merely external and materialist view of life, was unable to withstand the storms of war and began to come down with a crash.

251

Spiritual beliefs which were merely the result of wishful thinking, which were not based on impersonal and factual analysis of the human situation, were sharply challenged by the war and its aftermath. Those who held them had either to let them go and reconcile themselves to the real perspective or suffer vainly and uselessly for them. They had indeed to face the stark reality without any comfortable illusions. The medieval sleep which kept the eyelids of certain people conveniently half-closed to what was happening all around them was painfully ended. The era of destructive violence and brutal terrorism through which they have been passing marks the failure of orthodox religions and the futility of clinging to materialist ways of living in this twentieth century of light. The old ways are being left behind but the new way has not yet been found. There are those who have been looking for a new hope for mankind to arise out of the universal carnage and in contrast to its terrible background. The hope itself has varied with the temperament which entertained it. With some it is a new economic order, with others it is a religious revival, and so on. Meanwhile, the work of destruction continues apace. Although the world's tempo has been immensely quickened, the crisis in human thought and the distress in human life did not come upon us suddenly. There were forebodings, warnings, precursors, and indications.

252

The potentialities for moral evil which lay until lately within the world crisis would, if realized, have maleficently determined the worldly and spiritual fate of humanity for generations to come. This terrible possibility has only partially been averted by the defeat of the demon-obsessed Nazi leaders. The victory which came to the Allies was a physical one. It must also be completed by a mental one. For the seeds of greed, hatred, false-hood, and envy which the Nazis spread through the five continents are being further spread by the Communists. Violence and hatred have flared up anew and thus given the evil forces a fresh chance to destroy mankind.

253

So many men and women were forced to ask themselves why they had fallen into such a horrible situation. Such self-questioning, if done coolly and impartially, might have prepared the way for a better reception of philosophical views. One of its results would be that they were painfully aroused to their spiritual impoverishment. For the mere coming of war revealed the failure of the old order of thought.

254

Only when the war forcibly parted many of them from most of their possessions, both animate and inanimate, did they even begin to become aware of the tragic instability and transiency of earthly life.

255

The shattering events of war and its aftermath smashed some of religion's supports and weakened taste for metaphysical ideas. Values which were necessary to ethics were lost.

256

The sufferings of war did not have a morally purifying effect on all people but only on some people. On others they had a morally degenerating effect—on profiteers, for instance, and on those who sought relief in a lower sensualism than they had hitherto known. Again, if the war ennobled some soldiers with sacrificial ideals it brutalized others with violent instincts. Consequently, there are now two general groups, one which has advanced spiritually and one which has worsened spiritually. If the first is readier to accept such ideas, the second is readier to reject them. The position with which we are thus faced at the opening of peace is somewhat confused.

257

Since World War II the Orient as a whole has been moving away from its spiritual traditions and sources at a speed far more accelerated than the prewar one.

258

The realism of the terrible war conditions cannot therefore be without effect upon the character of the present writings. At least these conditions have moved us to bring down to earth the loftiest flights of thought, they have compelled us to insist upon all reflection having a practical bearing upon life, and they have made us recognize the duty of improving the physical surroundings of men no less than the more important duty of improving their minds.

259

The so-called peace is full of tensions: it is an armed truce.

260

The glamour of war-born idealism has gone. The apathy of peace-born realism has replaced it. Humanity has not generated a new incentive nor worked consciously for its own betterment.

261

During the war many men and women found stimulus to self-sacrifice and contact with an ideal but after the war they lost both.

262

Those who learned the spiritual lessons of this war by the time peace arrived were able to profit by mystical presences which manifest themselves. But those who missed these lessons have to share the responsibility for the further troubles which are occurring to themselves individually and to humanity collectively.

263

If the war has not matured their attitudes towards life, its agony has not been productive.

264

Fear and suspicion are filling the minds of whole nations in this postwar world, robbing the individual of whatever little peace of mind he had left.

265

World War II has forced the speed and strengthened the thoroughness with which inevitable changes in our personal lives must be carried through. This terrible, ghastly fact of World War II towers above everything. It is teaching us all better than any book. But alas, its lessons are negative. It cannot teach us what really IS. How petty are so many aims amid the unfolding of this gigantic world-drama.

266

The separation of the human ego from its divine principle has reached its utmost depth in our time. Hence we have witnessed, both in Nazi propaganda and in Nazi atrocities, an evil never before known. But the evolutionary working is causing an abrupt about-turn. The moment is ripe for the beginning of a new trend towards the attainment of the Overself consciousness.

267

The problem of how to keep moral integrity in a morally corrupting world has grown harder after the war, and not easier.

268

The fortunes of religious faith will not be geographically equal. In the democratic countries which fought for moral ideals and emerged victorious from the struggle, such faith will grow strongly and widely, whereas in the Axis countries which met with defeat, it will grow weakly and sparsely.

269

If some people have become more spiritual and others more sensual because of their wartime experiences, there are still others who have become more selfish. The war has lowered their ethical standard and increased their envy, greed, and malice.

270

Their faith has been unsettled but it has not found anything new to rest on.

271

How few people are really teachable? What has a decade of suffering taught humanity? The war is now a memory but millions of men and women are exchanging fresh illusions for old ones, millions of others are sharing bitter disillusions without any deep understanding of them.

272

There is one group which, tutored by horrible sin, has found that life is not what sentimentality-based religion led it to suppose, and another group which, tutored by horrible suffering, has found that it is not what progress-worshipping materialism led it to suppose.

273

The "peace" has become a breeding ground of moral despair and emotional resentment, of political chaos and spiritual degeneration.

274

We have only to take note of the ill-will and ill-feeling everywhere present to discover how greatly the past war and the present crisis have lowered the moral temperament of humanity.

275

In the war period, when millions were overborne by sorrow and loss and fear, the quest's practical worth in conferring inner serenity and outer courage justified it.

276

War tests character and reveals how far it has grown or how far it has degenerated. If the crisis smashed illusions and uncovered weaknesses, it also showed up surprising goodwill and revealed unsuspected latent strength. Even the horror and tragedy of this period left a train of effects not altogether bad. The comfortable inertia and prewar halfheartedness of the people Hitler disturbed, joined with the stimulus of opposition to him, roused some of their own latent forces into fresh activity and shocked them into the striving for their ideals. As the war proceeded they came to see that they must change their approach to many other problems too. They became conscious of other sins of omission—such as the economic and social. They began to think and talk of a better world which must be built after the war. Their triumph will consist not only in this but also in preserving the ethical values which the Nazis lost. If war came as the world's karma, its bloodshed suffering and destruction brought some mental illumination to those who responded to it rightly. Through such tribulations properly endured, the character of mankind begins to be purged and merely selfish motives to desert them. The new ideals which have passed through such pains of travail are themselves the heralds of a brighter, happier, and wiser new age of world history that will manifest itself in the not-too-distant future.

277

The close of war also closed Europe's lordship over the rest of the world. Her grand cycle has ended. The future is not with her. She has been exhausted by the effort of war and distracted by its aftermath of internal conflict. The political, economic, mechanical, and cultural initiatives of modern civilization are already falling from her faltering old hands and being picked up by young and vigorous hands. This is due, in part, to much of the best character and capacity from Europe being drawn off and collected in America.

278

The disappointments of this postwar era, which was expected to bring an era of peace but has brought only more threats of war, have turned more and more Europeans to seek comfort or guidance in religion, mysticism, or philosophy. This is noticeable in several countries but especially in England, France, Germany, Denmark, and Holland.

279

That the observance of religious practices largely declined before the war was a notorious fact. Their revival during the war should not have its real character mistaken. Suffering men and women felt the urgent need of religious support during the war's tensions. In many cases it has led to a durable conversion. But with the tensions relaxed, they feel the need of a more discriminating conversion. If they are to enter a period of spiritual seeking, this will be all the more reason for being somewhat wary of the spiritual offerings that will make their appearance. The new era is bringing new religious ideas, new spiritual attitudes. Many of them are valuable and constructive but others are wildly false and useless. Therefore critical judgement and not indiscriminate acceptance is needed here. Religio-mystic cults will have their vogue but will help us only to the extent that they are sound and balanced.

280

How much faith will remain in the sequence, after war and postwar upheaval, is yet to be seen. But of this we may be sure: that through this titillating process and its own wartime sufferings, postwar religion will become purer, truer, and more accommodating to modern needs. The toiling masses usually have little time for prayer and devotion, and still less time for mystical meditation and metaphysical study, so organized religion is a necessary way of taking care of their spiritual needs. In the fellowship of occasional public worship and through the sacramental means of grace, their emotions are uplifted, their hearts consoled.

281

The same churches which were filled during the nerve-shattering tensions of war, are being emptied by the softer relaxations of peace; the entangled superstitions, illusions, and exploitations which the converts had to accept hastily along with their reborn trust in God are beginning to dissolve, partly as an aftermath of the dissolution of wartime dangers or urgencies and partly as a consequence of the resurgence of a cooler, more discriminating judgement. The great spiritual revival which so many expected as the result of this latest war has not materialized. It is saddening to observe that so vast a flood of wartime misery and suffering flowed over humanity only to leave so little a mark of spiritual arousal behind it.

282

An important consequence of the inner significance of the war is that the external onset of peace marked the beginning of a new struggle. The unseen forces of darkness and enlightenment naturally re-arrayed themselves and re-aligned their supporters again inside all countries soon after peace had removed the former dangers which threatened them. The military victory has not concluded the war but only brought about a change in the external character of the conflict. The planet once more became a battleground between two rival attitudes, the stubbornly materialistic and the spiritually decent. The first will fight hard for domination, the second will enter the last trench and will defend itself and its future. At first it is assuming in most countries the aspect of nothing worse than a bloodless political strife. Yet it will be none the less bitter for all that, its later developments none the less bloodier. For all those who through selfish desire or materialistic miscomprehension wish to cling to the dying age and to resist the coming age of new ideas and a better life for mankind, the war's lessons will again have been of little avail. They will consequently have to bear the bitter karma which such resistance must necessarily generate.

283

What happened in the two years following the war's end decisively influenced what would happen in the next twenty years.

284

The outbreak of war, as well as the course which it took, led humanity into self-revelation, both individually and collectively. It forced millions, who were formerly satisfied with the pleasanter mere frivolities of life, to confront the grimmer and uglier realities of life. Problems which, through inertia or selfishness, individuals and nations did not want to face, were brought forcibly to the surface. The war widened men's outlooks, liberated them from narrow prejudice, offered the chance to expand their limited experience, correct their imperfect judgements and teach them what peace-time had never taught them. It could have awakened many out of their narrowness and widened their horizons and stretched their attitudes, but the chance was not taken. This terrible ordeal, by breaking up crystallized forms and weakening selfish organizations, gave a greater freedom to human intelligence to exercise itself and to new ideals to express themselves. But was this freedom properly used?

285

All this war and crisis offers a moral challenge to humanity, a last chance to choose the right road. Yet many have failed to perceive this and have "escaped" into sensualism and materialism. But it is only a false escape. Those to whom that great struggle was but a temporary inconvenience, who looked forward to a return backward to so-called normal times, are deaf to the twentieth century's voice, and blind to its significance. They may be too stubborn to learn its moral lessons, as they were too stupid to learn the lessons of the previous peace. They may try to resist them, but they will needlessly suffer.

286

The war mentality arising out of the killing instinct did not disappear with the proclamation of peace. The immense spiritual danger with which it menaced humanity did not end with the ending of war.

287

The evil forces which have inspired Nazism have been defeated. But tne defeat is not irretrievable. The military victory was essential but the mental victory will now be no less essential.

288

As in those momentous days that preceded the declaration of the war which it was a moral duty to wage against Nazi wickedness, so in these fateful days which have followed the declarations of peace, the situation in which humanity finds itself driven by the course of events offers it a choice of two alternatives. Two roads open up before it and each leads in a very different direction. Upon which of these diverging ways it is now taking depends whether it is going to rise or fall spiritually, no less than whether it is going to experience more prosperity or more poverty, ultimate war or peace. When war and crisis have so crushed humanity that its hopes have almost completely vanished and its outlook almost wholly blackened, it seeks sordid forgetfulness in drink and sensuality or noble relief in religion and mysticism. Thus the future of one large section is moral collapse and of another section, moral uplift. The confused postwar generation is being divided into two groups. The first comprises those people who are going down and becoming worse. This group, being more sensual and material, are becoming more brutalized, more addicted to violence. The second comprises those people who are going up and becoming better. Those who are only just entering it look for a guiding faith, an inspiring leadership, to enable them to rid themselves of uncertainties and futilities. Time will henceforth increasingly develop their character and aspirations. The world-crisis has brought about the first stirrings of spirituality in the hearts of these people. But to clarify and intensify these feelings, some time will be needed.

World War III

289

It is questionable whether humanity has learned enough from its ordeal in the last war and the present crisis. Since its return to a more spiritual outlook is foreordained, it may have to be accomplished at the price of a third world war.

290

The Mind back of things has not allowed the discovery of the atom bomb to be made just at this particular time without sufficient reason for doing so. Humanity is being prepared for the next fated move in its inner life. And that is a lessening of selfish materialism, an increasing of spiritual co-operation. The instrument used is a physical one though the net result will include a psychological one. Only if the fear generated by the unprecedented danger of this discovery attains such a tremendous magnitude that it overwhelms all other base emotions, is it likely to lead to the unshakeable determination to make the fresh moral start that is needed. The method of persuasion has changed radically. Where the spiritual teachers have failed to bring home their lessons to humanity, the atomic bomb may do so. It has forced these alternatives upon us: either the nations of the world must change their moral attitude towards each other or they must annihilate each other.

291

The atom bomb leaves no alternatives between self-reform and self-annihilation. Humanity's situation is critical urgent and grave. For human attitudes must be changed, and changed quickly. Yet human feelings are unprepared unwilling and unready to make this change.

292

Where the inner attitude of goodwill is lacking, there no real success can be achieved in the estrangement of war.

293

We were told the possession of nuclear bombs would act as a deterrent against aggression. But it could only be a temporary one. For arms races usually end in collisions, which themselves end in war.

294

Where are the purified characters, the ennobled minds, which have come out of the past two world wars? They exist, of course, but only as individuals. In the mass, more people were brutalized, more lost their faith in ideals and ethics than kept it. A third world war could produce only a still greater and graver deterioration. This is why the cause of peace must be helped—*now*, while there is yet time.

295

No nuclear war can be a righteous war. Its support can only be contrary to Christian ethics and its consequence to human welfare. It is evil, and nothing, no cause and no situation, can make it good.

296

They must recognize the fact that the only way to stop wars is the change of heart and mind from the state which breeds them.

297

It will be a war not merely for the triumph of one empire against another, but in reality a desperate struggle for the survival of true civilization, which would necessarily include the survival after the war.

298

It is astonishing that the terrifying peril into which the manufacture of atomic bombs has plunged the fate of mankind, brings from most people little more response than apathy.

299

If a nuclear war—so far unknown—should happen in our time and leave as its aftermath most of mankind dead and much of the planet devastated, nobody should complain about such a result. Everybody had years of warning but its deterrent effect was too small against immense stupidity, indifference, cruelty, short-sightedness, and wishful thinking. Neither the memory of past agonies (in two world wars) nor the imaginary picture of coming ones would then have been strong enough to teach us the dreadful lesson.

300

There is always a formula less costly than war if men of goodwill try to find it.

301

World war is not at any time a rigid preordained fatal inevitability, but only a probability.

302

The striking way in which the modern world is moving toward its doom is not accidental but predetermined. Yet this terrible inevitability is not imposed from without by arbitrary power. It arises from within, from the world's own characteristics.

303

During the First World War, a sex-ridden civilization which had sought intense pleasures found intense pain. Did it learn the implicit lesson? No! It plunged more wildly than ever in the quest of sexual joy, only to find still worse agony in the Second World War. The more it has wasted the gift of life, semen, the more it has lost the essence of life, blood. Semen is white blood. Nature has punished man's careless dissipation of the one with a forced loss of the other. The time has come to teach the lesson of sexual responsibility in clear words. If humanity refuses to learn and obey spiritual laws, the horror of a third world war, compared with which the second will be mere child's play, cannot be escaped.

304

It would be agreeable and pleasant to share such optimism about the non-inevitableness of war, but it would also be self-deceptive.

305

The year-and-a-half after Hitler disappeared brought the chance to make a new world or else the probability of having to prepare for a new world war.

306

When the terrors and horrors of one war fail to have the effect of arousing people to thinking for themselves instead of in a mass, that is to say, of seeking truth individually, then the war will repeat itself again and again.

307

If the war comes, it will have been brought by the erring nations upon themselves. If the war is not to come, they must change their ideas and their actions now.

308

Some believe that war might come in a few years' time; it might also come in only one year's time; but it would be folly to deny that it might not even come at all.

309

If no efforts at all had been made on *both* the physical and mystical planes to counteract the threatened conflict, it could have broken out in the Cuban crisis year. The situation is still an anxious one but it is not a hopeless one. Piety alone will not suffice to meet it, just as politics alone has already failed to do so. But the mystical efforts are being kept up. War is not inevitable. No one knows the outcome of the tremendous struggle going on between the atheistic hate forces and the constructive love forces on the mental level. The intercessory and contributory meditations of a few knowledgeable sages afford whatever real hope exists today. If the peoples and leaders fail to respond to those contributions, they will then have to carry the responsibility for its destruction.

310

It is folly not to see that war is inevitable, folly to blind oneself deliberately to what is coming merely because one dreads it.

311

While our human interest and nature shudder at the thought of such war, our human wisdom and insight have no doubt it will take place.

312

The danger is not only that a third world war will come, but that it will come during the old age even of those who reached manhood in the first world war.

313

None of the wars which mankind have hitherto suffered was Armageddon, for the last war was fought out fully and extended its devastations only in three continents and partly on the fourth, but the fifth was not affected in the same way. When Armageddon comes, it will devastate five continents.

314

The mass of people does not take to truly spiritual concepts. Extroversion, egoism, and preoccupation with personal or worldly affairs keep out any interest or attention in such concepts. Only the crushing shock of atomic war will provide an impulsion toward them from without.

315

Even the new polarization of attitudes which is emerging as a consequence of the war, is confused rather than clear-cut. The ghastly tragedy of this confusion would show itself at its very worst in Armageddon. In the Second World War the issues between good and evil were clear-cut and easily discernible. But in the third world war they would be confused, chaotic, and mixed.

316

It does not require much perceptiveness to perceive the inevitability of Armageddon. This fear haunts millions today and is one of the impulsions to the search for spiritual comfort, in one group, and the search for forgetfulness in pleasures, with the larger group.

317

We may face the tragic inevitability of a third world war with fear and gloom or with calm and resignation.

Constructive alternatives: collective

318

Politicians do not seek, and do not find, the real issues behind the apparent ones: this is one of the reasons why their very remedies merely cover up the causes, and repress only the symptoms. The time comes when what is evaded comes also to the surface and must be faced, when the illusions can no longer be hidden, when the chronic accumulated toxins break out all over the body politic, bringing severe troubles, maladies, and sickness.

319

So long as those who lead nations or rule peoples have wholly or partially inadequate understanding of the profounder significance of human existence, so long will those nations and peoples be led from one painful blunder to another.

320

This postwar world is hard to live in. We are paying the price for the visionless selfishness, the voracious greeds, and the stupid materialism of the past decades. It was for us to become aware of the new undercurrents of thought and feeling and to become conscious of their import. If we failed to do so it was because our intuition needed improvement. The distressing record during the past two decades of a leadership which lacked both realism and idealism partly explains the inevitability of this war. The blind incompetent and materialistic men who helped to write this record hugged their errors and deluded themselves into looking for the foe everywhere but in their own minds. The world is in such grim chaos because it has had materialistic leaders and no spiritual leadership.

321

Mankind cannot be fashioned in actuality into goodness or wisdom overnight—let alone the godlike exemplary image of which scripture speaks. Not even the most powerful adept can do that. Much of the preaching, most of the idealistic teaching, is hardly relevant to the human situation as we find it in the world today. Only clear thinking, and even clearer non-thinking intuition, can see the picture, not only as it is, but also in its wholeness. Without some knowledge of the World-Idea, those who hold public office, those who lead their countries, merely grope their way under the delusion that they see it. This does not mean that knowledge of this truth provides all the needed and perfect solutions of the problems. The egoistic attitudes and blindnesses, the narrownesses, the greeds, hates, prejudices, animosities, passions, and violent emotions of the people would still continue to block the way and obstinately obstruct the wisest and best of leaders, creating a karma that will have to operate, a destiny that brings back what is put forth. This is not to say that a fine leader's presence and power are as nothing; they mitigate the bad effects of mankind's own past making, and they initiate new constructive efforts which will penetrate the future.

322

The few statesmen, rulers, or politicians by whose decisions history itself is now being made, who control tremendous power, are the ones who need guidance and wisdom, prophetic warning and personal awakening if they are not to lead their nations—and with them all mankind—into the abyss of colossal catastrophe. If anything is to be done to save the world, it must be done through them—the masses of men will be more likely to follow where they go. If you say that the problem is too big for anyone to solve, you imply that nothing ought to be done to help these leaders find right direction. If you say, with Aldous Huxley's *Grey Eminence*, that "mystics who interfere in politics only make matters worse," I reply that unpractical visionaries, unbalanced fanatics, narrow sectarians, and inexperienced meddlers certainly do so, but practical, balanced, and mature mystics do not. History proves this point. Philosophy rejects both objections. Even where there is only a small hope of avoiding the tragic outcome of present conditions, it must take the chance offered.

323

When monsters devoid of human pity, inspired by terrifying hate, become leaders of a people, and are followed by them, the presence of the dark opposing principle in nature becomes very evident.

324

The fact is that a situation has arisen for which the military leaders are totally unprepared, one which was never foreseen in all their courses in strategy and tactics, and before which the political leaders also are bewildered.

325

In former times, compromise was a prudent and practical proposition. But in our time it will not succeed. The leaders of humanity must either adjust themselves to truth or find themselves, and their nations, smitten with disaster or catastrophe.

326

The makers of war cannot alter themselves suddenly into the makers of peace. It is useless to look to politics for the cessation of strife when it is itself based on strife. It is wiser and more logical to look to those who have found their own inner peace.

327

The need of a twentieth-century sage to guide twentieth-century people is plain. For people are seeking truth and yearn for happiness where it never has been and never can be found—that is, in materialistic thinking and selfish living.

328

The extent to which any single man is able to force world events today is small. Unseen forces of universal law are, on the contrary, using gifted individuals to control, influence, and fulfil the destiny of mankind.

329

No leader will appear to set the whole world in order for no man has any other answer that will be more effective than the Golden Rule, which mankind has known since before Jesus' days but failed to apply. If such a man is to be more successful he will have to demonstrate more spiritual Power.

330

The people who compose a community and the leaders whom they follow make its character as good or as bad as they themselves are. Only wild fanatics can expect to build a perfect society out of imperfect materials.

331

When the name of democracy is used as a shield to destroy democracy—while claiming its freedom—it is ridiculous to play the simpleton and ignore the reality of what is actually happening.

332

By using wrong methods, or even by using right methods at the improper time, the leaders of a nation attain the very opposite of what they strive for. It is for this reason that today the search after peace is bringing them farther from it. A very old Far Eastern text, the *Book of Changes*, declares, "If the military defense of a state is carried to such extreme that it provokes wars which annihilate the state, there is failure."

333

If the rulers do not respond to this last chance which has been offered them, they will not be given another. For there is a limit to the length of karmic rope which keeps the nations in an uneasy peace. But if they do respond to the warning uttered and accept the counsel offered, help will come—miraculous and abundant help. For if there is no tragedy graver than the tragedy of such rejected Grace, there is equally no blessing happier than the blessing of accepted Grace.

334

Too many of history's great leaders were at the same time mankind's great misleaders. For they took too many people down the easy but evil path of violence, which revealed destruction and dealt out death at its end.

335

A few months before he was murdered, at the end of that terrible period of Hindu-Muhammedan riotings, anarchy, and massacre, Gandhi exclaimed: "I do not want to live in darkness and madness; I cannot go on."

336

The dictator, the politician, and the journalist must take part of the responsibility for leading the masses to this lugubrious situation.

337

It would be a mistake to believe that salvation in any crisis depends on a quantitative element. Humanity could be helped by only a handful of men who found and lived in the higher consciousness, provided it were willing to follow the guidance and respect the enlightenment of these men.

338

If it were not for the presence of a few human lights in our world, and for their mostly silent but sometimes open activity, that world would have deteriorated spiritually, morally, to an extent far below what it has done.

339

Mankind has entered a new cycle, one wherein each man must learn something of the truth for himself. In former cycles he did not need to bear this responsibility. In the present one, he must accept it.

340

A time like the present should not be used as an excuse to escape into the past but as an inspiration to bring in the future.

341

The economic and political reconstruction of the world is a vitally important task, but its ethical reconstruction is immeasurably more important. The former touches the surface of life only, the latter touches its very core.

342

While our mental attitude remains what it is, no solution is possible. We meet hatred with hatred, suspicion with suspicion, fear with fear. Even nuclear disarmament would only ease the world's crisis and not end it, would only put off the urgency and acuteness and still leave the problem of enmity where it is. Among the ancients, Indian Buddha, Chinese Lao Tzu, and Syrian Jesus gave their solution. Buddha explained the operation of a higher law when he pointed out, "Hatred ceases not by hatred but by love." And the Western world has heard often enough (but does not practise) what Jesus taught on this matter.

343

The philosopher must look very far into human history and very deep into human nature when seeking the ultimate sources of human error and human wrong-doing. He must look farther than their social, economic, and political courses. This done, he will trace them to the animalistic instincts inherited from pre-human and primitive human incarnations. As long as these instincts remain undisciplined, and as long as the higher nature is not more eagerly cultivated, so long must we expect to witness the strife which produces war—whether between nations or inside them. It is quite proper to make the necessary remedial efforts through social, political, educational, organizational, and other means, but their benefits will disappear in the end if they are not made side by side with the effort to teach the necessity of liberation from these instincts by the appropriate mental and spiritual techniques. The more numerous the individuals who can find peace and joy inside their own hearts, the more will the dangers and horrors which threaten mankind be curbed.

344

There is no perpetual peace anywhere on this planet, only perpetual strife. But it is open to man to take the violence, the murder, and the war out of this strife. He may purge it of its savage beast qualities.(P)

345

The greatest spiritual needs of the modern world are more depth and more width. It needs to deepen its field of consciousness so as to include the true spiritual self and the divine laws governing life. It needs to widen out into loving thoughts and compassionate deeds. With right ethical ideals and sound nonmaterialistic ideas the external activities which will fill the postwar stage would then bring true progress to mankind. But with unworthy ideals and false ideas humanity would only fall into greater disaster and eventual destruction.

346

Without knowing the real and hidden causes of the malady of war, we cannot find the real and lasting cure of war.

347

The great Cuban crisis of 1962 resulted in a situation which brought about a postponement of the menace of World War III, but did not, fully and finally, avert it. All efforts to obtain peace may succeed or not succeed—the results are variable—but any effort to establish peace permanently cannot possibly do so fully and finally until the human race comes into a larger obedience to the higher spiritual laws.

348

If philosophy can do nothing for the peace of the world, then it is worth nothing. But it *can* do something. Indeed, if the politicians and militarists would recognize its inner worth, its private firsthand knowledge of the higher laws, it could redeem civilization from the evils and horrors of war.

349

We may find any number of excellent arguments against war. We may demonstrate conclusively that war as a process for achieving national aggrandizement is now entirely unnecessary, because applied science has opened the way for every nation to increase its wealth many times. But if arguments alone were sufficient to convince rulers, then war would have disappeared when the first flood of League propaganda was sluiced out on the world. The fact is that something more than the appeal to reason is required, for man contains passions, prejudices, greeds, and fears also.

350

You must batter down the barriers which wall in your view of life. You must stop thinking in terms of your own country alone. You must learn that the frontiers of England, of America, of India, lie far beyond England, beyond America, and beyond India. You must open out your philosophical horizon and bring your thinking up to date. Know that this century demands that the Indian peasant learn that his fate is inextricably bound up with the fate of the British factory worker, and both with that of the American trader.

351

When chaos and disorder, violence and materialism become widespread, the spiritual forces reassert themselves, restate the truth, and inspire a renewal of faith, religion, and mysticism.

352

A society which is based on a hierarchy of wealth, position, appearance, and worldly skill is unbalanced and cannot function properly or healthily or fully. It must look deeper and add inner spiritual correspondences to these things.

353

The political conferences to prevent or end war appear ridiculous; they are foredoomed from the start: selfishness and insincerity render them futile.

354

The hope for a lasting peace—so often unrealized—can become satisfied but only by looking for it in a new direction—within.

355

The world situation is very unpromising. Humanity has not learned as much as it ought to have learned from its terrible sufferings of recent years. Or, as in certain countries, it has even learned the wrong lessons and become more selfish, more brutal and violent, and more unco-operative. There is no escape, no new shortcut through political or economic change out of the chaos in which the nations find themselves, other than the oldest one in history—which is to avoid evil, to do good, to believe in God and the moral laws.

356

The deplorable state of the world today testifies silently to the widespread spiritual ignorance which is at the root of the trouble. Class hates class, group strives against group, selfishness is prevalent everywhere—this situation could only arise amongst creatures ignorant of the higher purpose on this earth. Consequently, to help make available knowledge of the truth and to elevate moral character constitute the noblest task to which any man could devote himself.

357

The way of arbitration—like the way of contractual treaties—for the purpose of avoiding war presupposes a loyal respect for promises and a level of simple honesty, an expression of obligations in deeds rather than oratory which, we know now from painful experience, does not exist in imperfect humanity. It is merely wishful dreaming to propose it as the practical alternative to war. The brutal realities of our situation have to be squarely seen without illusion. Nor is the bringing of the system of military naval and air defense to ever-increasing magnitude an effectual alternative. The same procedure is sure to be followed in the opposite camp. The result one day in some moment of emotional reaction to tragedy or of national cupidity will be an explosion of all these massed and concentrated engines of violence.

358

Sloppy sentiments about human brotherhood are not at all needed to pad out the plain fact that all of us ought to work with goodwill for the general good.

359

The dark possibility that destroys our future can give place to a brighter one only when enough philosophically illumined people are to be found in each country. Nor need they be many—a few in each city would throw out enough influence to bring about this change. It is the tragedy of our age that philosophical thoughts should be classed with idle dreams when they are the most practical of all today.

360

The present situation shows the utter failure of religion to control men; it will never be more than a temporary palliative; TRUTH alone can solve all national and international problems as much as it solves the personal ones. But truth is based on intelligence and mankind's intelligence still lags remarkably behind. So the adepts contribute their little bit towards enlightening others and wait with the terrible patience of those who think in terms of aeons, not years alone. The growth of intelligence will come through evolution, and then man will learn his personal responsibility for all deeds under the laws of re-embodiment and compensation; later he will learn that he cannot separate himself from the ALL, that the same Mind runs through us all, and that humanity is just a big family wherein the older members *are* responsible for the welfare of the younger ones, the rich for the poorer, and so on. Universal compassion will then be the only right outlook for a properly educated man. Where would Hitler's crude racial separatism or Russia's equally crude hatred of the bourgeoisie be then?

361

This divine consciousness dissolves inveterate prejudice and removes embittered passion. But no human will can manufacture it. The world must acknowledge a higher authority than fleshly desire and evolve by self-striving beyond its present materiality before the Overself's grace will confer such an exalted state.

362

Without trying to indulge in overoptimistic claptrap, it may nevertheless be predicted that, as the twenty-first century advances, human life will change both physically and culturally in an astounding way.

It is true that no particular war can possibly end all war. It is the untamed animal in man which causes all his personal fights, tribal aggressions, and national wars. It is the spiritual nature of man which urges him to live peaceably and harmoniously with his fellows. That man can rid himself of external bloodshed without troubling to rid himself of its internal causes within himself, is one of his intellect-born illusions. It may be kept at a

distance for a longer time than before but it cannot be kept there permanently while the passions of hatred, anger, and greed thrive in his heart. But
it is also true that his instruments of collective violence have now become so
destructive, so terrible, and so cruel that their very results are forcing him to
contemplate abandoning such violence altogether, and to turn towards
peaceful discussion for the settlement of his disputes. Human conflict has
reached its most violent expression in this war [WWII] of staggering
planetary dimensions and unheard-of scientific destructiveness. But it
helped to quicken the dawn of a day when the soldier's sword and the
airman's bomb will be found only in such places as the "Chamber of
Horrors" at Madam Tussaud's Museum in London. Such extreme violence
was an evolutionary necessity to convince him that he must cease to tolerate
war, that he must find a more refined—that is, more mental—method of
carrying on his struggles, that he must come into the consciousness of world
citizenship, and that he must create international institutions commensurate with such a broader consciousness.

Such thoughts have begun to circulate within his consciousness, but
they will circulate forcibly only whilst the horrors of the last war are still
easily remembered. It would be wiser and prudent to realize that a long
night must precede this full dawn. A fresh generation or two will not feel
the force of this remembrance, and then passions which breed war may
overcome it and prove stronger than whatever mechanical organization to
preserve itself society may have brought into being for its self-protection.
This is so because sustained thought is creative and returns to us, in part,
in the events which meet us as we travel through life. Nevertheless, we
have indeed started to move onward and upward to that degree of ethical
maturity which shall surely come when we shall have controlled these
passions sufficiently to fight our quarrels around a conference table and
not on a battlefield and which shall transform history from a record of
national warfare into a record of international welfare.

Is it really a paradox that the first practical step in forging an armour for
such self-protection against war must necessarily be a moral and not a
physical one? There must be deep unflinching sincerity behind the will for
peace. We yearn for a war-proof world; but when we come to consider the
practical means of protecting mankind from further wars, we shall discover that insofar as they are not counterweighted with ethical principles
and psychological understanding also, they may become as dangerous to
us through creating a false sense of safety as the old League of Nations
became for a similar reason. One of the half-conscious tasks which destiny

placed in the war's hands was to show the world's face to itself. In the result it unmasked a gargoyle before an affrighted audience. For instance, when Hitler denounced the League of Nations as a humbug, we turned our ears away. Yet he was not wrong as he was not quite right. For those who know what really went on behind its public conferences and pleasant speeches, know also that too much unscrupulous intrigue, political greed, and ethical insincerity were covered by its fine verbal facade of idealism and morality. The closure of Suez and its withdrawal of oil would have brought Mussolini's Ethiopian adventure, for instance, to an abrupt close. But this needed a sincerity which was lacking. The betrayals of Manchuria to Japan, of Ethiopia to Italy, and of Czechoslovakia to Germany were lapses in international morality whose consequences ruined the League. Its ethical failure was inevitably followed by its physical failure.

Not that the basic conception of a League of Nations was a bad one; on the contrary, it was magnificent! But it was one thing to invent machinery to check the outbreak of war and quite another to find the mental outlook large enough to work such machinery. For the new institution itself did not change their old outlook. Geneva witnessed both the birth of a great idea and the death of a grand hope. The League perished because it put heads together but not hearts. It was to be expected that a machine of the character of the League of Nations would work badly at first, but it was not expected that it would ignominiously fail to work at all. Only a few anticipated this failure. They were the few who comprehended that the mental reality behind a thing is more formidable and important than its material appearance, that the inevitable karma of so much past aggression, exploitation, cruelty, and selfishness could not be easily circumvented without a real change of heart.

The League of Nations was only an idea. It never came to life because it was never given the chance to do so. And it was never given the chance because each of its members thought of its own country first and the League second, because each brought its nationalistic interests right into the League chambers and kept them there as the foremost purpose of its presence, because none had the consciousness of really being what all pretended to be—a united commonwealth. We, however, have the splendid chance to make it something more than an idea. For most statesmen now realize that some kind of arrangement which will honestly carry out its task of preventing aggressive war and not merely talk about doing so, which will comprehend that the duty of stronger nations is to protect the weaker ones and not to exploit them, must paradoxically be one of the products of this terrible time. Thus Nazism, which was fundamentally opposed to the idea of a just peace, unwittingly and unwillingly contributed to its stabilization.

We must begin a new effort by realizing that the guns may stop shooting but this is not enough to make a peace. We need something more. We need a reconstructed society where the moral and physical causes which may ultimately set guns shooting again will themselves be liquidated. We must proceed by understanding that the historical and geographical accidents which divide one people from another, one class from another, one nation from another, have fostered dislike, suspicion, and even hatred in the past. The limited nationalistic outlook can no longer be accepted uncritically. The developments of modern scientific civilization have filled it with contradictions and imperfections, with dangers and inadequacies. In its prewar form it has become antiquated. It must now be revised and brought into line with postwar needs. Every major situation today is not only a national one but also an international one. Nations will have to broaden their outlook and give up some fraction of their nationalistic fervour not merely for the benefit of all but more so for their own individual benefit. And they will have to do this not only because the war's practical lessons have left them no alternative, but also because their moral evolution has left them no alternative. The necessity of curbing the power and authority of competitive nationality in the interests of international welfare is plain. Nazism and Fascism represented indeed in one aspect the last furious struggle of nationalism become aggressive and bellicose in an endeavour to save itself from impending and enforced limitation.

The animosities and prejudices, the rivalries and hatreds, of the old-fashioned nationalistic outlook must be replaced by the co-operative outlook of a new internationalism. Whether we like it or not, we are in the process of swiftly becoming a world community. The quicker we cut out the time-lag between the dissolution of our prejudices and the realization of our evolutionary needs, the less painful will it be. The sympathetic interest in foreign peoples, the feeling of connection with the wider human race, is something new in history but it is something which has come to stay. No continent can now afford to forget—as it has so often in the past—that it is a part of the same planet as the others. The great globe whose monstrous size frightened medieval minds has shrunk to a little ball which man now plays with. The war has taught more people more geography than any school ever did. This is not merely something to make us smile but also something to make us think. For it has forcibly brought home to them the fact that life today is an international affair, that they are being brought into ever-closer relations. We have to realize that we are approaching the middle of the twentieth century and not the middle of the eighteenth. Wireless, cable, telephone, steamer, railway, and printing press have made a new international relationship both necessary and possible but they have not yet made it actual.

The technological and commercial developments which have dissolved so many of the physical divisions in the present may be used, if we wish, to foster friendship, understanding, and goodwill in the future. The problems which have to be settled are now too large to be settled successfully on a prewar basis. A new international order must be instituted as being the only effective way to deal with them. Henceforth, the major events in every country must be looked upon as an integral and inseparable part of the planetary situation. The separate peoples are today too interdependent to carry on successfully with anything short of such an order. Every people is a part of a social organism and must share the general fate of that organism. If such a federation is still far off, it is near enough that a third world war will precipitate it overnight. For the difficulties of achieving it are really less than the difficulties into which another great war will plunge everybody. One must take a realistic view of the situation, yes, but one need not throw all one's idealism overboard to do it.

We have in the past enlarged the meaning of the word "patriotism" from a merely local to a tribal significance and then from a tribal to a national one. We must in the present enlarge it once again. It is no longer enough to be only Fiji Islanders or Frenchmen. We must also, and alongside of that, be world patriots. The political frontiers which separate one country from another separate them also from prosperity, peace, and advancement. The time will surely come one day to pull them down, when the United States of the World will come to birth as a single entity. The ultimate evolution will certainly be towards a universal humanity.

The immediate evolution is towards a consciousness that we are all human beings just as much as we are tribesmen or race members. This need not mean the total destruction of national sentiments and the total wounding of national vanities. It need not necessarily exclude an enlightened patriotism or a balanced devotion to a particular national or racial group. It would exclude, however, the hatreds, the prejudices, the dislikes, and the intolerant fanaticisms bred by false patriotism and narrow insularity. Just as a larger circle does not exclude the smaller concentric one contained within it, so loyalty to mankind as a whole need not exclude the lesser loyalties to race, creed, and class. What it does is to subordinate them. Each people could carry on its own autonomous existence and independent activities within the framework of an international association. The rights of freedom and self-rule need not be menaced by the broader rights of such an association. When the forms, interests, and arrangements of mankind become internationalized, the benefit will be moral as well as material. For group selfishness, false national pride, and racial prejudices will be forced down into second place behind human fellowship and common welfare. The administrative essentials of a fully developed new international order must consist of a world legislature, a world executive, and a world tribunal.

Most people are now much more ready for the widening in loyalties which world-order schemes would involve, but they are not at all as ready as they should be. Thus, they unnecessarily deprive themselves of the clear advantages of such an order and go on foolishly enduring the troubles of the old order. That we are moving toward some kind of single World Commonwealth is certain. That we are not emotionally ready for it is also certain. For the events and inventions which are pushing us forward are ahead of our ideas and ideals. The tragic needs of our time do not find a commensurate mentality to meet them. The Europeans, for example, cannot be persuaded to renounce their state sovereignties, cannot be made into common citizens of a frontierless continent against their will. How much more will this be the case with a world-citizenship scheme? But in the end humanity will find itself unable to keep the peace between its diversified groups without creating a separate paramount international association—be it central, federal, or league. A world organization which can legally settle international disputes and which possesses the armed power to enforce its decisions or to resist aggressions cannot ultimately be avoided. Men, in their present stage of moral evolution, cannot be effectively governed without the use of some kind of physical coercion nor can their national disputes be settled without some means of physically enforcing decisions. The peoples are being evolved from within and driven from without to the point where only a world association will fit their political needs.

Such an authority would possess the usual administrative powers. First, it would be a legislature whose jurisdiction would extend over the whole field of international matters and regulate by agreed laws the political, commercial, and cultural relations between the States. Second, it would be a tribunal where final judgement would be pronounced upon disputes, aggressions, and alterations of frontiers. Third, it would be an executive equipped to maintain order and enforce laws actually worked out to preserve peace. But besides the necessity of preventing possible internecine wars the practical advantages of such a common authority are so obvious that the administrations of the otherwise independent units will sooner or later be forced by developments to accept it. Such advantages would include a customs union, a common currency, a common transport system, and probably a common armed force. But the danger here is that a paramount supranational power may develop into a tyrannous suprastate. It may be that adequate checks and safeguards can be devised by statesmen against it, but in the end it can be overcome only by overcoming the moral and mental defects in men which could cause it.

If men are not evolved enough to support such an ideal institution as a world family of democratic nations, they are not so low that they cannot support the beginnings of such an institution. If a nation is unwilling to be its neighbour's keeper, it ought at least be willing to be its neighbour's helper. It is inevitable that as men become more truly spiritually minded they will become more internationally minded. And this is certain to reflect itself in turn in their political systems. The end of such a process can only be the formation of an international commonwealth. Hence, every political measure which promotes this end is a right one and every measure which obstructs it is a wrong one. But it must be also well-timed or it will defeat its own end. The League was ill-timed. The right time for a solely regional scheme was after World War I. Instead, too much was attempted by way of the League, which inevitably failed. But after World War II a regional scheme alone would likewise fail. The present suggestion adapts itself to this factor of proper timing.

It was predicted in *The Wisdom of the Overself* that the principle of cooperation would be the only principle to emerge from all the postwar conferences as being effective enough to solve their thorny problems. It will have many possible spheres of application but the first and major one will be in the direction of peace. So we venture to predict again that failure of international co-operative action to create and sincerely to sustain some kind of an assembly of representatives drawn from the different nations, will lead directly to the catastrophe of a third armed conflict more terrible than this planet has yet known. It could lead to this in one and a half to two decades. Metropolitan cities would not be able to escape heavy bombing and wide destruction. Such an honest and determined assembly of nations would be better protection for every country than any army, navy, or air force.

The ultimate evolution of the twenty-first century will be toward a democratic world association, acting through an international parliament, an international tribunal, and an international executive, which would impartially regulate, coordinate, and boldly envelop the entire economic resources of the planet as a whole. When all nations can thus share equitably in the common wealth and productivity, one of the prime causes of war between them would completely vanish. Past events have tragically proved the truth of these statements. Many of the calamities such as monetary collapse, trade depression, and labour strikes which descended on classes, masses, and nations were caused by their failure to recognize the immense power of the principle of mutual help and by their inability to meet the events of this historic turning-point with the understanding they demand. The first nation to recognize the one and to meet the other will do much, not only for herself, but also for all other nations. Both moral development and practical exigencies will require us in the end to subscribe to the fundamental truth that prosperity, no less than peace, is one and indivisible. But, unfortunately, we are not yet emotionally ready to climb such a height. We must expect, therefore, that different kinds of troubles will plague us from time to time as the penalty of our unreadiness.

363

We have to accept the solid fact that men do not change overnight, that starting new institutions and necessarily filling them with the same old faces that we already know, will not and cannot bring about a new world. Until we begin to recognize this and start working for new hearts and new minds even more than for institutions, we shall not come near to solving our problems.

364

Today, the mission of philosophy is a planetary one, for truth is needed everywhere, and for the first time can be transmitted everywhere. We speak here in terms of geographical fact, for vested religious interests and totalitarian political despotisms still continue to serve their masters, the darker forces of evil, by obstructing the contemporary planetary enlightenment.

365

Unless humanity recognizes that demonic powers are loose in its midst, are inspiring hatred violence suspicion and greed, it will not go down on its knees to ask help from a power greater than and beyond itself.

366

Unless we look behind the world's problems into the real and spiritual problems which they reflect, we cannot properly understand them or solve them.

367

The human situation which has emerged from the cataclysms and anguish of war and crisis, still shows insufficient spiritual awakening. And yet this awakening—and this alone—is the only instrument of our salvation that is worth looking for because it is the only one which is not doomed to be destroyed. All other instruments may be effective in ordinary times, but we are living in exceptional times. Today they can offer only the illusion of success or happiness with the actuality of failure or misery.

But so few people are fortunate enough to have the time, leisure, energy, and opportunity for spiritual culture, that the awakening from social lethargy is often the first sign of any awakening at all. The social awakening may nowadays be a troubled upheaval rather than a smooth progress. But human egoism and passion being what they are at the present evolutionary stage, this is inevitable. However, the awakening must be understood as the first part of a deeper awakening from spiritual slumber which is yet to come. We must see in all this social renovation a necessary preliminary and unavoidable preparation for the subsequent spiritual one. When the political, scientific, and economic reorganization of the world which is going on before our eyes culminates, when more settled conditions begin to prevail again, men will realize that materialism has brought them its best and worst. And realizing, they will turn to discovery of their inner needs. Therefore we may expect no general spiritual awakening in our own lifetime whilst this external new era is being established, but after that such an awakening will surely come because it is evolutionarily due. Thus there is room for both an optimistic and a pessimistic outlook; neither alone is quite true. If we look only at the next few years, there is gloom all around; but if we look through them to some decades farther ahead, there is light.

368

Those who believe in a sudden religio-mystical revival to change mankind almost overnight, are far from philosophy. But still they are only being foolish. Those however who not only believe this, but also believe that it is they or their particular religious organization that will help to bring about the revival, are also being self-conceited.

Just as the Germans were presented with the choice between Hitlerian revolution and democratic evolution as well as the chance of escaping a misery so much worse than the one Hitler offered to save them from, so humanity today has both choice and chance. The real decision is between obedience to a spiritual leading or denial of it.

With all too many people, both among the vanquished and the victors, everything within themselves remains as before the war. If anything, they are even spiritually emptier than before, because the negative feelings of bitterness, resentment, selfishness, suspicion, or violence have now taken hold of their hearts.

If we look the situation of contemporary humanity fully in the face, putting aside suggestion and propaganda, we shall have to confess that its salvation will never be brought about by the little mystical groups and large religious sects.

The "Kingdom of God on earth" is not a political concept but a personal one. Its realization will never be found outside but only inside the individual mind and heart.

369

The descent into materialism will be intellectually checked by science reversing its own nineteenth-century conclusions; the lapse into immorality by the vivid demonstration of its tragic results in recent national and individual history; the fall into irreligion by the uprise of a more personal and more mystical faith.

370

The first social goal which philosophy sets before its votary is the dropping of class race and creed prejudices—not, be it remembered, of their actualities. Although racial differences must be taken into account, cultural variations must be recognized and the contrasts of living standards must be noted; although the oneness of mankind is a metaphysical and not a physical fact and although its mystical unity is not its practical uniformity, all this is no excuse for racial prejudices and hatreds or for unfair partialities and discriminations. In the case of the colour bar, this has been particularly cruel in the past and will be dangerous in the future. He must be too wise, too tolerant, and too decent to be caught up by the fanatic nationalisms, the unashamed savageries, the battling brutalities, the social hostilities, the racial animosities and religious intolerances of unenlightened men. Whoever breathes the rarefied atmosphere of truth can only regard with sorrow those who insist on breathing the murky fogs of overweening race nationality sect or colour discriminations. Whoever practises the philosophic discipline is walking the path to the consciousness of being a world citizen. He cannot help but be a confirmed internationalist. This is a logical and practical result of his knowledge and attitude. He sees clearly that we are all children of the same supreme Father, all rooted in the same infinite Mind, all brought together on this planet to carry out the same noble tasks of self-regeneration and self-realization.

Consequently he is friendly to men of all nationalities, all races, all countries. They are not disliked suspected or hated, ignored neglected or ill-treated because in the flesh they happen to be foreigners. He sees that the truth is there are no Englishmen, Frenchmen, or Germans but only human beings harbouring stuffy mental complexes that they are English French or German. Nevertheless the man who has liberated himself from this fleshly materialism need not cease thinking of himself as a citizen of his particular country. But he will alongside of that think of himself as a citizen of the world.

371

In devoting time to spiritual reform, we go to the root of all other reforms. If men get rid of their spiritual ignorance it is inevitable that they will more quickly get rid of undesirable conditions in every other department of their life. Nowadays we must especially guard ourselves against the one-sided unbalanced doctrines, the selfish degrading ethos, and the false materialistic ideas which have so widely permeated the political, cultural, commercial, and religious terrain of our time. No Marxian magic and no financial wizardry can turn a planet peopled by men and women still dominated by hates, greeds, selfishnesses, and lusts into a physical utopia. Ultimately the experience of all history, both individual and national, teaches the lesson that physical well-being alone is not enough. It contributes towards the true happiness of man on earth but does not complete it. The welfare of the body is not an end in itself but only a means to a higher end. Hence philosophy, in its consideration of the methods to be used to achieve such an end, says that external re-arrangement of social forms will not of itself bring about fully satisfactory results. A re-arrangement from within is equally if not much more necessary.

372

Only those who refuse the lessons of mankind's historic past can suppose that peace, which it has never had for more than short periods, will suddenly bloom all over the earth and remain here continuously, in defiance of the violent and destructive instincts which still lurk in mankind.

373

The opportunities to wage war can be brought under international control by external means, and within our time they will be so brought when mankind is driven by necessity to take such a measure for the sake of the race's own survival. But the psychological causes that urge men to wage war—these remnants of the animal left in man—can only be dealt with by internal means.

374

This drawing-together of the different peoples out of their earlier isolation, which modern civilization has brought about, has not only increased their knowledge of each other but also increased their effect upon the lives and fortunes of one another. Out of this has grown the complexity of contemporary political, economic, and racial problems. What one nation does is liable to affect not only its neighbours but also far-away nations to the point of actual war. Therefore, there is much greater need of learning for what purpose all the human race has been placed on this earth than there was in earlier and more isolated times.

375

Not any military, political, or economic preparation—whether defensive or aggressive—has any hope for mankind's true protection, if it does not include learning and obeying these higher laws. There are healing, restorative, guiding, and protective forces amid us even today, trying to reach the human race and to penetrate the dense, dark conditions surrounding it. If they are recognized and received in time, it will be saved from a frightfully destructive event. But if human blindness and inertia prevent this from happening, the penalty will have to be paid.

376

In the heart's deepest place, where the burden of ego is dropped and the mystery of soul is penetrated, a man finds the consciousness there not different in any way from what all other men may find. The mutuality of the human race is thus revealed as existing only on a plane where its humanness is transcended. This is why all attempts to express it in political and economic terms, no less than the theosophic attempts to form a universal brotherhood, being premature, must be also artificial. This is why they failed.

377

None of the Powers, great or small, has been able to resolve the world crisis. It drags on through the years, getting aggravated with each year. This is because all the Powers try to resolve it against the wrong background, using ideas and methods which may have formerly been right but now are obsolete and inapplicable. This is the Nuclear Age. It requires a totally new approach.

378

If God's in his heaven and all's well with the world, are we in error to attempt reforms where they are obviously needed or to right wrongs where they are heavily oppressive? No—this is no error, for the attempt itself will then be induced by the divine presence.

379

Men who have lost the sense of life's spiritual significance, and who do not even have any insistent questions about it, will not respond to such events in the correct way.

380

Hitherto religion has provided the ordinary man with the truth in a form he was capable of comprehending. But owing to the wider spread and quickened evolution which he has undergone in recent centuries, he has become capable of comprehending more deeply that which was formerly kept apart from popular religion and reserved for mysticism, the next higher form. Consequently it is no longer enough to limit him to merely religious dogmas and practices; these must now be intermixed with mystical doctrines and practices also. It is a fact that war and crisis have multiplied by many times the number of mystical seekers. But the new group is still, relative to the total population, extremely small, insignificant and uninfluential. Yet the benefits of mysticism could be of untold help to countless others. The temporary forgetfulness from current turmoils and personal burdens which mental quietism offers its votaries should prove attractive to quite a number of persons in these times. For the need of personal, firsthand experience of the soul is greater today than ever before. Therefore the importance of this work is unquestionable.

381

So many are discussing the new economic world which they hope, expect, or demand to emerge during the postwar period, and so few the new spiritual world without which it can only be a failure. The truth is that both are needed, that one without the other will be an imperfect incomplete thing.

382

Because we live in an era of flux, we need a better-exercised intelligence and intuition to negotiate it aright.

383

The real war today is within the human mind. The real choice is between allegiances being made there. As individuals give themselves up to, or cleanse themselves from, the base emotions, they carry on *this* inner war.

384

The interminable quarrels over ownership of countries will always produce recurring wars. So long as Nature's proprietorship is ignored and unacknowledged, so long will men and nations stake out their selfish claims to perpetual possession.

385

It is an inexorable fact, which no politician can controvert by other facts but only by windy oratory and glib promises, that the causes of international tension friction and war will never be removed except by removing the egotisms, the greeds, the wraths, and other negatives from man's nature. Until then, we shall get rid of one old cause only to find a new one springing up in its train.

386

Until they inwardly recognize and publicly realize the overriding importance of thought and feeling in these matters, their remedies will be illusory, their hopes denied, and their forebodings fulfilled by the course of events.

387

Those who are led by religious enthusiasts to expect a miraculous conversion of mankind to goodwill peace and wisdom overnight, expect the impossible and are preparing themselves for bitter disappointment. Human character grows gradually; it does not improve by magical transformation. It is better to be realistic, to face the unpalatable truth, than to surrender ourselves to wishful thinking and be deceived thereby. For emotion and passion are still the real rulers of mankind, say what you will.

388

Human society has always had its problems and even more so in our times. But the larger the number of problems the larger the number of agencies seeking to solve them grows. Why do we have to solve every problem with which the world is confronted? Why can't we leave them alone, indifferent, and attend solely to our own problems? Why must we meddle in affairs we ill understand? The answer is that we fail to see that the world is itself the great problem for which there is no solution.

389

There can be no perfect solution to the world's troubles because there can be no permanent one. All changes, all is transient.

390

There would be more peace in countries and between nations, in families and between neighbours, if people stopped meddling in other people's affairs or interfering in each other's lives or fanatically forcing their doctrinaire ideas and beliefs where these are repugnant.

391

Most eloquent of all is Emerson: "Love is the one remedy for all ills. We must be lovers and at once the impossible becomes possible. Our history for these 1000 years has not been the history of kindness but of selfishness.

Love would put a new face on this weary old world, in which we dwell as enemies too long. Love will accomplish that which force could never achieve. Once or twice in history, kindness has been tried in illustrious instances, with signal success."

392

Lao Tzu wrote this parting advice to the civilization he forsook:

Love is victorious in attack
And invulnerable in defense;
Heaven arms with love
Those it would not see destroyed.

393

Censorious minds have doubtless much to pick on which is wrong or rotten in our society, but until they have something better to replace it with, some really worthwhile alternative, of what use is the destruction and liquidation of that which has been built up?

394

The spiritual progress of man winds upward by devious routes, by slow wanderings, and by periodic lapses. But its ultimate character as progress remains assured. Slowly, out of all these wartime reflections and peacetime crises, these dangers, agonies, and calamities, the world is becoming aware that it must find for its day-to-day activities a strong support, a better faith, and a truer ideology.

395

Many leaders such as Churchill, and even the Pope, have talked of a new world to be built. Their aims are excellent but it will not suffice to change things externally alone; people must be educated aright, which means they must be educated in truth. The time to sit in seclusion or to enjoy one's inner peace all alone will then have gone. Service and Action will be the keynote. The justification of the higher philosophy is what it can *do* ultimately, not merely what it can think. It alone has a sane view because it alone knows the need of a sound foundation in correct thinking plus an active effort afterwards, erected on such a foundation. How hard this ultimate teaching is as a way of life until one becomes habituated to it! For he has to feel that all the world is but a dream, even horrid wars, and yet he will have to know it as actual and act as though it were real. For ultimately it is real. Just as all the events, people, and objects of a dream are after all nothing but Mind, in essence, because they are ideas and Mind is their reality, so in this world we have to understand that that which is regarded as Mind, unified, all around us *is* the real. It is because ignorant people concentrate only on their material beliefs, taking body and environment as matter, and regarding everything as individual and separate, that they can never get at this higher realization. If he remembers that all golden rings, watches, tie pins, and so on, are in essence only one substance—gold—so he may remember that all bodies, things, and events are in essence also one substance—Mind. The sage is the person who holds firmly to this double "vision" or rather understanding and has made it his or her own by unremitting effort.

396

So much progress that men hope for from a science-based, politically guided civilization turns out to be a chimera. There is no good that science gave them without its costly price, no promise held out by political shifts without its revelation of the evil in man. Real peace, true progress, genuine prosperity can come only by a different road.

397

Those utopians who look for a quick abatement of human selfishness—and a consequent quick abatement of all the ghastly evils, sins, and crimes which come out of it—look in vain. But what cannot come quickly on a mass scale can, and will, come from scattered individuals.

398

First the killing instinct will have to go, then the fighting instinct will have to follow.

399

To eliminate the frictions in the world it would be necessary to eliminate those between human beings.

400

Those who do not know that human evolution moves through double rhythms of ascension and declension, talk cheerfully of an increasing spiritual revival moving triumphantly to the complete change of our species. But the fact is that what we see are vestiges of medieval faith rather than a rising spirituality.

401

Even if the world crashed in a nightmare of hate, evil, and ruin all around us, those who gave their allegiance to Goodness and Wisdom were not wrong nor their efforts a total failure.

402

The nations can use nuclear energy to explode bombs or they can use it to power engines: they must choose between these two alternatives. If they try to evade the choice and to have both, they will end by losing both in the annihilation of nuclear war.

403

An age which has found a surer and swifter way to destroy the human species has done so because it gave so much enquiry, so much thought, to the nature of the atom. Why cannot it give a fraction of that enquiry and that thought to the nature of mind, when the consequences would be so much more useful?

404

Is there, can there be, such a thing on earth as a paradise without sin? The answer is that it does not now exist and that it can exist in the future only if it is also a paradise without any people!

405

It was the Stoics who wrote that the wise man will not waste his energy and years in futile political endeavours if he finds his environment too corrupt.

406

One need not be a materialist to reach the conclusion that perfect solutions of social, economic, or religious problems simply do not exist; there are only palliatives, not panaceas.

407

The quietude on this planet grows less and less; the noise and turmoil more and more. The need of this inner life becomes greater but the possibility of realizing it becomes smaller. Yet the problem is not a new one; only a recurring one. Two thousand five hundred years ago the gentle old dreamer Lao Tzu wrote of it.

408

The course of nihilism, as travelled by the intelligent classes of our time, ends either in bitter communistic materialism or unprincipled anarchic amoralism or retrogressive Catholic or Hindu mysticism. But do any of these neurasthenic terminals offer an adequate solution of the modern man's problems, a comfortable home for the modern consciousness? Whoever is fully alive to twentieth-century needs and trends, cannot say that they do.

409

What can we gain by moving back in time? The crossroads at which we stand must be faced, not run away from. The attempt to renounce our times and leave our century will be severely defeated by the grim facts of these times, the harsh events of this century. There is no sanctuary in medievalism.

410

Neither reason nor goodwill were able to force Europe to adopt a wiser and purer form of religion, so utter impoverishment and bloody war had to force her to think. Only an overwhelming realization that such a change is supremely urgent, supremely essential, and supremely fundamental, if civilized society is not to break down completely, will compel this reconstruction. And the situation created by entry into the postwar period provides this required but dearly bought realization. And what is true of Europe, which suffered most during the war, will be true in a lesser degree of other parts of the world.

411

A highly exaggerated mystically sponsored Golden Age of the remote past is as supposititious as a materialistically sponsored one of the near future is unrealizable.

412

It is a silly mistake which some mystically minded enthusiasts fall into, that everybody is soon going to follow mysticism! The only basis they have for this assertion would appear to be that they move within a tiny circle where everybody is following mysticism and that they are judging the larger world outside by what is happening inside the circle.

413

The pathway of greedy acquisition upon which humanity now stands must be left for wise co-operation. The old motives will not work today.

414

Destiny is at work and all the multitude of prayers to God are not going to save humanity from what it creates for itself. Nothing could have been more ironic than the bombs falling on Warsaw Cathedral when more than a thousand worshippers were inside praying for God's protection on Poland.

415

The war period has shown how uncertain are all materialistic standards, how much they are at the mercy of military political and economic shifts. It must therefore articulate in thoughtful minds a quest of higher standards which shall transcend such uncertainties and shifts.

416

Because humanity must find the solution to their troubles within themselves, all the so-called solutions offered from without have proved disappointing. And because the attempt to find scapegoats in other men, other political parties, other doctrines of belief, and other nations is really an attempt to relieve themselves of this personal responsibility, they have so far failed to find an end to their troubles.

417

Those inspirers of evil-doing and racial animosity who fondly believe that they can protect themselves against the forces of spiritual evolution which are stirring within the consciousness of mankind, are dwelling in an atmosphere of futile make-believe.

418

To outgrow the instinctive cravings of the primitive animal-man and to supplant them by the noble aspirations of the well-advanced truly human being, is the only way to *guarantee* peace on earth.

419

We shall have to renounce this fetish of achieving absolute agreement and full unity among those who differ from each other in fundamentals. Human nature and human mentality being in the present unregenerate and diverse condition as they are, it is futile to pursue an unrealizable ideal.

420

The attempts to prevent war and unify the nations can meet with no success while we make no attempt to discipline the violent impulses and greedy calculations which cause war. Only when human evolution has gone farther, and the brute's instincts have been sufficiently disciplined in us, shall we drop war. But the clash of egoisms will still remain. Our frictions and battles will continue; their outer form will, however, change for the better and be lifted to a plane more truly human and beyond the merely animal.

421

If present-day world misery demonstrates anything at all, it demonstrates the failure of the materialistic outlook, the futility of expecting peace and prosperity from purely material sources, the danger of ignoring the stubborn fact that personal character counts most in the making of a people's happiness. The old way of sheer materialism has been tried and found to end in a dangerous morass. The new way of a nobler life and deeper faith does not look so tempting. Yet other way there is not except to sink in a still deeper morass.

422

Communism could be defeated and Socialism avoided if the appeal they make to the discontented could be eliminated. This in turn requires the cause of discontentment be itself eliminated. That cause is the too unequal distribution of (a) profits (b) income and (c) capital. The remedy for (a) is to make labour an equal partner with capital in the sharing of profits by a system of co-partnership. The remedy for (b) is to fix maximum and minimum incomes. The remedy for (c) is inheritance reform.

423

Whatever benefit has come from politics physically has had to be paid for spiritually, for it has poisoned human relationships.

424

In the end society is only a society of separate persons; in the end we come back to the individual human problem.

425

There is much demand today for various rights in their totality. Can the right to freedom be fully given to maniacs and murderers? Can the right to free expression in speech and writing be given at those who spread hatred or immorality? Can the right to education be given at a level beyond the capacities of those who make it? If life is to be orderly, if crime is to be contained, then there must be limits as well as rights.

426

There is no other way left for us today than the way of looking right through the facts of the contemporary situation, to their underlying significance, their foundational cause, if we are to understand it aright. We must have the courage to acknowledge them for what they are. We must have the strength to be pessimistic if pessimism is required by truth. We must have the humility to confess our errors.

427

When we understand the forces which work behind the curtain of history, we stop groping.

Crime and punishment

428

The punishment of crime should be of such a nature as to be materially useful to society and morally useful to the criminal.

429

Crime and Punishment (Essay)

When men misuse their liberty to commit crime, we withdraw it and put them in prison. But legal punishment has two grave defects: it makes no provision for moral re-education alongside of the physical punishment, and it makes no difference between the repentant sinner and the nonrepentant one. The criminal is simply a man who has misinterpreted life, failed in self-discipline, accepted the suggestions of an evil environment, or been hurt by a hard social system. It is not enough to enforce retribution. Society must help him straighten his life-pattern, improve himself, and re-establish his ethical sense. Prisons should be not merely penal institutions but also educative ones. Every prisoner should be brought under some system of instruction that would elevate his character—instead, as often happens, of debasing it still further.

It is far easier to degrade oneself than to uplift oneself. Every criminal knows that. The process of manufacturing a criminal is simple and easy. He commits his first crime and then, in order to save himself from its effects, he has to commit a second one. Once again he has to save himself from the effects of this one in turn and so commits a third crime. In the end he slides down a long slippery slope and becomes a hardened criminal! Only forethought for others or fear of the consequences for himself will save a man from taking the first ominous step. It is because men have insufficient forethought or insufficient knowledge of the consequences that they become criminals.

Or else, after the first punishment, instead of trying to understand the lessons of their sufferings, they nurse under-surface resentments which later explode and injure their whole life. It seems to offer an easier way out than the sterner path of moral repentance and honest endeavour. But they fail to foresee that it is no way out at all, that the selfish new crimes merely revive and worsen the hateful old tribulations. With every wrong step they take, they walk nearer and nearer to that calamity. What their befooled minds do not know is that even if they pass from successful crime to successful crime, nevertheless—under karmic and evolutionary law—they will later pass from painful retribution to painful retribution.

All this can be as true of nations as of an individual. Instead of meditating on the defeat that overtook them, they actually meditate on the victory that they themselves nearly overtook. Even when punishment is catastrophic and overwhelming, the very immensity of it creates a strong egoistic passion for self-justification, leaving room for only few and faint signs of any real change of heart. Such moral declension is as low and saddening as it is too often repeated by history. Every criminal nation which is at all curable must be brought to understand the moral degradation into which it fell when it blindly followed a path of pillage or violence. They learn little, understand little, and take to themselves few lessons from experience. They suffer, but their suffering is misread and misinterpreted. Here, for those who still doubt the truth of reincarnation, is one more argument in its favour. No single lifetime is enough to provide the necessary range of varied experience and to bring human development to an optimum of moral perfection—not even twenty lifetimes would be enough.

All aggressive persons and antisocial criminals reveal by their attitudes that they are still children in the understanding of life. There are two schools of thought as to their treatment. They have done wrong and must be punished. They have done wrong but must be forgiven. To state the problem in either of these drastic ways alone and let it go at that is dangerously to oversimplify its complications and difficulties, nay, is indeed misleading. For both these statements are true yet are so only in their own places. The first, presented by the cynics, advocates rigorous punishment. The second, presented mostly by the religious idealists, advocates a complete forgive-and-forget policy. The first is sadistic, the second sentimental. Both are unwise. Philosophy avoids such extremes and finds a sensible middle way between them. It says we must not push the criminal farther down the road of wrong-doing by evoking his spirit of revenge through unduly harsh treatment. Yet we must not let him walk down it of his own accord by letting him believe that wrong-doing brings no retribution at all.

A merely sentimental view of this problem will not really help us or them. A thoroughly psychological view will not only save us from further depredations but also save them from falling again into their own worst self. A misplaced adherence to emotional upsurges will, however, prevent us from correctly perceiving the true facts of this complex problem. It is the dictate of wisdom that we shall not forget, but it is also the dictate of compassion that we shall forgive. Little sectarian minds can only oppose these two as antitheses, whereas large philosophic minds can hold them harmoniously together. There is some confused thinking in the minds of pious people about the question of forgiveness. Criminal aggressors—whether they be single individuals or whole nations—need to be punished as much for their own moral benefit as for the physical protection of society. If through sentimental emotion they are left unpunished, then we render them a disservice. For they will fail to learn the age-old lesson that crime does not pay. Not that they will really escape from the inevitable come-back of karma, but when perpetration of crime is swiftly followed by proportionate punishment, the moral lesson involved is brought home to the wakeful consciousness much more effectively than when the same lesson is brought home to the subconscious at a later period or in another birth. There are times when a naughty child asks for and deserves spanking. Just as we do not hate a child even when performing such punitive operation, we ought not to hate the erring criminals who have put their energies into wrong channels even when we are restraining or punishing them. It should be done in the spirit of education, impersonally, calmly, without hatred, but with firm inflexible determination to teach them the lesson of their own experiences—the truth that barbarity does not pay. There are brutes in human shape. That all the links between the baboon and men have not been lost is plainly proved by the very existence of these creatures. They will respond only to a language which they can understand: disciplinary punishment, firm repression. Their twisted minds must be surgically operated on, which means that they must be made to feel something of the pain which they made others suffer. Therefore those who through false sentimentality or wrong religion would here use kindness make a profound mistake.

But, object some religious and most mystical persons, ought we not to show mercy? Ought we not to forgive a sinner? Yes, we ought to forgive because we should comprehend that he sins through ignorance of life's unwritten laws. But the scriptural injunction to forgive enemies is often misconstrued. We ought to show mercy and forgive sinners but we should do the one at the right time and the other to the right person. Otherwise, we merely misplace these virtues and thus convert them into vices. It *is* our duty to practise compassion but it is *not* our duty to misplace it. We should show mercy only when there are signs of real repentance for having perpetrated the crime and in proportion to the actual degree of such repentance. For example, those who commit murder commit the greatest of crimes. They must make the greatest of repentances. They must turn themselves into penitents, sincerely disavowing their past evil and convincingly demonstrating their change of heart by tangible proofs.

When we witness the return to life of a criminal's sleeping conscience, the remorseful recognition of wrong-doing, and the honest admission of guilt, when he expresses genuine sorrow over his crimes and shows forth sincere repentance, it will be right and proper to treat him mercifully and forgivingly. In the moment when he truly repents, to our joy and his profit, in that same moment we must extend forgiveness and help him start a fresh and better life. But those other individuals who do not do any of these things, who merely smart with resentment and thirst for revenge, their treatment must be stern and punitive. Unless and until they do repent thoroughly, wise justice has no option but to treat them firmly. This treatment is helpful to their purification. A sentimental neglect to administer this tart medicine will only morally harm them in the end, let alone expose the world to a repetition of their crime.

The guilty must learn that everything has to be paid for. But the dearness or cheapness of the price they must pay should depend partly upon the measure of spontaneous repentance and amendment which they themselves bring forth. For there is always the divine message which, if they will tardily heed and obey it, can mitigate their unhappy lot. And that message says, "Repent, and be redeemed!" But repentance must run deep, into open deeds and secret thoughts, if it is to be karmically effective. Its reality must be proved by abundant evidence. The criminals have to pay today for what they have done yesterday. But if they have acknowledged their error, if they are genuinely remorseful, repentant in heart and mind and deed, if they strive spontaneously to make what amendment for the past it is still possible to make, then in that case new karma will manifest itself side by side with the old and thus modify their miseries. For although it is true that part of their future already exists even now, owing to karmic causes which they themselves set going, it is equally true that until the events of that future crystallize into the space-time world they are always liable to be modified by any fresh karmic causes which are introduced into their own domain.

How many can take this essential step of a moral about-turn? Can we awaken a criminal in jail to a sense of his personal failure and moral shame? Because he has suffered the humiliation of retribution, there is always the probability of comprehending that there is a better way. And because he is a human being, there is always the possibility of ethical recovery and moral improvement. Those who believe that they can solve such a problem as criminality on a merely practical basis alone are wrong. Experience will teach them that it is inseparable from a moral one, too. For if the criminal really repents, then our duty is to forgive him. A moral shift on his part should lead to a practical shift on ours.

We may forgive criminals and yet punish them for wrong-doing, if that be our duty, or place them under such external limitations as will prevent their further wrong-doing, if that also be our duty. The two are not contradictory. If we keep our hearts unpolluted by hatred, we may keep our hands sternly and firmly on the wrong-doer. This is included in what the *Bhagavad Gita* means when it defines the higher yoga as being "the skilful performance of action." The skilfulness here meant is obviously not the technical kind but rather the mystical power to remain inwardly detached whilst doing worldly duty. During the war, it became necessary for philosophic students to learn how to fight a cruel aggressor in the right spirit; they had paradoxically to learn how to deliver without anger or hate hard blows against him whilst feeling profound pity for his moral darkness.

But philosophic students are few. It is useless to ask humanity in its present state of evolution to behave on this high plane. A sage (and perhaps those who try to follow him) would not find it difficult to extend his compassionate goodwill to all criminals—indeed he would find it difficult not to—but it would be too much to expect that everybody else is capable of extending it.

430

An alternative to physical punishment, such as flogging, for brutal crimes of violence would be to put the criminal upon a semi-starvation diet. His bodily weakness would then affect his mental aggressiveness, would reduce and counter it.

431

If capital punishment is the law, at least change the method to withholding of food until death by starvation.

Pacifism: general, non-nuclear ethic

432

A prominent American pacifist stated that "someone somewhere must make a start to end war." This is true and laudable and certainly a needed reminder to mankind of its higher goal, but the problem involved in the current world crisis is not solved as simply as that. Just as in philosophic practice the ultimate view has to be coupled with the immediate one, so here with human nature in its present stage of evolvement, the recognition of the basic difference between a just and an unjust war must be given.

433

A philosopher is a pacifist in the sense that he does not practise violence against other living creatures. But he is not an uncompromising pacifist. He does not consider the use of arms wrong in all circumstances. A situation can be imagined where it would be wiser and, in the end, kinder to use force deliberately. Yet the general fact remains that the history of warfare is a history of the manifestation of man's lower nature, his bestial nature, and his evil nature. As he grows spiritually he will organize more and more for peace, less and less for war.

434

He allows other creatures the right to live, even to the point of eating no meat, but if they encroach on his own right, and endanger his own survival, then he will defend himself as resolutely as other men. Nor is the situation changed if these creatures are not animal but human. Pacifism is useful as a protest against human proneness to resort to violence, so he sympathizes with it in specific cases. But its usefulness ends when unscrupulous aggression seeks to triumph and needs the education of defeat.

435

The pacifist movements naturally attract intellectuals and artists, ministers of religion and humanitarians. But they also attract the sinister and subversive elements who try to direct, guide, or secretly control them, to make them serve their own antisocial destructive purposes. The presence and prominence of genuine idealists along with these pretended ones create confusion in the public mind. How can a movement be bad which is supported by such good men? That they are being used as a cover for the activities of bad men who spread falsehood and preach hatred is not so easily seen.

436

The classic objection which was so often thrown at Gandhi, is still a sound one. "Would you stand by, in your adherence to the ethic of nonviolence, and allow your wife, mother, or sister to be raped without lifting an arm to protect her?" The man who pushes the nonviolent attitude so far that he will not even help save the victim of such an attack, is a doctrinaire, the victim of his own misapplied fanaticism. Nature (God) can be very violent at times: it is not always peaceful.

437

On the mystical level, all war is evil and all pacifism is good. On the philosophical level, the universality of this rule vanishes. We there rise from a judgement based on pure feeling to a judgement based on its integration by intuition with pure reason, the result of which is intelligence.

438

If pacifism is to mean the acceptance of evil then it cannot be enough.

439

Gandhi's advice to the young man that he should still practise absolute non-violence if someone attacked his sister, is not perfect. He would better have advised the use of force unless the young man were so developed that he could successfully defend her without it and unless the assailant were so sensitive that non-violence would bring out a response in him. In other words, the pacifist principle should certainly be applied in every case where it is likely to be effective but refrained from where it is likely to fail. It is not a principle of universal applicability.

440

Men whose temperament is naturally given to violence in speech or deed, or those who always stir up agitation, extremism, irreconcilation, and intransigence, must be firmly and unflinchingly ruled. Weakness would be folly.

441

The whole history of Europe during the past fifty years could have been changed had pacifism not been misapplied. After Lenin seized power in Russia the leader of the Socialist Revolutionary Party, which not only had a majority in the Constituent Assembly but controlled more regiments than the Bolsheviks, refused to put up any resistance. He said, "Russian blood must not be shed." *If strong action had been taken then Lenin could have been thrown out and the loss of freedom in so many countries—half the world—prevented from happening.*

442

It may be asked why the counsel to practise nonviolence was ever given at all by saints and prophets. Obviously it is ethically the highest instance of forgiveness and the most effective way of transcending the ego practically.

443

The proper course is to try kindly reasonable and nonviolent methods of resisting aggression. If they fail then forceful ones become the only alternative. But they should not blur the goodwill which must be felt towards all men, including enemies.

444

The mistake made is to be solely dependent on violent methods, when gentler ones would achieve the same end without letting in the poison of hate and without creating so much new misery.

445

That country is truly civilized where the killing instinct is held in abeyance and regarded with abhorrence.

Pacifism in light of nuclear threat

446

With the world as it is and in mankind's present evolutionary condition, it would be imprudent to reject violence at all times and during all events. But to reject the violence of nuclear weapons would be the highest prudence.

447

In earlier eras the duty of armed resistance to armed aggression was both a practical and moral one. In the present era changed conditions require a revision of this duty.

448

The evil passions of men produce wars which, in this nuclear age, can end only in destroying both sides alike. Therefore for rulers even to talk of the possibility of taking part in such war today is sheer madness.

449

The threat of nuclear bombing has created a situation so entirely new that the old ideas about defense have to be scrapped. Formerly it was logical and morally right to meet violence with violence, but now it is suicidal and morally wrong to do so.

450

In the past, international aggression accompanied by force had to be met by national defense accompanied by force. The resultant war was, unhappily, inescapable. It was bad, but it was better than surrendering to evil. In the present, this is no longer true. The use of nuclear forces in war is a completely immoral act. It is so not only because the scale on which it annihilates men, women, and children alike is unheard of, but also because the aftermath which succeeds it will be so savage as to be worse than the communism or capitalism such a war sets out to destroy. The means used being wrong, the end result will be equally wrong, besides being unwanted and perhaps unexpected.

451

What the Bomb has done is to show up war for the evil thing that it is. Are its warnings to pass unheeded simply because we do not wish to be troubled by such sombre morbid thoughts?

452

The greatest value of the atomic bomb, after its compulsory prevention of war, is its compulsory abolition of frontiers. It renders them meaningless. It makes a world authority inevitable. It renders a merely international league insufficient. Only a world federation and world authority will suffice to meet it. With this change in media, all military manuals became obsolete overnight. What gunpowder did to the bow and arrow, atomic bombs have done to gunpowder. The political struggle to secure strategic frontiers has now lost all meaning. For there are none.

453

We are told that adequate means of defense must be maintained, else the evil powers arraigned against us will overwhelm the liberties, the justice, the religion, the decencies we hold dear. We are told further that the policy of unilateral nuclear renunciation is a policy of surrender to those powers. The answer is that those who support the traditional way of defending those liberties—the military way—are today the real enemies, since the traditional way will lead inescapably to war, which in turn will lead to their total destruction, and our partial destruction. Those who claim that the next war will not necessarily be a nuclear one, talk like fools. When such power is within the reach of men, they will act like human beings, with all the weakness of human beings to resist great temptation, to grasp it. If it is not rejected now, in the calmer atmosphere of peace, it will certainly not be rejected later in the tenser atmosphere of war. If the unilateral policy is not accepted now, the penalty will inevitably follow.

454

War is no longer the same. The revolution which has taken place in it is so absolute that it has not merely destroyed an old form of war, but war itself. That which will take its place is the murder of half of mankind and the suicide of the murderers.

455

The weapons of physical warfare are also the symbols of man's hates or greeds, suspicions or fears. So far as the first of these negative emotions is concerned, Buddha neatly put the point: "Hatred ceaseth not by hatred; it ceaseth only by love." This lesson of two world wars must be extracted, and extracted quickly, if a third world war is to be avoided. And in the face of atomic extinction, the practice of nonviolent pacifism, which is the outer expression of love, is not mere sentimentality but the highest rationality and practicality.

456

The nonviolent way to bring peace to the world is today the only way even though in the pre-atomic age it may not have been. For under this menace of nuclear weapons war cannot be prevented, nor peace attained and maintained, by the traditional arms race.

457

Is it practical and realistic to turn this earth into a gigantic incinerator? Yet that is just what those leaders who insist on making and piling up atom bombs are doing. Nothing could be more practical than throwing all those satanic bombs away—if in the meaning of practicality we are to include actions which promote our survival.

458

The practice of nonviolent pacifism at this juncture of history where the menace of atomic warfare is so unprecedented, is not mere surrender. It is a new way of fighting which uses spiritual weapons instead of physical ones. But whereas atomic warfare would destroy both antagonists and bring barbarism, this new way will save both. It will save their lives and their civilizations. More, it will give a tremendous spiritual boost to the side which tries it first and ultimately give some uplift to the other side too.

459

In renouncing war for such reasons we do not necessarily renounce evil for good. We simply choose between evils and abandon what has now become the greater evil for a lesser.

460

So long as this enormous distrust of each other remains, so long will the desire for disarmament on both sides fail of realization. There is no likelihood that it will not continue to remain. Therefore if this failure is ever to be brought to an end, what cannot be reached by both sides agreeing together must be reached by one side acting alone. That is, the goal of full disarmament can only be reached by stages, and this is the first stage. It has some unsatisfactory and disconcerting features, it raises new doubts and fears, but all that is outweighed by the enormous gain of preventing a nuclear war.

461

We are confronted by the power of evil in formidable array and menacing guise. We cannot ignore it for it forces itself aggressively into our lives. We may not, without being untrue to our ideals, respond to its crude and cruel emotional and intellectual attacks with the same weapons, with hatred, greed, contention, with the rejection of God, morality, and truth. This we admit. But to its threats of physical attack we consider ourselves entitled to use the same physical weapons. We refuse to let ourselves be dragged down to evil's own low plane inwardly but we are willing to let ourselves be dragged down outwardly. Why this difference? If the one is wrong, the other is also wrong. A sharp logic requires us to hold firm heroically in nonviolence, and not to copy the ways and weapons of our antagonists.

462

If the course suggested here offers great risks, as it does, it is justified by the incontestable fact that to hold inflexibly to the old one offers immeasurably greater risks of spilling death upon us all. The pattern of fighting in war has been followed since history began. It is a familiar one and was safe enough to follow in the past, for both antagonists survived. But now in this nuclear age, it has lost its safety, for both know that they are unlikely to survive a nuclear war. A new and unfamiliar pattern is needed and must be created, and that quickly. Time is running out.

463

The alternative choices are both evil, but not equally evil. Either we disarm and seek peace on the best obtainable terms—no matter how crushing they may be—or we continue the nuclear armaments race until it eventually and inevitably ends in nuclear war. Under the first choice we may find ourselves—if the worst happens—in a situation hardly short of virtual surrender. Its consequences may include atheistic education for the young and the disappearance of all that is fine in our civilization. But it would continue to survive and after some time reciprocal influences would begin to appear. Under the second choice, in fighting to defend our way of life by atomic weapons, we would be using an evil means to attain a good end.

464

There will be risks either way, so why not take the risk of peace rather than of war?

465

History will continue to repeat itself so long as men believe that force and violence are the only ways of achieving security, so long as no nation has the moral courage to apply spiritual truth.

466

In one sense our time is a challenge to change old ways of thinking about war. It is a time to draw on spiritual resources until we see it in a new light, a spiritual light, which should induce us to banish it once and for all. It is a chance to avert calamity and create opportunity. There is no escape. If we do not rise to the new requirement, much of our civilization will be eclipsed and most of us will vanish from the scene.

467

Since war can no longer serve as a useful instrument of either attack or defense, it should be dropped from all thinking and planning for the future, regardless of what other nations do.

468

Is mankind to be condemned forever to murder on a national scale, is war to become an eternal state of affairs? Or will some nation be heroic enough, wise enough, to break the vicious circle?

469

The saying, "War is not so burdensome as slavery," was correct but only pertinent to all eras prior to the present one.

470

The first nation which will dare to apply this truth to its own affairs and relationships will draw a dividing line through the world's history. It may have to suffer although not in the same way, nor to the same extreme extent, as did Telemachus, who was stoned to death in Rome's Arena but accomplished his mission of putting an end forever to combats between man and beast. But this nation will prove that the vicious circle of war unending can be broken, that bloody combat of people against people can end.

471

If pacific and nonviolent methods will fail to produce, in most circumstances, any immediate successful result, they cannot fail in the long run, if patiently practised, to impress the adversary by their example—hitherto unknown to and unconceived by him.

472

Nuclear war is immoral. This alone is sufficient for one side to refuse to engage in it, whether or not the other side takes advantage of such refusal.

473

In the absence of an impartial and effectual world-authority, the only alternative to war as a means of settling disputes is renunciation of the right to kill.

474

Man has been forced against a wall built from the results of his own actions, that is, karma, and made to face two alternatives: either he goes on preparing defensively or aggressively for war or starts the new course of preparing for peace.

475

The remedy is simple to formulate, although political and military leaders who find it unpalatable will assert that its result would be worse than war. It is this: cease manufacturing both atomic bombs and other atomic weapons; cease using the atom for military purposes in any way. This may seem startlingly unrealistic but it is the only way to escape an otherwise inevitable fate, too terrible to describe even in outline.

476

What Napoleon, Tamerlane, Genghis Khan, the Caesars, and all the aggressive warrior-rulers known to history combined could not kill during their entire lifetimes, can be killed in less than a minute by the weapons of twentieth-century man.

477

The only way to put an end to any possibility of atomic conflict is to put an end to atomic weapons. It is as simple as that.

478

The way of disarmament may fail to be accepted but it is the only way open to us that could avert war, within the very limited time available.

479

What is the opposing quality to the violence of today? Not merely nonviolence—a negative one—but gentleness—a positive one.(P)

480

Is the true patriot only the man who puts his faith in brute force, harsh violence, and tragic destruction? Is there no love of country in gentler ways? I venture the claim that the man who keeps himself above war passions, who seeks and finds the Overself's inner peace and then distributes it in his country's mental atmosphere, is worth more to the State than the man who places his reliance on murderous weapons.

481

What Gandhi did for India we need someone to do for the whole world. The freedom from colonial status which he achieved by nonviolent means is a small thing compared with the freedom from the menace of atomic warfare which must be achieved if civilization is to continue.

482

The problem of our proper reaction to war is a difficult one. The duty of defending ourselves against, or rescuing the victims of, a murderous assault seems to be a moral one and just as applicable to an international scale as to an individual one. It seems right and reasonable to believe that open aggression should be resisted and even, to a certain extent, punished.

But with the advent of the atomic and hydrogen bombs the method of fighting for any cause, even a righteous one, has become the greater of two evils where formerly it was the lesser. Where self-defense may lead to certain and suicidal self-destruction, we begin to pause, to consider, and to hesitate.

Any investigation of the destiny of nations from a philosophic point of view shows that the appearance of an aggressive invader on a people's borders must have some underlying karmic cause deeper than the obvious political or economic one. Just as the appearance of a certain unpleasant event in an individual's life is often due to corresponding faults or weaknesses in him which need to be remedied, so the invader's appearance points to deficiencies or errors in the invaded nation's inner life. They too need correction. There is no escape from this inner duty, and so long as the weaknesses remain so long will troubles appear or assaults threaten.

Until the nations achieve this moral development, they can hope only to restrict the violence and area of war, not to eradicate it. Such a restriction can be brought about by external means only by an international policing army, just as society's crime is restricted by local police. This single army to replace the many armies implies some kind of a world government. Yet national feelings are everywhere still unwilling to sacrifice themselves to a supernational government, and there is some ground for the refusal. There is no other prospect of its arrival than through a third world war, whose aftermath would unquestionably be the birth of a world government to control international relations, leaving the separate peoples free to pursue their own policies in regard to internal ones. This is the only alternative path to peace, terrible though it be.

Meanwhile what is the duty of the spiritually awakened individual, as apart from the unawakened nations? Has the time come for him to practise a new approach? Does the old one of meeting violence with violence belong to the animal world? Then what is the new one which belongs to the human world? Must he cease to take life, withdraw from this course of endless slaughter, and seek protection from the higher powers by offering up even the will to live itself if needs be? The individual alone can test the truth and worth of this newer moral concept. For support of it offers no early likelihood of attaining sufficient strength as a political power. Philosophy can give no lead in the matter. The decision is a personal one. Each must decide for himself.

Constructive alternatives: individual

483

There are positive and negative forces in the world and therefore in human beings. If a person cannot eliminate his negative qualities (and most people find it almost impossible), he can, however, bring them into a neutral point and thus establish a state of equilibrium or balance.

484

Living in a society where there is so much folly and ignorance, evil and unbalance, he must protect himself mentally, emotionally, physically, and even psychically.

485

In a world seething with negative thoughts, murky in several areas with suspicion and even hatred, inflamed with violent feelings, he who knows the truth must hold all the more to inner and outer calm, to goodwill and faith in the Overself's presence.

486

Evil is strong in the world and sometimes people who aspire to the good become discouraged and depressed. It is at such moments that they need to recall whatever glimpses of the Real they have had and to remember that all things pass away, including the evil.

487

We live in apocalyptic times, as history is already revealing. The call today is a penitential one, a solemn recall from earthliness to holiness, from frivolousness, grossness, and madness to remembrance of life's higher purpose. Those who feel in their own hearts some sort of a response, however feeble, should cling to this precious intuition and let it guide them until they are saved.

488

The failure to persuade either the masses or their leaders to change their way of life and thought is not a reason for abandoning either the inner or outer work as useless. Even though any marked and visible result may not now appear, it may yet do so at a later date. We must have a moral concern which instigates acts aiming at conversion or makes proposals even if they will obviously fail.

489

Questions about man's future and civilization's prospects trouble us. More pessimistic answers are gloomily given than optimistic ones. It is not easy to do otherwise, when the facts are so tragically plain and when they lie so plentifully all around us. Philosophy least of all can afford wishful thinking. It too sees the night falling but whilst counselling stoic resignation it does not discourage constructive resistance. And it reminds the individual that society's catastrophes should urge him all the more to seek and find the one necessary refuge—his own sacredness.

490

If anyone wants to see a better world he must make his contribution toward it. And this demands inexorably that he begin with himself and make his character and conduct better.

491

The prudent man learns by observation or by experience, or more often by both, that there is spiritual ignorance in the world and in man: he must often conceal the greater portion of his wisdom and his power. This is necessary for his own protection and security. It was a similar caution and desire for personal safety which induced the writers of ancient Hindu texts and medieval Italian ones to advise those who lived under a brutal tyranny to emigrate. This did not mean going to a new country but to a new district.

492

There is not much that an individual can do in time of great general catastrophe, such as the mass horror of war. But even then, the hope and faith of an existence higher than the present one is not without its value. At such times one must lean back, draw a deep breath, and remark as Abraham Lincoln did during the blackest hours of the U.S. Civil War: "This too will pass."

493

The coming of war brings its own anxieties. This is when he has to draw upon his spiritual knowledge to get the strength and courage to endure bravely special trials and tribulations. It is only at such times of crisis that all higher interests get the chance to prove their solid worth, for without their inner support and some kind of understanding of what it all means, life becomes most inhumanly alarming. He may have found glimpses of inner peace from time to time and now he has to insert these into his external life and try to stretch them out through constant remembrance of the Real. Such frequent communion and intelligent remembrance can give him the strength to go on, the peace to put up with frustrations, doubts, and fears, and faith in what is still beyond his conscious knowledge, the satisfaction that the years are not being wasted. All other duties become better fulfilled when he fulfils this supreme duty of realizing the ever-present reality within the heart. Indeed they cannot be separated from it for through them Reality can express itself.

494

It is not palatable to hold the thought that humanity is so bad, or else its rulers so misguided, that little or nothing can be done to save it. Yet if it happens to be a true thought, we ought to be strong enough to accept it and acknowledge that there are times when such a defeatist outlook is justified and necessary.

495

It does not usually pay to be pessimistic but that need not prevent our facing unpalatable facts.

496

The evil he has no opportunity to fight in the larger world outside, he has every opportunity to fight in the smaller world inside his own person.

497

With destruction awaiting modern civilization, it is useless to look for a safer refuge than in finding the peace and strength of the Overself. For if we do that, we shall also be led by it to do what may be physically needful too.

498

If greater knowledge brings greater power, it also brings greater responsibility. The more he receives from the Overself's grace, the more should he give to humanity's need.

499

With so many people in the world today whose outlook is negative, whose emotions are twisted and thinking is warped, it is more needful to stand firm in one's own spot of positive thinking than ever.

500

Whoever doubts the truth of this message, thereby deprives himself of its benefits. But this is equally true of the believer who fears its truth. If the future holds distress and suffering, blows and disasters, it is to be met with courage sought and asked from the higher self. According to our faith, it will be given us.

501

It is not a question of what we like or prefer or believe. It is a question of accepting quietly, or else defying vainly, the course of events and the trend of destiny.

502

If catastrophe and obliteration threaten humanity and if the individual is hopeless when confronted by them, it is logical to conclude that although humanity might not be able to save itself, the individual can save himself from these disasters if he believes that inner salvation is at least a possibility where outer salvation is not. Yes, you and I can save ourselves from within even when we cannot save ourselves from without. That at least is a better lot than the one of the man who can save himself neither from within nor from without and puts his faith in political action alone. For politics is merely a system of human bargaining actuated by self-seeking. It can invoke the aid of no higher power because it does not rise higher than this self-seeking interest itself. But the individual is free to lift himself above this sordid plane and therefore he is in a position to invite the attention and aid of higher powers.

503

He who consciously inhabits reality will live independent of the mutations of fate, the catastrophes of history, and the crises of an epoch in dissolution. Even in crisis of war, where danger or even death is lurking, philosophy reveals its immense practicability. For the philosopher can meet them with the utter calmness, effective capacity, and resolute heroism with which his studies, reflections, disciplines, and ideals have formed his character. Amid the surging tides of postwar chaos he sets the example and shows the value of philosophic discipline and the power of philosophic principles by standing firm as a rock. Just as he kept cool in the very midst of global conflagration, so he now keeps clear-sighted amid the gloom of its dusty aftermath. In the very midst of world confusion, he becomes a little oasis of strength and peace, wisdom and certitude, calm and holiness. If he has to live in a chaotic disordered environment, the sad heritage of war, he still lives his own constructive ordered pattern of existence. The very example of such a man keeping steady and balanced thus silently helps some others who are bewildered or aimless.

4

IN THOUGHTS, FEELINGS,
VIOLENT PASSIONS

Their presence

There is too much criticism abroad today, too little affirmation. Millions of men think and live largely on negatives.

2

It is because all humanity is approaching the threshold of a new era, a better era, that all the devils of the old era put forth their fiercest efforts, whilst there is yet a little time, to degrade human character, to drag it down into the hells of the worst forces and emotions—hate, envy, aggressiveness, and brutality.

3

If there is physical pollution in the atmosphere, the water, and the earth, there is another kind in humans, a moral depravity and mental baseness not less repellent.

4

If there is so much friction, violence, and tension in the world, it is only because so many individual persons themselves are inwardly experiencing these things. They fill the world's aura with bad thoughts which, if sustained, prolonged, and strong enough, break out on the physical level into undesirable or evil happenings. If there is so little real peace in the world, it is only because there is so little real peace in the individuals who live in the world. Their thinking, their emotions, and their passions have affected the mental atmosphere of the world.

5

The most violent selfish passions and the most aggressive of emotional urges abound in this decade only because they have been brought up to the surface the better to attack and curb them.

6

Just as association with a master throws the disciple's virtues and vices to the surface, so contact with the higher forces being released in the world brings both great evil and great spirituality to the surface. The evil, in the disciple's as in humanity's case, must manifest itself so that it may not lurk untouched but may be got at, grappled with, and eventually destroyed. Let us not misunderstand appearances, therefore. Since last century, things have been getting worse only to get better. Today most people feel frustrated, restless, and discontented. They search for happiness here and there, in this thing or that thing, through one person or another, or by moving from excitement to sensation. All this is their unconscious reaction to the new spiritual forces arising in their midst and destined to be vigorously active in a couple of hundred years.

7

Today humanity has largely lost faith in itself, doubts its goodness, worries about its future, and is bewildered about its present.

8

Compulsive fears and corrosive anxieties, enfeebling doubts and neurotic complexes trouble the minds of so many millions in our age, as thwarted hopes and enchaining environments depress their hearts.

9

Idealism presses them to become servants of Good; passion distorted into destructive violence deceives them into becoming servants of Evil.

10

The thoughts which have gestated unspoken in men's minds and the feelings which have fermented unexpressed in their hearts have been and are being thrown up to the surface through the upheavals of our times, externalized, as it were, in their events.

11

Humanity did not come into its present grievous situation by chance. The whole picture of thoughts and their consequences, passions and their evils, acts and their effects, must be seen under the light of immutable karmic law.

12

The policy of fear and suspicion has not brought peace nearer; but, on the contrary, pushed it farther away.

13

We live in a world which, today, is populated with too many madmen, too many unbalanced maladjusted persons. But because they are not actually raving and jumping so as easily to be identified for what they are, this is seldom understood.

14

Racial antipathy leading to actual violence is not limited to man, although it is only the less evolved humans who resort to it. In the tropics one sees black ants fighting the red ones, mutilating and even killing each other.

15

This is the final tragedy of Man: that he lets himself go along with destructive forces which in the end could gravely injure the whole species, when he could go along with the constructive ones.

16

This fleshly body, in which we live and move and have our being, has, through sex and sport, become a cult to the modern world. We fall in our millions, prostrate votaries at its shrine, forgetful that its quick growth is followed by quick decay, that our idol is doomed to crumble. Too many moments of highest enthusiasm on the part of youth are often reserved for the new religion—sport. A whole theology has been built up around the strokes of a bat and the throws of a ball; hard hitters are now canonized as saints. He who throws his ball far enough may yet send himself, with it, to the new heavenly Jerusalem! And as for sex, the passions and emotions of the young are deliberately stimulated by the arts of literature, journalism, cinema, and advertising just at the age when they ought to be disciplined.

17

How little men collectively learn from the past is shown by every textbook of history, which teems with constant repetitions of the ugliest passions.

18

The world-wide condition of the human mass, its hates, ignorance, and violence, brings despair to many a thoughtful mind.

19

Violence is a destructive force which in the end and when excessive destroys even itself.

20

Among the negative emotions we must include prejudice and bias.

21

The negative emotions include arrogance and vanity, cowardice and moral weakness.

22

All the negative thoughts and feelings show a misuse of mental power.

23

Temptations and beguilements, illusions and deceptions, beset the path of ordinary life just as they do the inner life of the quest. But in the latter case they may also assume a subtler form. Here there are telepathic, psychic, spiritualistic, and neurotic possibilities.

24

There are times when a person is more vulnerable to attack by negative thought than at other times. In great emotional excitement, anger, or passion of any kind, we are most susceptible.

25

The symptoms of neuroticism have been well analysed by psychiatrists. They all sum up to a single thing: intensity of egoistic emotion. This is disturbing to the mental balance of the neurotic person and tiring to those who have contact with him.

26

The negative thoughts and feelings include: excessive or constant criticism, pride, and conceit.

27

Pride may prevent the self-confession of a shortcoming or a blunder. Thus it does the ego's dark work.

28

The inhuman and destructive attitudes, unsympathetic and unpitying, are a sign of the evil presence at work in our midst.

29

While men seem permanently estranged from their spiritual selves, we need not wonder at the despair and hopelessness, the cynicism and selfishness, which enter into the moods of so many people today.

30

Ignorance breeds violence and violence in its turn breeds further violence.

31

If our desires choke the inner peace which might be ours during times of prosperity, our fears choke it during times of adversity.

32

There are men who are in a cycle of going down deeper into selfishness, illusion, spiritual ignorance, and extroversion. They have yet to touch the bottom of this descent, a contact which many older egos have also made before, but long ago left for the upward climb. Although the redemptive return of these unseeing entities is assured, for they cannot eternally and ultimately deny their own inmost nature, nevertheless they will respond to the blackest evil during the present phase of their descent. They are called "the Asuras" in the *Bhagavad Gita*, "the men of hatred, greed, and lust."

33

Lost religious faith is one link in a chain of which degraded morals is the next.

34

The hopelessness which mankind's situation naturally leads to is not less divinely-intended than any other effect of destiny's turn.

35

Many people in Europe must feel they have no future to live for and only an apathetic present in which just to exist, not live. Since God permits this, evidently God perceives its value in the evolutionary scheme.

36

Yes, there is odious evil in the world—much of it petty but some of it quite monstrous. It takes its genesis in the thoughts of men.(P)

37

Mentalism says that most of one's misery is inflicted on oneself by accepting and holding negative thoughts. They cover and hide the still centre of one's being, which is infinite happiness.(P)

38

Whereas all the great prophets like Jesus and Krishna make a religion out of love, the demonists make a religion out of hatred.

39

Those who constantly indulge in savage criticism of persons or principles, who are saturated with negative thoughts and feelings, have never seen the Light nor felt its peace.

40

There is something in the old Zoroastrian doctrines after all. Ormuzd and Ahriman are ever at war for the world: Stupidity and Wisdom are ever struggling in battle. Every great truth has to fight its way anew. Enemies are obstinate and entrenched, while the memory of man is weak.

41

The mind's power is being unscrupulously misused when it seeks to influence others against their own interest and for its selfish purpose.

42

Where there is fierce hatred or monstrous cruelty, be sure that evil forces are present too.

43

You may dispense to others only what you have yourself. If your mind is steeped in nihilism, it will be despair which you offer them at worst, or selfish cynicism at best.

44

Men who are otherwise capable of correct judgement and sane conduct, as in their business activity, will reveal a paranoid imagination or pernicious delusion when racial, class, religious, or aesthetic prejudice gets into their head or eyes.

45

The use of blood in animal sacrifices is a legacy from Atlantean sorcery. It is evil, and found only among peoples who have not attained the refinement of consciousness and development of conscience which accompany a higher conception of God.

46

The terrible fact is that millions of so-called sane men and women are so unbalanced, so hysterical, and so obsessed, that they are really half insane. They are dangerous to themselves and to society.

47

The average person who thinks he belongs to the human species, has still a long way to travel before he becomes a full member. Only half of him has become human. The rest is still an animal, in whom the killing instinct is still active enough to punctuate his history with fighting wars and his diet with eating flesh.

48

His animal ancestry has provided man with the killing instinct. His human cleverness has provided him with the most effective weapons to express that instinct. His spiritual aspiration has not evolved to the level where it should be—above the other two and restraining them.

49

There are other manifestations of this killing instinct, this lust to slay another living creature. We see it in the child who tears wings off a fly.

50

Brutality and cruelty are especially linked with the minds and actions of those persons swayed by evil forces, whether physical or psychical.

51

There is enough unpleasantness or evil in the world in which we have to live. We should avoid getting involved in it so far as we can. This applies to activity and also to receptivity through reading, through entertainment, and other uses of leisure.

52

When adult people begin to accept, and their young children to demand, entertainment by the daily portrayal of sadistic violence or obscenity, when those who feel outraged by this situation have become a small minority, we have to assume that decadence, bad manners, and low moral standards are triumphant.

53

The school of journalism and periodical-filling these days is preoccupied with the ego, with personality: the universal and impersonal does not attract or interest. Moreover, it is only the bestial, the negative, the petty, and the surface characteristics of the ego which hold their scribblers' attention. Prying, meddlesome, trivial gossip and pulling others to pieces is a favourite sport.

54

There *must* be censorship in an era of annually increasing crime. How many films and stage plays, books and magazines are let loose on an undisciplined world packed with detailed suggestions for immorality and criminality. This is not entertainment: it is evil. So many composed pieces are almost textbooks for the susceptible imitative young on how to start self-destructive, antisocial, selfish careers, how to yield to fleshly promptings without exercising the slightest restraint.

55

We would not allow full freedom of movement to plague-carrying rats in our kitchens and homes. Yet we allow these human carriers of mental plague the freedom to print and publish, declaim, and propagate their poisonous suggestions and negative ideas, their pornography and violence, their hates and moral subversion, their evil.(P)

56

The young worshippers of new art forms in the pop and rock world are the same ones who contributed to the ranks of drug takers and, later, hatha yoga. They need violent thrills to sustain their interest. That is, they are primarily pleasure-seekers, not spiritual seekers. They are governed by moods and impulses.

57

The romantic rubbish which fills the ears and attracts the eyes of the modern young through the communications media leads them into false pictures of the life which awaits them and so into false values.

58

When a civilization finds its pleasure in witnessing plays which explore all aspects of pornography, seeing films exploring all aspects of brutality and crime, permitting sports as cruel as fox-hunting, it has become low in morals, vulgar in taste, and self-destructive in its karma. It will fall, as Rome fell, as feudal Japan's last phase fell.

Ways of responding

59

These negative emotions are just like physical ills: they too require treatment, and are not to be left in neglect.

60

These negative thoughts have a habit of pushing themselves into his consciousness. He must just as often resolutely push them out again.

61

In every human difficulty there are two ways open to us. The common way is familiar enough: it consists in reacting egoistically and emotionally with self-centered complaint, irritability, fear, anger, despair, and so on. The uncommon way is taken by a spiritually minded few: it consists in making something good out of something bad, in reacting selflessly, calmly, constructively, and hopefully. This is the way of practical philosophy, this attempt to transform what outwardly seems so harmful into what inwardly at least must be markedly beneficent. It is a magical work. But it can only be done by deep thought, self-denial, and love. If the difficulty is regarded as both a chance to show what we can do to develop latent resources as well as a test of what we have already developed, it can be made to help us. Even if we do not succeed in changing an unfavourable environment for the better, such an approach would to some extent change ourselves for the better. We must accept, with all its tremendous implications for our past, present, and future, that we are ultimately responsible for the conditions which stamp our life. Such acceptance may help to shatter our egoism and that, even though it is painful, will be all to the good. Out of its challenge can come the most blessed change in ourselves.(P)

62

Truth twisted into service of the lower purposes or even the evil forces must be carefully inspected, analysed, and lastly corrected or rejected.

63

Whenever a strong impulse becomes uppermost and inclines him toward some deed or speech of a negative kind, he had better scrutinize its source or nature as quickly as he can.(P)

64

A young officer working on a ship wrote that he would awaken during the night and discover himself under an undesirable physical and mental condition. He seemed to be clearly in a mesmerized condition, caused by someone or something giving the powerful posthypnotic 'suggestion to wake up and obey. The remedy is to use the same technique *in reverse.* That is, practise auto-hypnosis, give the self-suggestion that on waking up there will be full consciousness and full rejection of the negative idea.

65

If he must hate something, let him hate hatred itself.(P)

66

The storms of violent passion are to be resisted as the smoothness of inner peace is to be invited.(P)

67

To keep one's temper in a single provocative situation may be easy, but to keep it consistently equable is a real feat.

68

Life is a conflict. He must not let these negative feelings take up lodgement within him longer than a single moment.

69

All mankind must awake from its materialistic apathy and cast out something of its selfishness. It is called upon to renounce its violence and meannesses, its intolerances, unkindnesses, and injustices. It must either emerge from its animal brutality or else suffer itself to be extinguished by it. It must come out from the shadows of ignorance, selfishness, and materialism. Only then will it find the sunshine of a larger life that awaits it.

70

It is not always he himself who acts in a particular way at a particular time. Impulses from lower sources or outside contacts may be strong enough to push him into deeds which are regretted afterwards. But then intuitions from higher levels or outside sources may influence him to wise choices which bless his future.

71

We must not hate those who are born of the same divine essence as ourselves but we may hate the sins they perpetrate and the evil they radiate.

72

The seeker has to contend not only with limiting environments but also with internal enemies. Apathy delays him, depression obstructs him, and loneliness frustrates him.

73

The more he becomes sensitive, intuitive, responsive to the spirit, the more he is unfolding exceptional passivity. But this puts him in peril, for he feels the negative presence too. Hence the more he must restrict his contacts until his strength is above them.

74

It is prudent to escape from a situation where there is much pressure to commit a foolish action or to make a foolish decision leading to calamitous results—and not continue to stay in it until the danger materializes.

75

One whose presence is felt to be odious, whose personality is regarded as distasteful, is better left alone.

76

He should never allow the actions or words of ignorant men to arouse in him reactions of anger, envy, or resentment.(P)

77

The years are too few and there is too much to be done—both on oneself and for oneself—to waste them in negative, resentful thought and decaying, neurotic emotion.

78

When he comes to understand its importance, he will begin to exercise some vigilance over his thoughts.

79

Resist beginnings—that is the most practical way to deal with negatives.

80

The destructive thoughts of fear and self-doubt which whine at your door, whine at the door of every man. But you can make them powerless to hurt you. For—

> There is no chance, no destiny, no fate
> Can circumvent, can hinder or control
> The firm resolve of a determined soul!

81

If the negative thought persists then he has to wrench himself away from it with the assent and use of all his being—feeling, reason, intuition.

82

His own attitude towards events holds the power to make them good or bad, whatever their nature of itself may be.

83

Those who are unable to think correctly about this tragic world situation must be pardoned, but those who refuse to think correctly about it do not deserve pardon.

84

The counsel of Jesus to "resist not evil" does not apply to other men's acts but to our own thoughts. We are to turn aside from a negative thought-habit by the simple method of substituting the opposite and positive one. We need not spend our strength resisting the thought of misery, for example. We are to substitute hope for misery, whenever the latter appears.

85

Wrong-doing will be avoided not because it is punished by the law of recompense even when it is not punished by the law of society, but because of the strong inner conviction that right-doing is its own reward, its own satisfaction.

86

The beautiful is allied to the good. If we cultivate beautiful feelings, evil ones begin to get dissolved.

87

He will not risk rebuffs by expressing his views and describing his experiences to the uncomprehending or the unsympathetic.

88

It is cowardice to refuse to face the fact that one has made a mistake and to continue following the same course because it is difficult to stop it and return to the right road. The easier way is too often the worse way, leading to trouble for one's self and others.

89

There is a limit to the extent of concessions to prejudice; we must not move beyond it.

90

Beware of those whose mind is vindictive and whose speech is venomous.

91

It is of little use to meet irrational arguments with rational statements if they are born of emotional prejudice or passionate bias.

92

The old Chinese saying that where goodwill exists agreement will not be hard to find, still remains true.

93

The crowds which delighted in the gladiator shows of ancient Rome and, to a lesser extent, those which delighted in the bullfights of modern Spain, do not seem to understand how bestial they allow themselves to become at such times. The true human being, the fully evolved man, must have the quality of pity in him if he is to be distinguished from a member of the animal species.

94

Do not attempt to fight evil with evil. Overcome it by calling on a higher power to bring out the good in you wherewith to meet it. In this way you obey Jesus' counsel, "Resist not evil."

95

Synesius (fourth century): "This would be the most extreme of ills— not to be conscious of the presence of evil. For this is the condition of those who no longer try to rise. . . . for this reason repentance is an elevating means . . . [but] both deeds and words [must] lend a helping hand."

96

A philosopher may not ignore the negative side of his or another's life: he *has* to deal with it because circumstances force him, like everyone else, to do so. But his way will be different, because he will use all his faculties and capacities: intellectual, practical, and intuitive. He will keep calm and not let passion or negative emotion carry him away. But all that done, he hands over the results to the higher power (which includes destiny). His mind must stay in That which transcends negativity, sin, evil, even if he must grapple with them.

97

Philosophy will not disregard the bad in others, and the sin in ourselves, but having seen them clearly it does not react negatively in useless condemnation. Instead, it reacts constructively in trying to realize the meaning of evil, the consequence of sin, and then proceeds to cultivate the opposite quality, the good of that particular evil—as honesty where there is dishonesty and so on.

98

We may regret the existence of these faults in others, but we may not refuse to recognize them if practical dealings are involved.(P)

99

Amid all the pessimistic reflections which the state of the world so easily induces in the thinking man, he may yet be buoyed up by the hope which the eternal verities must again and again give him, that is, the hope that the end of it all will be immeasurably better.

100

The existentialist view—so popular with so many younger people to-day—that we begin with oblivion and end with annihilation, that what comes between is either meaningless or mysterious, with no solutions to problems, no answers to questions, is a view which the tragedy and evil and catastrophe of our times tempt us to accept. But religion and philosophy release us from this despair.

101

In such critical times as these even some faith in the existence of a higher power, and some aspiration towards serving it, has protective value.

102

Trust, not tension: trust in the higher power producing serenity rather than tension; because of the pressures of life this is a great need today.

103

However dark or desperate world history may seem at times, we must always remember no one can disrupt the divine World-Idea, or spoil its manifestation, or prevent its glorious outcome.

104

Fear of the power and cunning of these evil opponents causes them to rely on obvious but ordinary human forces and weapons for protection. They forget the divine forces they could, and should in this crisis, call on—and neglect the superhuman and extraordinary.

105

To express a half-amused contempt for the intelligence of our time is not at all the same thing as to make a jaundiced indictment of it. To witness the magnificent parade of a civilization of almost unredeemed triviality is less likely to arouse bitterness in the soul and more likely to give it a good half-hour's amusement.

106

On the one hand, carried away by the idealistic enthusiasm and millennial promises of merely emotionalist cults, some believe that a spiritual teaching has only to be propagated and it will spread triumphantly everywhere. On the other hand, confronted by the formidable spectacle of a whole world plunged in ignorance, conscious that the ordinary individual can do so little to uplift it, others drift into bewildered defeatism and actually do nothing at all. But this second attitude, although much more sensible and much more justifiable than its opposite one, is not quite philosophical.

107

According to the old classical fable, we had to look for truth in the bottom of a well; today we have to look for it in the bottom of a bitter disillusionment.

108

In the dismal world conditions of today it is a paramount necessity to obtain some glimpse, however meagre, of the divine plan which is working out for all our lives. Only in this way can we co-operate with it understandingly and adequately.

109

Instead of relying on flight into the unknown and uncertain, it is better to rely on God. In the first case he may be making a false escape and duping himself, but in the second case he opens the way for true guidance in the matter.

110

With peace in the mind and harmony in the feelings, both completed by knowledge of the universal presence of divinity—who could harbour evil thoughts, hatreds, or destructive plans?

111

Every evil person who crosses our path provides an opportunity, in the injury he attempts to do us, to keep ourselves from being provoked into retaliation, anger, or resentment. If we succeed in overcoming our own feelings, we mount upward a step.

112

In a negative situation, where negative criticisms and negative emotions are rampant, other persons may try to involve him in it, or at least get him to support their attitude and endorse their criticism. But a feeling may come over him preventing him from doing so. If so, he should obey and remain silent. With time the rightness of this course will be confirmed.(P)

113

When Confucius was asked his opinion of the injunction to return good for evil, he answered, "With what then will you return good? Return good for good, but justice for evil." Is this not wiser counsel? Does not the other push goodness to an extremist position, rendering it almost ridiculous by condoning bad conduct?

114

Inner and outer difficulties are often related. What appears to be an ugly state of affairs may well be a definite attack of certain evil forces using interested human instruments. In such a situation, the individual should never practise nonresistance in any way, but, on the contrary, should fight them off as hard as he can. At the same time, he must remember that weakness in self-control can give these evil forces an opening which they might not have had otherwise. He must be on his guard if he wishes to emerge victorious in the struggle. If he does not throw off this condition, he, himself, unwittingly erects a barrier through which the divine help sent him finds it difficult to penetrate. Although the temptation to seek release at such a time through, for example, the easy way of drink is understandable, he must nevertheless remember the duty he owes to his spiritual life, to his personal interest on the relative plane, and to others.

115

Although the student must forgive those who mistreat him, he need not think that forgiveness implies he has to associate with such people thereafter. Whenever the thought of them, or their abuse, comes into his mind he must exert his willpower to drive it out, and immediately direct his thoughts toward God, or toward any inspired individual in whom he has faith.

116

Only the sage is entitled to dismiss evil and to deny its existence: all others must look it in the face, understand it, and overcome it by slow gradations.

117

It is better to keep out of the way of evil men, especially when they are in power as Buddha advised, until or unless we are driven by the necessity of circumstance or the inward voice of duty to oppose ourselves to them.

118

It is always a certainty that the practice of active goodwill directed toward those who regard him harshly will benefit his own development, while it is always a possibility that this practice may dissolve the harsh feeling against him. It is all gain and no loss. This is one part of the case for Jesus' advice to return good for evil.

119

It is a technique of this evil power to paralyse its intended victims by frightening them. If we give way to fear, we give aid to its effort. It cannot be beaten without open defiance and ready valour.

120

You must remember that you will meet with those individuals who are themselves the bearers of antagonistic forces, instruments of darkness— sometimes consciously, mostly unconsciously, people used by evil forces.

So far as possible you must avoid such people. Certainly never enter into intimate association with them, whether the relation be business or personal. If you do you will find that sooner or later some of their unfortunate karma will tumble on you and you will have to suffer with them. These people are opposed to your quest and all that it stands for, although they may talk as believers in spiritual things—indeed, they often belong to some cult or other. But they do not understand truth or live it. They cannot help you and you are not strong enough to carry them. So leave them alone. And that is not always easy, because often they are people of a kind that force themselves into your life. Sometimes you can know them by this hallmark, by this aggressive way which they try to entangle you. It may even be necessary at times to deal with such people with a firm hand, even mercilessly and relentlessly. If so, do not hesitate, but do it without any personal feeling of any kind.

121

Men who are wholly selfish, cunning, combative, ambitious, and unscrupulous represent the dark principle and become dangerous to society.

122

Sentimentality is not spirituality. It is true we give our goodwill to all mankind, and so we give it to those who are the instruments of dark forces. But that does not mean weakness or foolishness in our dealings with them. Life will teach them. Leave them alone.

123

"Brotherhood? No, be the thought far from me. They are Adam's children—alas, yes, I well remember that, and never shall forget it; this rage and sorrow. But they have gone over to the dragons; they have quitted the Father's house, and set up with the Old Serpent; till they return, how can they be brothers? They are enemies, deadly to themselves and to me and to you, till then; till then, while hope yet lasts I will treat them as brothers fallen insane."—Carlyle, *Latter-Day Pamphlets*

124

Those who have scientifically engaged in psychical research know that a psychological belt wherein a host of evil earth-bound spirits are congregated surrounds this planet. Psychical researchers are aware too that such obsessing entities become most active at night, as anyone may discover by watching the conduct of a possessed person.

125

A human being can be infested astrally with psychic vermin as he can be with physical vermin.

126
The wise man refuses to accept removable evils and avoidable sufferings.

127
If he finds himself brought by circumstances into the society of evil-minded people, the first step to self-protection should be to switch the mind instantly into remembrance of the witness-self and to keep it there throughout the period of contact. To turn inwards persistently when in the presence of such discordant persons is to nullify any harmful or disturbing effect they might otherwise have on our thoughts.(P)

128
This instant and unhesitating turning inward is also an effective method of insulating oneself against the currents of fear, despair, and weakness which misfortune often generates.

129
If the student feels evil forces have attacked him from time to time, let him pray earnestly every day for self-purification and make the sign of the cross whenever he becomes aware of their presence, at the same time invoking the help of whatever power or personage he feels inspires him most.

130
In times of terrible danger he should stick to his faith in the divine power as a protective talisman. Whenever he is in difficulty he should drop all fear and trouble temporarily from his mind and imagine himself handing them over to his higher Self, thereby surrendering himself to its will, help, and protection.

131
When there is evidence of being obsessed by a spirit-entity, the only radical cure is exorcism. Unless one has the guidance of an adept, the following is suggested: First, he should try sleeping with a green-coloured night light burning throughout the night. It should be placed not more than eighteen inches from the bed. If this fails, then an ordinary non-coloured electric bulb may be substituted, thus giving a stronger light. The inconvenience of trying to sleep with the bedroom illuminated will only exist for a few days or a few weeks and will vanish as the eyes become accustomed to the new habit. It may even be averted by covering the eyes with a black silk bandage. In addition to this, he must pray, and combine this with creative meditation, wherein he actually pictures the freed condition desired during the night. He should also pray and meditate prior to retiring.

132

One must learn to control his thoughts—deliberately driving out the memory of undesirable psychic experiences or of any individual possessing "evil powers." He should take the protective words "Lo—I AM With You Always" and repeat them to himself, trying to realize their truth and meaning.

133

The student who has got involved with sorcery or black magic must cut off every possible connection and communication with the source of evil. Then, he must destroy or get rid of any articles or writings in his possession coming from it. He must express repentance for his errors of judgment and pray for guidance in the future.

134

He needs for such psychic encounters the faith, the courage, and the knowledge which may come with time and growth. He needs such an attitude as George Fox had when, thrust into a cell haunted by the ghosts of men's murderers, he exclaimed, "I told them if all the spirits and devils in hell were there, I was over them in the power of God, and feared no such thing."

135

He who is confronted with a choice of evils must call in the help of the higher power.

136

Even trouble can be turned to self-educative uses, and some kind of benefit gained out of the experience. But this can happen more easily and more quickly only if the willingness to learn is there, and only if a corresponding surrender of self is present. It is then that so-called evil is converted to so-called good.

137

What Jesus taught nearly two thousand years ago, and what the Buddha taught nearly five hundred years before him, is still true—even more true, if that could be, for it has the proofs afforded by all history during that time: hatred cannot end by being returned, nothing will dissolve it save a generous and patient goodwill.

138

A friend who has turned against you and become an enemy can be met in a better way. Instead of getting angry or resentful for his unkind words or actions, try to turn him over benevolently to the higher power. If you succeed in entering the Stillness for a period with your last thought being such a wish for him, this will be, in the end, more effective. It will make it possible for his attitude to be modified and for your own hurt feelings to calm down. The more you *forget him in the Stillness*, the better the result will be for both of you.

139

Zoroastrian religion associates grief with the evil principle, and therefore shuns it.

140

Summon the strength to refuse to receive other people's negative opinions. Say plainly that they are certainly entitled to their views, but you would rather not discuss them and would prefer some other subject—providing it is positive.

141

Instead of hating your enemy, and meeting bombs with your bombs, his sin with your sin, try another way, Christ's way. This involves real risk, moral courage, and mental flexibility. It requires willingness to endure and suffer for what is right, a trust in spiritual principle rather than in brute power.

142

He is competent to deal with life who equips himself to deal with its darker sides as well as with its brighter ones, with its difficulties and sufferings no less than with its joys and successes.

143

We cannot ignore the spirit of our times without inviting failure, and we cannot despise it without inviting danger. We must needs face its reality.

144

Throw out negative feelings, expel resentments against other persons, and you will be a better and happier person.

145

Every negative thought about others nip at once by a smile to yourself, looking at your higher Self dealing with it.

5

THEIR VISIBLE AND
INVISIBLE HARM

At the heart of every atom of every universe there is Spirit, divine and deathless. It is for this reason that any human society based upon its denial has no future and cannot survive. As long as man exists he will need to satisfy inner hunger, to find spiritual comfort, to receive holy communion, and to hear words of eternal truth.

2

The sight of evil men rising to power over stupid or stupefied masses has brought good men to despair. But the universe has room for both. It is a school for all and the outcome of its instruction is yet to be seen.

3

It may well be that those who have banished the religious faith of childhood from their hearts and replaced it by the scientific scepticism of adulthood, followed by the political cynicism of maturity, will end by banishing hope, too. The perversity of mankind, the hypocrisy of its leaders, and the presence of materialistic society may well seem to justify it.

4

Through ignorance of destiny's laws and through weakness in his psychological being, man creates the conditions which must finally express themselves in violent conflict with his fellows.

5

Most people have failed to recognize that the forces of destiny are back of these events. Even the powerful impact of such stirring events as history has recorded in our own times has not been enough to bring about this recognition. Yet they sense their own helplessness, although they do not understand that it is the very inevitability of their karma which has made them feel this helplessness.

6

Some men radiate animosity as others radiate goodwill. The unfortunate members of the first class are victims of their own negative thinking.

7

Those of us who have been born and brought up in democratic countries like England and the USA rightly resent the idea of living under oppressive dictatorship. Yet we tend to overlook the fact that even in such countries the State is itself becoming more and more formidably dictatorial as it becomes more and more centralized. Those of us who value individuality and freedom are coming into inner conflict with it—some of us even into outer conflict.

8

Men who are scarcely sane, who are either pathological cases or in need of psychological treatment, become heroes and leaders among the young.

9

Confronted in actual firsthand experience by the terrors and errors, the tragedies and sufferings of these decades, the serious mind could lose its balance enough to declare life an unmitigated evil.

10

The disciples of Materialism say that the execution of 3000-odd persons in the French Revolution was a small price to pay for the beneficial reforms which it brought about. But only the philosopher can trace the line of connection between its hatred and violence and the Napoleonic wars which soon followed it, taking a half million French lives and hundreds of thousands wounded, mutilated, or crippled French bodies; these too must be added to the cost of hatred, the price of violence.

11

Cunning criminals and brutal plotters have found whole nations willing to follow them.

12

These sinister figures seek, and often get, key positions in politics, organized groups, etc., and from there manipulate the mass and use them as blind unwitting tools.(P)

13

When we examine the forces which are active in the heart of sick humanity today, we must report little hope for the patient's future if we are to report faithfully at all.

14

Spiritual faith is stronger in a few individuals but weaker in the great masses. The future is bright for better machines yet dark for better morals. A moral awakening and religious renewal was hoped for. That, unfortunately, is not the situation which has actually developed. Humanity has suffered but has not been prepared enough by its sufferings to let the new spirit have entry into its heart. Nothing is gained by blinking at these facts.

The end of the war did not bring that new spirit amongst mankind which is the prerequisite to a better era. The social, political, and economic structures now being erected will not succeed without it. It is a waste of time to enter any public activity which is foredoomed to defeat.

15

The disadvantage of attempting to avoid sufficient consideration of these truths and of shutting his eyes to their consequences, is that the pleasanter time thereby gained is much more than offset by the immense worsening of the climax when it does come.

16

Too many find their work boring, their careers futile, and their lives aimless. The result is spiritual torpor.

17

In other times what they sought from drink or sex, ambition or adventure, was happiness. But in these times what they seek from them is— short of killing themselves—refuge from unbearable hopelessness and fatiguing uselessness.

18

They must be uneasy whose hearts are spiritually empty but whose world is full of menace.

19

The past has become a grave of buried hopes, the present a dulled waiting for better times, and the future a bitter blankness which will not bear contemplation.

20

Just as the introduction of poisons into the human body harms it, so the introduction of unsuitable materials and forces into the earth's body will harm it too. Nature brings its own retribution to its dwellers for what they do to the planet. This applies just as much to the introduction of mental and psychical pollutions into the invisible atmosphere or aura.

21

The magnetic relationship between the two earth poles has been disturbed by the excessive amounts of radiation poured lately into space, with great weather disturbance as a result.

22

A despondent outlook can be an effective obstacle to hearing the Overself's voice.

23

History, both ancient and modern, shows that there is much evil in mankind, that its stupefying effect leads not only to an unwillingness to listen to truth and an unreadiness to understand it, but also to a hostile malignity against it expressed through vituperation and opposition.

24

Resistance to the spiritual forces and rejection of their message must lead in the end to the destructive penalties of which war, pestilence, and flood are instances.

25

"Conscious of danger in its depth, I would not preach the Law of Laws to men." Thus Buddha told his disciples of one of the reasons why he first refused to make public his discovery of ultimate truth. To whom was this danger? If to himself, he was above fear. It was to his own generation. He expressly declared, on another occasion, "I have seen these things before, yet I did not reveal them. I might have revealed it, and others would not have believed it. Now, had they not believed me, it would have been to their loss and sorrow." Buddha meant—and his meaning is further eluci-dated by other sayings—that those to whom he offers mystical truth and reject it, will bring hurt upon themselves by the very act of rejection. Such truth is accompanied by great power. It cannot be separated from its sayer. The sage doubted is the truth doubted. The sage rejected is the truth rejected. When this happens, the accompanying power—which would have blessed and helped if believed in—still affects those it touches but affects them adversely. It is like electricity, which is so useful a servant of man but so dangerous when not rightly treated, which may save life or destroy it altogether. The Prophet of an age or a continent knows these facts, as the law that brings him into birth knows it too. Consequently he appears when humanity has passed through such tremendous self-earned sufferings that the risk involved in saying the Word and thus showing them the only true way out, becomes an act of mercy by contrast.

26

When man becomes insensitive to the sacredness within himself, he is lost.

27

It is a sin to deny the Power from which his body draws its life, his mind its consciousness and intelligence, his soul its very existence. It invites punishment, which comes through being left alone with the opposing force in Nature, with its physical, intellectual, psychical and subtle forces, unguided by the intuitive and unprotected by the divine. Man then tries to live by his own light alone. He fails, stumbles, falls and suffers. This is his position today and this is why there is a world-crisis of stupendous pro-portions. This is his hour of real need. This is when he must turn, as in

Biblical history, to his true Deliverer. Every other way out except this one is closing for him.

28

Atomic Energy. What the scientists have done is to *destroy* the atom, the stuff which God made and used to make the universe. They have released destructive forces into the world and degenerative forces along with them among mankind. Even the peaceful commercial use of nuclear energy in reactor-installations brings these evils among us and the precautionary safeguards fail to overcome them.

29

Man's intellect, when not balanced by intuitive feeling and when directed by his animalistic and egoistic impulses, can only lead him to self-destruction in the end. In a total sense, this will not be permitted by the World-Mind. Therefore, its course will be hindered and he himself restrained as soon as the time is appropriate.

30

The physical starvation or privation which afflicts so many millions in Europe and Asia is deplorable but the spiritual starvation or moral degeneration which afflicts many more is really a worse evil. This idea may seem strange, even repulsive, to most people. For its truth can become evident only after carefully thinking out the causes and consequences of both situations, although it is evident in a flash to those who have enough intuitive insight.

31

There is a grimmer prospect than overpopulation. By destroying his home, man as species is destroying himself, not to mention animals and plants who will pass with him. If this planet dies a new one will be born, yes, but he will carry the moral guilt.

32

In an unsympathetic society, what is deep in a man's heart may be deliberately denied expression and not allowed to come out.

33

The large cities have become large blots on mankind's inner life and outer health. They are marvels of ingenious arrangements but monstrosities of nervous strain and psychoneurosis. Their inhabitants follow an artificial existence under the delusion that it is a human existence. Everything within them is abnormal yet custom and cowardice, ignorance and selfishness have proclaimed it normal. The air is filled with chemical poisons by travelling vehicles and factories and industrial plants. Their water flows through miles and miles of sediment-lined pipes. Their food is stale, devitalized, adulterated, and often disease-breeding. The unnatural living and high tension of millions of city-prisoned people exposes them to physical and nervous sickness.

34

It becomes harder with each year for the inhabitants of modern London or modern New York to achieve this gentle receptiveness to intuitive spiritual moods.

35

Science has not served the world if its industrial constructions have turned wandering streams into foul gutters, green fields into filthy slums, and pleasant valleys into mean joyless streets. Worse is the poisoned air and food, the mechanized worker.

36

In destroying woods and forests, in building over glades and dells, men have been destroying one of their principal resources of spiritual welfare. The message which their loveliness and silence could give is lost; the benefit to feeling and thought is not received.

37

Bafflement in the face of the world problem produces inertia and paralyses initiative.

38

We all are suffering the evil effects of dispersed radioactivity even now. The dosage is small but cumulative, worsening with every year that passes.

39

An exhausted people may become too tired to believe in anything or to hold on to principles, may live from moment to moment in weary opportunism.

40

Despite delusions about their progress in conquering Nature all men are still controlled by Nature's higher laws. Violation of those laws always brings suffering but the present-day violation will bring disaster.

41

An ethically blinded world may not perceive the actuality and factuality of karma. Hence, it may not comprehend that it was Europe's remorseless collective karma which compelled Neville Chamberlain—pacifist though he was—finally to declare the war for whose avoidance he had dedicated the work of a whole decade. There is no other God pulling historic strings than the karmic laws of retribution and re-adjustment. And let us not forget that this destiny is not an arbitrary tyrannical power; it is self-earned by the nations as by individuals and thus self-called into operation. The sufferings it brings to peoples are really the reactions of their own near or remote deeds. They are visited by the consequences of their own making. Karma works in its own time to set straight all crooked things, not in ours. Nevertheless we can sometimes see it move quickly enough to teach a vivid lesson both to those who suffer its consequences and those who observe that suffering.

42

Because sufficient people were unable or unwilling to learn the proper lessons of the first world war, they had to suffer the consequences of this failure in a worse form—the second world war. If the latter's lessons are in turn also left unlearned, then those consequences will come in the worst possible form—a third and atomic world war.

43

When a civilization becomes so mechanized or brutalized or sensualized or materialized as to be quite insensitive to the higher values of life, it invokes its own slow passing away or abrupt disappearance.

44

The violence and vice of our times are the direct consequences of the irreverence and materialism of our times.

45

When men who have spent their whole lives harbouring destructive ideas are given a constructive teaching, they are naturally impermeable and unreceptive to it. There are materialists who are impatient at hearing philosophic truths and even irritated by them. Such persons may even become quite violently abusive. This happens because they have completely lost their capacity to practise calm unprejudiced abstract thinking, and because they have crushed the feeling of veneration before something higher or nobler than themselves—whether it be a beautiful landscape or God.(P)

46

The hard, almost callous, insensitivity of so many moderns, their sceptical, contemptuous, sarcastic, and conceited attitude when confronted with the finer and subtler things of life, show how deeply atheism, or materialism, has eaten into their souls, how ignorant they are of the higher laws governing life.

47

We naturally and normally shrink from entering into the study of spiritual mysteries, so materialized have we become.

48

Man is more miserable, more restless and unsatisfied than ever before, simply because half his nature—the spiritual—is starving for true food, and the other half—the material—is fed with bad food.

49

Whilst so many are obsessed by materialistic outlooks, it is inevitable that they should lose the moral sense and commit blunder after blunder and consequently suffer distress after distress. Yet of the worst result of these obsessions they are not even aware. And that is, to live so remote from their own inner core of divinity as to miss the most worthwhile values and meanings of life itself.

50

Without knowledge of these higher laws, men blunder into sin and suffering. With the increased power to hurt others which the advances of science have brought them, the need of this knowledge has become acute. For the fear and hate which they have brought over from their animal phase of evolution will still motivate the use of this power.

51

The search for truth is impossible in a society where freedom of thought is forbidden, where public activity on behalf of mystical truth is totally forbidden and on behalf of religious truth progressively throttled.

52

It was not a moralist or religionist, but an economist—J.M. Keynes himself—who looked back on life and confessed that "in truth, it was the Benthamite Calculus, based on over-valuation of the economic criterion, which was destroying the quality of the popular ideal."

53

Higher values vanish, morals disappear, and character becomes baser when the shallow atheism replaces superstition and imposture masquerades as religious faith.

54

Their faith in a higher purpose of life having failed, it is not long before the labour of correcting and purifying human nature will seem unnecessary.(P)

55

The suffering which people have gone through has not awakened them sufficiently, and spiritually people have even declined. This is a grave problem everywhere, and has its roots in a materialistic obsession with a merely external life.

56

The worth or worthlessness of a materialistic attitude towards life will come out not only in dealing with the ordinary questions and everyday problems but much more in special difficulties, emergencies, and crises.

57

The danger today is that most men are not only unaware of their true relation to Nature but also obsessed by their deceptive materialistic illusions about it.

58

The very sense of an inner lack which exists in so many people today, is itself a recognition of their spiritual deficiency.

59

A world without meaning, a life without purpose—this is the miserable consequence of materialism!

60

The number of awakened individuals must be compared with the number who still remain asleep in ignorance and materialism. Then it will be realized how greatly the latter rules humanity.

61

Millions of people seem to carry on their lives quite comfortably and form their opinions quite easily without the necessity of troubling themselves about the place in one for spiritual laws and in the other for spiritual truths. It is as if such things simply did not exist. The realm of spiritual truths has become like a foreign country to them, the spiritual life like a queer eccentricity. It is not that they are incapable of understanding the truths, for many of them have fair intelligence, or that they are too distant from the life, for many of them are good in heart and conduct. But when so many people are so unaware of, or so indifferent to, the higher purpose of life it requires no special foresight to forecast what gloomy changes will take place in their future course. Those whose interest in life begins and ends in their little egos, who cannot believe in and immediately reject the need of putting a higher purpose into all their activities, naturally fall into unavoidable error and experience avoidable sufferings.

62

Both the protagonists in our contemporary international scene have really fallen into the same soul-sickness; the chief difference is only in the way and the extent to which they fell into it. Both have sold their spiritual birthright for a mess of materialistic pottage, the one through temptation and freedom and the other through blindness and compulsion. The goals of both civilizations are similar, only their methods and atmosphere differ, and differ widely. Both seek the mechanistic and materialistic life, but one only partially, the other wholly. Hence the real struggle is between two varieties of materialism. The only correct conclusion is that this is not so much a conflict of clashing ideologies as of two different variants of the same ideology—a good variant and an evil one. This leads to a confused rather than a clear issue. The clean-cut difference in ethical values, aims, and ideals which made the war against the previous incarnation of the aggressive spirit a defensive struggle against obvious evil is still present today, but the metaphysical issues are somewhat chaotically distributed on both sides.

But how far is it enough from the point of view of higher culture? Will they learn to appreciate the values of truth, goodness, and beauty or despise and trample on them? For the juncture of social justice with mechanical development could provide them for the first time with more freedom every day. What use will they make of this enlarged or even new freedom? We may not let such questions hinder us from creating the *opportunity* to think about higher matters. What use or abuse will be made of it is history's concern.

If, as we believe, it be true that history moves in cycles, the world is now entering a new cycle. The old Chinese culture featured this theory of collective fortunes moving through a series of phases, whilst a similar doctrine has long been held in India. We well remember one evening many years ago listening at a riverside village near Gaya, where Buddha attained Nirvana, to one of those melancholy Hindu melodies whose monotonous repetition of the same low wailing notes depresses most Westerners. We complained about this to our cultured companion. He was an extremely old man who sat twice a day in the yogi posture of intertwined ankles—so pleasing to behold, so difficult to perform—with his gaze fixed into space and the fading sunlight playing in quivering undulating waves around his figure. The sacred cord of the twice-born, the white triple thread of the Brahmin, hung around his neck. He did not answer for a full two minutes, for he had been wedded by long habit to silence. Then, without turning his head, he said slowly:

"My son, among our people it is otherwise. We are not, like the Westerners, afraid of truth's sadness, while welcoming its joy. We know that the scenes of this world come and pass like a dream of the night. And this is true of all the events and fortunes of a people's life also—more especially now that we live in the Iron Age, which is ruled by frequent death and covered by spiritual darkness. You know that we measure the world's history in great epochs, each divided into four successive lesser epochs and each endlessly departing and returning on itself like a wheel. Do not blame us, then, if our minds fall quickly into despondency and if our music reflects this sadness. We accept it resignedly, and through such resignation find contentment. We know that karma is always active and we try to accommodate ourselves to it.

"Once I brooded for long over the strange prophecies to be found in an ancient Sanskrit book, a *Purana*. In it I found this passage: 'When the earth is bound by iron chains (are they not your railways?), when men speak to each other across immense spaces (is this not your telephone without wires?), and when materialism rules supreme (has history shown a less spiritual age than ours?), in that time there will incarnate Kalki, the Slayer of Men, who (it is written symbolically) will carry a flaming sword in his hand.'"

63

The negative and undesirable traits of character will tend to reproduce themselves in undesirable and inharmonious forms of experience.

64

The rule of casting out all negative thoughts, and keeping them out, is an absolute one. There are no exceptions and no deviations. Such negatives as hate, irritability, and fault-finding make poisons in the body and neuroses in the mind. They irritate the nerves, disturb the proper movement of the blood, distort the internal secretions, and destructively affect the chemical composition of tissue cells. Nor is this the end. They provoke like emotions in other people with whom we are constantly thrown in contact. We then have to suffer the effects as if they were echoes of our own making. Thus the discords inside oneself throw up disturbances outside oneself. One's anger provokes the other person's anger, for instance.

65

Negative emotions and memories hold accumulations of worthless, even self-harming material, useless debris that serves only to hinder progress.

66

Fierce intense hate blinds the eyes of reason, hurts the hater, and creates delusion.

67

Whoever holds fiercely to his hatreds not only can never enter the kingdom of heaven, but will certainly never enter the kingdom of truth.

68

The man who is happy only when he hates will one day be tutored by having to experience the results of his own destructive feelings.

69

He who slanders others attracts slander to himself.

70

If these negative traits are too strong, they may not only hinder the appearance of "the flash" but also the progress in meditation. This is one of the reasons why the medieval mystical authorities laid down a ruling that cleansing of the heart, purification of the mind, must precede or at least accompany the practice of meditation. That they often carried this process too far and enjoined a rigid extreme asceticism does not invalidate the excellence of their ruling.

71

Arrogance and pride not only prepare the way for a fall, as history so often tells us, but also make a man stick more stubbornly to his deviation from the correct way.

72

The compromise with evil leads in the end to confusion and weakness, a gradual decline of standards, a wavering fealty to opportunism, and a fatal contradiction of principles.

73

If a negative emotion is strong enough, it may not only colour his reasoning faculty, but even preclude its use altogether.

74

It is hard for a man who is filled with bitterness about a situation in which he is involved to be strictly objective toward it.

75

We are weakened every time we give harbourage to snarling thoughts about other people and whimpering ones about ourselves.

76

The negative person too frequently expresses criticism, disapproval, or anger. This contributes to his own bad health.

77

When the lower passions of violence, aggression, and greed are more developed than reason, they enslave reason and put it to their own selfish service. Excessive greed and unscrupulous ambition easily distort the straight shapes of rational truth and put plausible disguises on ancient errors. The defect in all such thinking is that it has not been pushed far enough. It stops too short and too soon. It stops working when confronted by ethical considerations and it will not go on to reckon with the existence of retributive karma. The defeat and failure of its wrong-doers illustrates the eventual defeat and failure which always overtake wrong-doing in the end.

78

Those who find nourishment in tales of horror and drink in reports of crime open their minds to evil suggestion. In strong characters and truly adult persons the influence may be but slight, but in weak ones and mere adolescents it is more serious.

79

His stumblings and his fallings may depress his heart and reduce his aspiration. They may deter his will from further endeavour.

80

For those monsters of hate and cruelty, either utterly materialistic and God-denying or fanatic and taking the name of God in vain, there is no shelter where they can hide once they are forced across the barrier of death.

81

The qualities of determination, intelligence, and persistence—so useful in philosophy—can be used for good or evil. They can make a more successful criminal as well as a better philosopher. The upsurge of well-thought-out, daring, resourceful, and highly ambitious crime in modern times is a sign of misapplied powers, while its violence is a sign of merciless egocentricity. The end for such persons is commensurate. Then may come a crippling deformed future birth, or a sudden and radical awakening to the grave peril toward which they are heading—and a change of course to a better life.

82

The unfortunate experiences which sometimes befall an individual's worldly life are, or may be, partly induced by his own psychic practices of the period immediately preceding them. One may have been drawn into a vortex of psychic evil which has harmed his spiritual life and brought suffering into his worldly existence.

83

What are the inner causes which can produce these dismal outer effects? Here are some of them: shock, worry, fear, resentment, anger, excessive criticism, condemnation of others.

84

The English woman novelist named Ouida, who wrote during the earlier part of this century, was so successful that she became the highest-paid fiction writer of her time. Yet when she died she was alone, penniless, half-blind, and dwelling in a back alley of Viareggio, Italy. Why? She was brilliant, fluent, and vibrant in her style, but most of her written work was scathing, bitter, highly critical, filled with prejudices and even hates. To what extent did a mind and heart holding so many negatives contribute to these unpleasant results? Yet she was unquestionably a lady in manners, breeding, dress, and way of life. She wrote her letters and even her manuscripts on the finest quality paper. She was highly independent and refused an offer to write her own life story, even though a substantial amount of money was the prize. Her reply was that it would be lowering herself to feed her own egotism and vanity to do so!

85

It is quite true and utterly obvious that bad physical conditions make their contribution also, but it is even more true that bad inner conditions are the fundamental causes which turn outward remedies to disappointments in the end.

86

Blind selfishness brings mutilated lives and ugly minds.

87

Pessimism is practical defeatism and psychological suicide. It is the child of despair and the parent of dissolution.(P)

88

Long ago Buddha said that if we make room in our minds for negative, bitter thoughts of complaint, outrage, or injury against those who mistreat us, we shall not be free and will remain unable to find peace.(P)

89

Beware of giving birth to thoughts of hate, envy, malice, or wrath and sending them to another person. For they will reach him, yes, but will then return like a boomerang to their source.

90

The Sanskrit proverb which says that wicked men may gain the fruits of their aggressions and desires, may win victories over others, also says, "But at the end they are destroyed at the roots."

91

The coldly calculated torture of animals in the name of scientific progress must be paid for in different degrees by those who allow it as well as by those who perpetrate it. The practice of vivisection is a sinful one. The men who do it will have to pay the penalty one day, quite often by being born into a maimed and hurt body. Some among them, who gradually lose every vestige of pity from their character, become heartless monsters.

92

Through violent aggression whereby impassioned men seek to destroy others, they work their own destruction—at first moral, in the end, physical.

93

These undesirable thoughts and feelings are bad for others as well as himself, besides wasting so much of his own energies.

94

An evil man's mistakes sometimes strike back at him later when he least expects them, and can least afford them.

95

Is it prudent to heed all this talk of coming calamity? Is it a mistake to read material speculating on its likelihood or imagining its horrors? Each person must answer such a question for himself, but the philosophic person approaches it in a different manner. On general principles he dislikes negative thoughts and repels them. He seeks a clear recognition of what is happening in the world around him, but he trains himself—disciplines his mind and detaches his emotions—to do so without picking up the accompaniments of panic or depression. He practises living with complete calm in the face of provocations and irritations, keeping his head, when others all around are losing theirs.

Index for Part 1

Entries are listed by chapter number followed by "para" number. For example, 1.8 means chapter 1, para 8 and 3.69, 75, 86, 89 means chapter 3, paras 69, 75, 86, and 89. Chapter listings are separated by a semicolon. Please note also that, for the reader's convenience, the first number in the right-hand running heads throughout the text indicates chapter number.

Index for Part 2

Entries are listed by chapter number followed by "para" number. For example, 3.132 means chapter 3, para 132 and 3.122, 313, 315–316 means chapter 3, paras 122, 313, 315, and 316. Chapter listings are separated by a semicolon. Please note also that, for the reader's convenience, the first number in the right-hand running heads throughout the text indicates chapter number.

The 28 Categories from the Notebooks

This outline of categories in *The Notebooks* is the most recent one Paul Brunton developed for sorting, ordering, and filing his written work. The listings he put after each title were not meant to be all-inclusive. They merely suggest something of the range of topics included in each category.

1 **THE QUEST**
   Its choice —Independent path —Organized groups —
   Self-development —Student/teacher

2 **PRACTICES FOR THE QUEST**
   Ant's long path —Work on oneself

3 **RELAX AND RETREAT**
   Intermittent pauses —Tension and pressures —Relax body,
   breath, and mind —Retreat centres —Solitude —
   Nature appreciation —Sunset contemplation

4 **ELEMENTARY MEDITATION**
   Place and conditions —Wandering thoughts —Practise
   concentrated attention —Meditative thinking —
   Visualized images —Mantrams —Symbols
   —Affirmations and suggestions

5 **THE BODY**
   Hygiene and cleansings —Food —Exercises and postures
   —Breathings —Sex: importance, influence, effects

6 **EMOTIONS AND ETHICS**
   Uplift character —Re-educate feelings —Discipline emotions —
   Purify passions —Refinement and courtesy —Avoid fanaticism

7 **THE INTELLECT**
   Nature —Services —Development —Semantic training —
   Science —Metaphysics —Abstract thinking

8 **THE EGO**
   What am I? —The I-thought —The psyche